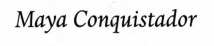

Maya Conquistador

MATTHEW RESTALL

Maya

Conquistador

BEACON PRESS

BOSTON

BEACON PRESS
25 Beacon Street
Boston, Massachusetts 02108–2892
www.beacon.org

Beacon Press books are published under the auspices of
the Unitarian Universalist Association of Congregations.

03 02 01 00 99 98   8 7 6 5 4 3 2 1

This book is printed on recycled acid-free paper that contains at least 20 percent
postconsumer waste and meets the uncoated paper ANSI / NISO specifications for
permanence as revised in 1992.

Text design by Christoper Kuntze

Library of Congress Cataloging-in-Publication Data
Restall, Matthew, 1964–
    Maya conquistador / Matthew Restall.
        p.   cm.
    Includes bibliographical references (p.   ) and index.
    ISBN 0–8070–5506–9 (cloth)
    1. Mayas—History—Sources.   2. Conquerors—Mexico—History—Sources.
        3. Mexico—History—Conquest, 1519–1540.   I. Title.
    F1435.R493   1998
    972'02'—dc21   98–15751

TO ISABEL

who was born when this book was begun

and would now love nothing more

than to tear out its pages

and eat them

Contents

Maps and Figures

List of Abbreviations

TCH Title of Chicxulub, aka Chronicle of Chicxulub, aka Crónica de
     Chac-Xulub-Chen, aka Códice de Nakuk-Pech
     [Cited numbers are page numbers on photostat of nineteenth-
     century Regil manuscript, Tozzer Library, Harvard University, and
     Latin American Library, Tulane University]

TULAL Latin American Library, Tulane University, New Orleans

TLH Tozzer Library, Harvard University, Cambridge
     [Note that many of the cited items in TLH were formerly held by
     Harvard's Peabody Museum and are referenced accordingly in older
     publications]

TT Tierras de Tabi
    [Cited numbers are folio numbers of manuscript, Latin American
    Library, Tulane University]

TY Title of Yaxkukul, aka Crónica de Yaxkukul
    [Cited numbers are folio numbers of original 1769 manuscript, Latin
    American Library, Tulane University]

XC The Xiu Chronicle, aka Xiu Papers, aka Chronicle of Oxkutzcab
    [Cited numbers are document numbers in Roys's 1941 transcription,
    Tozzer Library, Harvard University; original manuscript and bound
    photographs in Tozzer Library]

Preface

The enduring images of the Conquest of Mexico are powerful ones: the Spanish conquistadors are bloody but bold adventurers; the Aztecs are noble savages lamenting their broken bones and spears.[1] The tale told again and again is the sixteenth-century epic of Cortés the conqueror and Cuauhtemoc the last emperor, of the tragic Moctezuma, the Aztec ruler who let the Spaniards into his capital, and the legendary La Malinche, the enslaved noblewoman who became Cortés's interpreter and later his lover. The story of siege and sacrifice, of sad nights and days of destruction, continues to overshadow all others.[2] This view of the Conquest, primarily from the perspective of the Spaniards, goes all the way back to the narratives of Cortés himself, whose letters to the king of Spain became best-sellers in Europe in the conquistador's own lifetime.[3] And although there have been recent popularizations of Nahua accounts of the Spanish Conquest of central Mexico,[4] little attention has been given to the Conquest of the rest of colonial Mesoamerica (or New Spain, as the colonists dubbed the region).[5]

Yet there are other stories, compelling and surprising, to be told. This book presents one of them: the Spanish Conquest of the peninsula of Yucatan, at the southern end of what has become modern Mexico, and the creation of a colony there. Only this tale has a twist: the courageous conquistadors are not Spaniards, but Mayas—noblemen of the indigenous race of the region. In fact, the tale has many twists, for the Maya texts reproduced and discussed here offer neither the view of the victors nor a uniform vision of the vanquished, but rather the multiple perspectives of various Maya accounts that range from the end of the Conquest period (the late sixteenth century) to the last decades of colonial rule (the early nineteenth century). Yes, there are broken bones; but this is more a story of survival, of a society whose vitality and complexity reconstituted itself not just in a singular post-Conquest moment but over and over again in numerous ways as it adapted to the colonial experience that was the Conquest's outcome.

This book is divided into two parts. In the first part I introduce and discuss the topic of the Conquest and Maya perceptions of it. Chapter 1 provides historical background; it begins with the tale of the Spanish Conquest, told primarily from the Spanish viewpoint, and goes on to argue the relevance of two pre-Conquest periods in Yucatec history, the heydays of the cities of Chichen Itza and Mayapan. Chapter 2 offers an analysis of Maya perspectives; it examines why Maya accounts played down the role of violence, explores the Maya emphasis on historical continuities through the Conquest period, and suggests that the multiplicity of Maya views is rooted in the nature of native identity—which was based not on ethnic consciousness but on the allegiances of class, family, and municipal community.

In the second part I present a series of texts, translated from Yucatec Maya into English, that contain Maya accounts of various aspects of the Spanish invasion. These sources are published together in English for the first time (some have never been published in English before, others have previously been available only in obscure, out-of-print editions).[6] The book's purpose is thus to make valuable and unique ethnohistorical sources accessible as never before, as well as to offer a compelling new perspective on the Spanish Conquest.

The book is not just about the Conquest of a region of colonial Mexico, but through the expression of many voices, talks of many conquests—within Yucatan, Mexico, and beyond. Furthermore, in emphasizing the reaction to conquest by the "conquered," rather than the details of the conquering process, the book—following the Maya sources themselves—is ultimately about colonialism and its complexities, with conquest functioning as a muted and multifaceted metaphor for the colonial experience. For the Spaniards, their conquest of Yucatan was a singular, monolithic event that took place in the 1540s, marking the beginning of a long period of benevolent colonial rule (which ended in 1821). For the Mayas, however, conquest and colonialism were not so easily separated, either chronologically or conceptually. Both were part of the ongoing process of negotiated relations that was the nature of political, economic, and social life. Thus in telling us about the coming of the Spaniards, Maya authors are revealing to us their memory and perception of the Yucatec past before, during, and after the Spanish invasion; more than that, these sources open up to us Maya views of their whole world, past and present.

From Emiliano Zapata to my own family, many other people helped make this book possible. When Zapata was asked why he and his fellow peasants were fighting for the Revolution, he pointed his finger at a box of old colonial land titles.[7] This book follows Zapata's finger to old colonial land titles—specifically examples of the genre known as *títulos*, or primordial titles, as well as other Maya-language sources. My interest in these documents was sparked some years ago while I was doing research at Tulane University's Latin American Library, greatly assisted by the late Martha Robertson and inspired by Victoria Bricker (especially her approach to the Books of Chilam Balam).[8] To my surprise I discovered that, the Books of Chilam Balam aside, Maya sources on the Conquest were not readily available in published form or in English translation. The publication of James Lockhart's *We People Here* further inspired me to do something about this. The sources that I eventually collected and translated for this book—primordial titles, annals, petitions, and other materials—were found archived in the United States, Mexico, and Spain and were selected for their perspectives on the Spanish Conquest, although the texts are rich in many other kinds of historical and anthropological information. In the course of various research trips, I built up a great debt of gratitude to the directors and staff of the Archivo General de las Indias in Seville, the Archivo General de la Nación in Mexico City, and the various local archives in Merida, Yucatan (especially those under Piedad Peniche Rivero and Michel Antochiw), the Benson Library at the University of Texas, the British Library in London, Tulane's Latin American Library (under Guillermo Náñez Falcón), and Harvard University's Tozzer Library, where Greg Finnegan and his colleagues were tirelessly helpful. While the scholarship and comradeship of dozens contributed indirectly to this book, the following colleagues and friends contributed directly to the project's progress and fruition—John Coatsworth, Alexander Christensen, John Drayton, William Hanks, the Holmes family, Dana Leibsohn, James

Lockhart, Tsubasa Okoshi Harada, Steve Patterson, Sergio Quezada, and Pete Sigal; Felipe Fernández-Armesto, Frances Karttunen, Patricia McAnany, and Susan Schroeder were especially generous in offering extensive comments on the manuscript. Much of the research and writing time was made possible by Boston College Research Incentive Grants and in particular by a one-year fellowship from the National Endowment for the Humanities. I could not have asked for better than Beacon editor Deb Chasman, copyeditor Susan Meigs, and cartographer John Cotter. Finally, I would like to thank Helen; as always, she supported my endeavors without question or reserve.

M.B.R.
Belmont, Massachusetts
March 1998

PART I

Contexts & Conquests

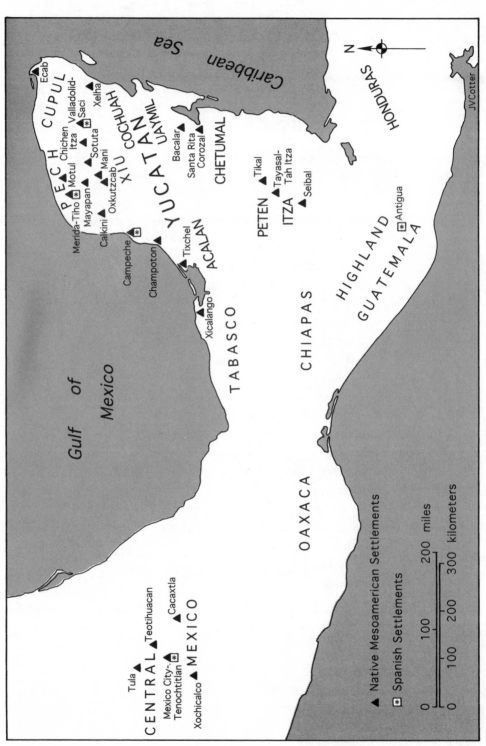

Map I. *Mesoamerica*

CONQUESTS

CHAPTER 1

When Alonso Canche was a boy he witnessed an extraordinary scene, one that he would never forget. Later he would hear the story told over and over again by his father and the other elders of the community, or *cah*. Later still, long after Canche had been christened Alonso, and when he was an officer of the ruling council of the *cah*, he would relate the tale to the town notary and see it written down for posterity.

The scene took place in 1541 in Alonso's home *cah* of Calkini, in the plaza that stretched from the front patio of his family's house on one side to a great ceiba tree that overshadowed a large and ancient well on the other side. All the elders and most of the people of Calkini, including Alonso's father, Napot Canche, who at the time was serving as *cah* governor or *batab*, turned out to welcome the foreign visitors.

More than visitors, the men who lined up in the plaza were well-armed invaders from central Mexico, commanded by their bearded captain, named Montejo, whose small force of compatriots (Spaniards simply called "foreigners" in Canche's account) was supplemented by a larger number of Nahuatl-speaking warriors from central Mexico— whom Alonso and his fellow Calkini residents called Culhuas. The ostensible purpose of the occasion was for the people of Calkini to present the foreigners with a bountiful selection of the fruits of the land— honey, corn, turkeys, cotton. The real purpose, the meaning behind the offering of tribute, was for the Maya rulers of the district to acknowledge openly the authority of a new higher power, one whose long-term local presence was as yet uncertain.

3

But the Canche boy could hardly have been aware of all this. What he did see was a well-ordered and solemn ritual turn into a barbaric free-for-all—and the disdain of the Maya witnesses can be detected in Alonso's account of decades later—as the foreigners broke ranks and grabbed what they could of the precious goods prepared by the people of Calkini. Then, to add insult to injury, they seized some of the men, many of them local officials, who had presented themselves along Napot Canche's patio; and, with this additional human booty, they left.[1]

This scene, whose details are drawn almost entirely from the Maya-language account included in what I call the Title of Calkini (see Chapter 5) prompts a number of questions, few of which are answered by the text of the document. For example, when in the sequence of Conquest events did this scene take place, and why is no date given in the Maya account? Did Calkini residents offer no resistance to the foreigners, as the account seems to suggest? How might the people of Calkini have interpreted the event, then and later? Why were Spanish invaders accompanied by central Mexicans, and why did the Mayas have a name for these natives of a distant region of Mesoamerica?[2]

I would like to address these questions by turning from the small Maya community of Calkini to the colonial Spanish city of Merida and then to go briefly back in time to the pre-Conquest Maya cities of Chichen Itza and Mayapan. The broader purpose of this voyage is to provide the reader with some historical context for the Maya accounts (discussed in Chapter 2) of what I shall call, for convenience's sake, the Conquest. My specific intentions are, first, to tell the tale of the Conquest in a way that offers the reader an outline of events and at the same time, for comparative purposes, privileges the Spanish perspective; and, second, to examine the significance of Yucatec history, particularly the precedents of conquest and conflict, in the centuries before the Spanish invasion.

MERIDA: SPANISH SACRIFICES

Almost two decades before Alonso Canche saw a Spaniard named Montejo in Calkini, Spaniards had invaded central Mexico. There the Spanish followers and central Mexican (or Nahua) allies of Hernán Cortés had destroyed the city that had dominated most of central Mexico, the Aztec (or, more accurately, Mexica) capital of Tenochtitlan, founding upon its ruins Mexico City. In the years that followed, a first and second generation of colonial settlers sought not only to consolidate their hold on the central valleys of the region but also to subjugate the peoples of northern and southern Mesoamerica. Hence the passage of Cortés himself across the foot of the Yucatan peninsula in the mid-1520s, re-corded in the first of the Maya accounts presented below (Chapter 3). Hence too the appearance in Yucatan, beginning in the late 1520s, of Spanish expeditions of conquest led by associates of Cortés, men of the Montejo family whose endeavors eventually resulted in the creation of Merida.

The Spanish colonial city of Merida was founded on the Maya site of Tiho in 1542, a year after the tribute ceremony in Calkini described above. For the Spaniards, and for most of the historians writing in Spanish or English over the subsequent four centuries, Merida's year of genesis was the end of the Conquest and the beginning of colonial rule —in the most partisan minds, the dawn of civilization in Yucatan. Yet for the Mayas the founding of Merida was neither a beginning nor an end, but merely an event that fell, not just in the middle of an ever-protracted Conquest, but somewhere between the beginning of their history and the present. The Spanish creation of a new provincial capital is but one small entry in the Annals of Oxkutzcab (Chapter 4); it does not even merit mention in the annals of the Book of Chilam Balam of Mani (Chapter 7) or in the Title of Calkini (Chapter 5).

Thus the significance of Merida to the tale being told here is its potential as a symbol of the difference between Maya and non-Maya views of the Conquest; it offers a stepping-stone into a brief analysis of the Conquest from the Spanish perspective (just as Chichen Itza and Mayapan will be used later in this chapter to survey the precolonial Yucatec experience of external and internal conflict).

From the Spanish perspective, the Conquest was structured around a series of expeditions of exploration and invasion, each named after the Spanish captain who led the effort. As has been detailed elsewhere in Spanish America,[3] these were not modern-style military campaigns staffed primarily by professional soldiers, but expeditions of armed settlers from a variety of occupations and origins, whose actions were often given royal sanction only after the fact. They sought economic opportunity, and, even if they survived the conquest of an inhabited region, often spent the rest of their lives competing with their compatriots for the Crown's recognition of their endeavors. Some returned to Spain or moved on to other conquest enterprises.[4] Others settled permanently in newly founded native-built Spanish cities and towns, such as Yucatan's Merida and Campeche. Such settlers in Yucatan would eventually forge a regional Spanish identity. But during the early sixteenth century, the peninsula was but one of many lands seen by Spaniards as a potential source of wealth and a future imperial province.

The Spanish Conquest of Yucatan can be divided into three stages: the first, of 1502–27, was little more than a series of Spanish-Maya encounters, albeit mostly hostile ones; the second, of 1527–45, might be termed the Montejo stage, in which Spaniards, under the leadership of a trio of men sharing the name Francisco de Montejo, mounted a series of campaigns that resulted in the founding of a colony; the third stage, beginning in 1546 and lasting, depending on the region and one's perspective, through the colonial period and possibly beyond, consisted of ongoing campaigns of violence against Mayas by Spanish settlers and officials, incidents not traditionally characterized as part of the Conquest.

The first Maya-European contact appears to have been an encounter in 1502 off the coast of Honduras, when Christopher Columbus and his crew picked over the contents of a Maya trading canoe and seized the captain.[5] Not for another decade would Europeans set foot on Yucatec soil, and the first time they did it was not by design. Between 1511 and 1519 there were four Spanish expeditions to Yucatan. The first, following a shipwreck, was unplanned. The other three sailed from Cuba with licenses to trade and explore, not with permits to conquer the peninsula, and none made any major forays into its interior. These encounters and expeditions had little immediate impact upon the indigenous inhabitants except for the small numbers of Mayas killed in coastal skirmishes. But the impact of the diseases they unknowingly introduced was devastating. By the time the Spaniards returned in 1527, smallpox had swept through the population, to some extent softening the Maya for conquest, as one historian has put it.[6]

Two men from the 1511 expedition survived both the shipwreck and their early encounters with the local Mayas;[7] both went on to play prominent roles in the Conquest, at least from the Spanish perspective. Gerónimo de Aguilar lived as a slave for seven years, was purchased back by Cortés in 1519, and became an apparently crucial link in the chain of communication between Cortés and the native leaders.[8] Gonzalo Guerrero was also enslaved at first, but then, according to several second-hand Spanish accounts, he was "converted into an Indian and become much worse than an Indian." As, according to Aguilar, Guerrero married the daughter of a local Maya lord and had three children, he is celebrated today as the father of the first Mexican mestizos. At the time, however, Guerrero horrified his compatriots, who became convinced that he had become a war captain and was responsible for various Maya attacks on Spanish parties, dating from the Córdoba expedition of 1517 and continuing through the 1530s.[9]

From the Spanish viewpoint, Francisco Hernández de Córdoba's 1517 expedition discovered Yucatan. It landed twice, first at Ecab, at the northeast corner of the peninsula, and then near Champoton, on the southwest coast, where a Maya attack fatally wounded Córdoba and forced him to retreat back to Cuba. The next expedition, also from Havana, was led by Juan de Grijalva, who landed on Cozumel in 1518. Grijalva claimed the island for Castile and then led his four ships along the same coastal route Córdoba had taken the previous year; he also was attacked at Champoton and twice engaged Maya forces at Campeche.[10]

Before returning to Cuba, however, Grijalva pushed further along the Gulf Coast than his predecessor had and obtained material evidence suggesting that central Mexico, not Yucatan, was the greatest source of wealth in the region. Because Pedro de Alvarado (to become infamous for his roles in the conquests of Tenochtitlan and highland Guatemala) had been sent ahead with this news, the governor of Cuba was already planning a fourth and far larger expedition by the time Grijalva returned. This was led by Cortés, who was joined by Grijalva's former lieutenants, including Alvarado and the elder Francisco de Montejo, one of the future conquistadors of Yucatan. Cortés also drew upon his predecessor's efforts in another way; using reports of the Grijalva expedition for guidance and encouragement, Cortés made a brief stop on Cozumel before sailing straight around Yucatan to Tabasco.[11] From there he would go on to central Mexico, and, after a two-year campaign, destroy the regional power of the Mexica and their capital of Tenochtitlan.

Only after this would Cortés and Montejo return to Yucatan, the former in 1525 (see Chapter 3), the latter in 1527, as head of the first Spanish expedition armed with a royal license to conquer the peninsula. Accompanied by some five hundred men, Montejo sailed straight to Cozumel, the island he had stood upon eight years earlier. In the interim he had spent several years in Spain promoting the interests of Cortés while the latter was besieging and destroying Tenochtitlan and consolidating Spanish control over central Mexico; Montejo's reward, upon reaching the newly founded Mexico City in 1522, was a handful of *encomiendas* (grants of labor and tribute from indigenous communities), including Atzcapotzalco, a large *altepetl* (Nahua community, equivalent to the Maya *cah*) near Mexico City. This success only encouraged Montejo to do what Cortés had done—throw off his patron and conquer a province of his own under direct royal patronage. Thus when Montejo was sent back to Spain in 1524 to represent Mexico's conquistadors, he began to prepare his own venture, formally requesting Crown permission to conquer Yucatan in 1526.[12]

Once on Cozumel, Montejo continued to imitate Cortés; he claimed the island for Castile, and then, having crossed to the mainland and founded a town near Xelha, he scuttled his ships. This measure was made necessary by the dismal state into which the expedition had quickly fallen.[13] "Since the men were new in the land, many fell ill and were ailing with the efforts of its settlement and pacification," the group's priest, Juan Rodríguez de Caraveo, wrote later. According to Montejo, "Many of the men soon died."[14] The campaign of "pacification," as the Spaniards called their conquest endeavors, had brought only disease and warfare to Yucatan; it was thus fitting that illness and the hostility of the local Mayas threatened to end Montejo's expedition before it had hardly begun. Although after two months Montejo's men were able to move out of their camp north to Ecab, when they attempted to advance west they were forced back by Maya warriors. Retreating to the coast, the survivors boarded a ship that had come from Santo Domingo and sailed south to Chetumal; the bay seemed a good base for a conquest effort, but Montejo now lacked sufficient forces, and so, in 1529, he returned to Mexico.[15]

Begun in imitation of Cortés, Montejo's first *entrada*, or entry, had ended with none of the success of the famous central Mexican campaign. Yet Montejo remained optimistic, writing in his first letter to the king in 1529, "I heard many reports of gold and precious stones which are in the land; I am very hopeful that with the aid of Our Lord I shall pacify the land in a short while."[16] Montejo's resolve was further strengthened by his son (the second Francisco) who joined him in planning a second official *entrada* and who seems to have convinced his father to use the Chontal region of Acalan, not Chetumal Bay, as a stepping-stone to the seizure of the peninsula. The younger Montejo had accompanied Cortés on his 1524–25 expedition to Honduras, and both he and Cortés were enthusiastic about the wealth, cooperative inhabitants, and convenient location of Acalan.[17]

As it turned out, competing Spanish claims on Tabasco so mired the Montejos in political disputes that by 1531 they had resolved instead to establish a base at Campeche. Over the next three years the elder Montejo concentrated on consolidating a grip on the Campeche region, while his lieutenants Alonso Dávila and the younger Montejo did the same to the east and north respectively. Although all three were faced with almost incessant hostility from the Mayas, none was forced into full retreat as previous expeditions had been. Yet they were disadvantaged by two factors, one which slowed their advance towards colonial consolidation, the other which brought the campaign to an abrupt halt in 1534.[18]

The first factor was the tendency of these conquistadors, in accordance with normal Spanish practice, to institute the *encomienda* with excessive haste and often with brutality. Despite the inherently exploitative nature of the *encomienda* (which gave a Spaniard the right to demand labor and goods from entire native communities), its imposition and maintenance would prove to be tenable once the colonial régime had won the cooperation of native community governors and had established some semblance of legitimacy; after all, systems of labor and tribute provision, both local and regional, were hardly new to Mesoamerica. In Yucatan in the 1530s, however, that time had certainly not yet come. In all three cases—the Montejos in the areas of Campeche and Chichen Itza, and Dávila in the southeast—most or all of the local Maya leaders initially accepted the Spanish intrusion without violence. Their position of guarded diplomacy even included, in some cases, the offer and payment of tribute goods, supplies which the Spaniards sorely needed and whose donation was taken by the Spaniards, to some extent correctly, as a sign of political submission. However, the Spaniards' intention to impose a permanent system to exploit local resources was not immediately apparent to the Mayas, not until, that is, the Spanish captains distributed *encomiendas* and their followers leapt to make good on them.

Consequently in all three regions Spaniards were faced with the greatest opposition after *encomiendas* were given out. It was three or four months before the Canul, Canche, and other Maya leaders in the areas around Campeche and Calkini organized an assault on Montejo's position. Dávila had two months respite before being attacked by the leaders of the Cochuah, Uaymil, and Chetumal regions (today's southern Quintana Roo), who had not opposed the Spaniards at first but who had then been faced with *encomienda* demands. In the north the Cupul and other leaders also appeared to accept the Spaniards' demands until their permanence became apparent; sporadic resistance and passive non-cooperation were soon replaced by an open and organized Maya campaign to eject the younger Montejo and his men, who were forced from Chichen Itza back to Campeche. Not until Montejo returned with his father and a far larger force in 1534 did the Spaniards establish a tentative hold on the peninsula's northwest.[19]

The second factor to undermine the *entrada* of 1529–34 was an external one; "with the great news that came of Peru," Montejo would later write to the king, "all the men went away and depopulated all the towns of the land."[20] Fray Lorenzo de Bienvenida, also in a letter to the Crown, put it this way: "Because there is no gold or silver here, and because of the news of the riches of Peru and the slight resources which the governor, Montejo, had, they were unable to maintain themselves in it."[21] As a result, there was a withdrawal of all Spaniards from Yucatan (with the exception of a marginal settlement at Champoton).

As Montejo and his followers would tell it, and as historians have continued to suggest, the news of Peru came just as the completion of the Conquest was imminent. I suspect that this view is partly rooted in the promotional campaigns of the Montejos—as they struggled in the late 1530s to re-recruit followers to the Yucatec cause—and partly influenced by hindsight. For in reality the Spanish hold on the peninsula was highly tenuous, dependent primarily on the continued goodwill of allied noble families such as the Pech and the Xiu (a subject explored in subsequent chapters). Furthermore, as the above Bienvenida quote implies, the Peru factor was really a symptom of a longer-term Spanish problem—the lack of precious metals in the peninsula. This rendered the settlers utterly dependent on the efficient, large-scale provision of low-value local resources (the colonial economy would become based on the extraction primarily of cotton cloth and wax).[22] Such a need clashed with the decentralized nature of sixteenth-century Maya politics (discussed below), a circumstance that was probably aggravated by Conquest-era warfare. With or without Peru, the Spaniards were forced by Maya leaders to proceed painstakingly through a prolonged series of negotiations and renegotiations, punctuated by episodes of violence and alliance, retreat and return. The miserable state of the Spanish settlement at Champoton after 1536, on the verge of starvation and massacre by 1540, might have been that of other settlements had they remained in the late 1530s.[23]

If the Spanish hold on Yucatan had been so tenuous in 1534, how, when the Spaniards returned in the 1540s, did they establish a permanent colony so quickly? A number of factors are relevant here. The first three are interrelated. First, during the Spaniards' six-year absence the Mayas were further weakened by smallpox and other diseases that the Spaniards had brought with them in the early 1530s to parts of the peninsula where they had previously not set foot. Similarly, the second Montejo *entrada*, in attempting to use one indigenous group against another (a standard Spanish practice), had stimulated rivalries among Maya regions and their ruling families; in the six-year interim these rivalries broke into open civil wars. Including the massacre at Otzmal (see Chapters 4 and 8), these conflicts further undermined the Maya ability to resist the third Montejo campaign that began in 1540. Third, a severe drought and a plague of locusts, exacerbating a food crisis that had begun during the earlier wars against the Spaniards, brought disaster; according to fray Diego de Landa, "such a famine ensued that [the people] fell dead on the roads, and when the Spaniards returned they did not recognize the country."[24] Being absent during these years, of course, the Spaniards were spared the effects of this famine.

Fourth, the Spaniards who returned in 1540 enjoyed advantages that were unavailable to previous expeditions. The younger Montejo and other veterans of the campaigns in Yucatan were now familiar with much of the peninsula (taken for an island before the 1520s and largely unknown in its interior before the 1530s). The lessons learned from earlier campaigns were clearly laid out by the elder Montejo in instructions written for his son in 1540.[25] The instructions emphasized the importance of earlier alliances with Pech, Xiu, and other leaders. They also stressed the need for a judicious and select use of violence. Montejo's men were not to "injure or mistreat" those natives who "have always wanted the Spaniards to settle in those provinces," but were told, "if some do not offer obedience, you shall go to war." In this way the younger Montejo succeeded in forcing other leaders to submit to Spanish demands. The rulers of Calkini are one example; what the Calkini account (Chapter 5) omits is that their leaders had refused a 1540 request for tribute and submission, complying the following year only after the younger Montejo's cousin (the third Francisco) had taken forty or fifty men on a quick slash-and-burn campaign through the region.[26] Another advantage in the third Montejo campaign was the increased use of Nahua auxiliaries from the elder Montejo's Mexican *encomiendas*; their role is downplayed in Spanish reports, but their presence is clearly noted in Maya accounts such as that of Calkini.

These factors—the Mayas decimated and weakened, the Spaniards reinforced and strengthened by experience—go a long way to explaining how several hundred Spaniards were able to establish a permanent colony in the peninsula. That explanation becomes clearer still if these factors, relevant particularly from the 1540s on, are combined with two others that affected the entire course of the sixteenth century: the

Spanish technological advantages of steel blades and crossbows (and, to a lesser extent, the use of muskets, horses, and war dogs); and the tactical discrepancy between the Spaniards' willingness to kill large numbers of Mayas indiscriminately, and the Mayas' preference for person-to-person combat and the taking of captives.[27]

Finally, the third Montejo *entrada* was not as speedily successful as Spanish accounts suggest. Certainly within two years the city of Merida had been founded on the Maya site of Tiho, and its presence was to be permanent and secure. By 1542 the core of the colony was also established, a strip running along the west coast and half way round the north coast of the peninsula; this strip had been pushed far enough inland by 1545 to create a secure zone around and between Campeche and Merida. For the conquistadors, it was important that these events —Merida's founding and the securing of its environs—represented a completion of conquest, a fait accompli. Rewards and offices could then be claimed, rivals shut out, and resistant Mayas enslaved or otherwise brutalized as rebels. This position has consequently passed into history as fact. For Landa, writing in the 1560s, Yucatan was a Spanish possession from the moment the elder Montejo declared it to be so on Cozumel in 1527, and it was conquered by his son in the 1530s and 1540s. The seventeenth-century chronicler López de Cogolludo ends his narrative of the Conquest at 1545, but its completion is effectively announced with Merida's founding three years earlier; in his history, the early 1540s were more about Spanish politics and the establishment of administrative structures than the details of Maya-Spanish conflict.[28]

Postcolonial historians took the same line. Yucatec bishop Crescencio Carrillo y Ancona, in a catechism on Yucatec history published in 1880, describes the January 1541 offer of allegiance by Xiu and Chel lords as the event that "almost completed the conquest"; it was "completed entirely with the victory gained in the battle of San Bernabé of June 11, 1541, against the army of Cocom, king of Sotuta, who was the only one who had not offered obedience."[29] Tozzer and Chamberlain, both North American historians writing in the 1940s, remarked respectively that in 1546 "the country was finally pacified" and "by mid-1534 Montejo had solved his basic military problems and, while there was still much work to do, the conquest as such was fundamentally achieved." Chamberlain dated the colony from 1541, described the Conquest events of 1546–47 as "The Great Maya Revolt," and ended his book-length study at 1550.[30]

In classifying the bloody conquest war of the late 1540s in the northeast as a rebellion, Chamberlain was following a historiographical tradition going back to the early colonial period, to Cogolludo, to Landa, and to the conquistadors themselves, who later depicted the war as a series of atrocities by Maya rebels.[31] Montejo, for example, described the war as a just suppression of an Indian uprising incited and lead by the Maya priests or prophets called *chilam*, who "told the people . . . that God said that all the Spaniards had to die and that none should remain in the land." He wrote that the principal *chilam* "confessed many evil things that the devil had given him to understand."[32]

The characterization of the 1546–47 eastern war as a rebellion reveals the profound Hispanocentrism of the contemporary Spanish perspective. The Maya attempt to roll back the Spanish presence was undeniably a Conquest event, part of the ongoing resistance to Spanish demands. In Montejo's interpretation, however, this was a revolt not only against Spanish settlers but against God; because the Spaniards had declared their colony established, opposition to it was unjustifiable, inspired by the devil and by "fanatical hatred."[33] Maya violence, which resulted in the death of fifteen to twenty *encomenderos* and some members of their families, was thus diabolistic and atrocious; the Spaniards' subsequent killing of hundreds of Mayas, the enslaving of two thousand more, the burning of half a dozen native priests, the execution of captured warriors, the hanging of women, all of this was necessary and legal punishment meted out, according to Montejo, "with the least possible harm and prejudice."[34]

The eastern war was not the only case of a continued campaign of conquest through and after the 1540s. The east remained permanently scarred by the Spanish invasion and presence,[35] with the region between the Spanish town of Valladolid and the island of Cozumel never fully incorporated into the colony. Meanwhile, in 1545, Franciscan friars began to arrive in Yucatan.[36] Their presence was seemingly benign compared with that of the conquistadors. Yet in the summer of 1562 their head, fray Diego de Landa, instituted a brutal campaign of persecution in which over four and a half thousand Maya men and women were tortured, about two hundred of them to death, while hundreds of others were permanently injured; some also committed suicide.[37] Landa's intention was to extract confessions of idolatry and other heresies, such as the use by Maya priests of a Christian-style crucifixion in combination with the Mesoamerican heart sacrifice. He won such confessions by applying the full range of Inquisition torture methods, such as suspending victims by their wrists while they were whipped, burned with hot wax, or weighed down with stones, or tying them to a wooden frame, the *burro*, and then assaulting them. The Maya response was such (see Chapter 9) that the colonists, including Landa's opponents within the Church, feared a full-scale Maya reprisal and moved to have Landa removed from office (he would later return as bishop). Although the veracity of the confessions was accepted by Spaniards at the time, and subsequently by scholars, it has more recently been questioned.[38]

The 1562 persecution might be taken as the final event of the Conquest. Certainly within the colony there would be no more Spanish acts of violence as institutionalized, condensed, or widespread as this. Yet the Conquest of the peninsula as a whole dragged on for the rest of the colonial period, as the border between the colony and the unconquered territories shifted to the southeast only extremely slowly. These unconquered lands were dubbed *despoblado*, "uninhabited," by the Spaniards, but this was wishful thinking on their part, a euphemism that disguised the incompleteness of the Conquest. The *despoblado* was doubly inconvenient to the colonists. It provided a refuge for Mayas seeking to escape, temporarily or for good, the burden of Spanish economic demands. It also divided the bulk of the colony to the northwest from the southeastern portion of the colony centered on the small Spanish town of Bacalar. This southeast corner of the peninsula had once been densely inhabited by Mayas, but the Spanish invasion of the sixteenth century devastated the region. The fiction was that the Pacheco family conquered the Uaymil and Chetumal districts in 1543–45, and that the Spanish military activity in those districts in 1546–47 was the suppression of a rebellion. In fact, the Spanish campaigns of the 1540s were possibly the bloodiest and most horrific of a long series of Conquest actions, ranging from Montejo's *entrada* of 1528, to the incorporation of the Peten Itza into the colony in 1697, and the forced resettlement of the Tipu Mayas in 1707.[39]

The Spanish sources on the Conquest are both primary accounts by Conquest-era Spaniards, from the reports by the Montejos and their compatriots to the famous *relación* of Diego de Landa, and secondary histories, ranging from López de Cogolludo's seventeenth-century chronicle to Chamberlain's 1948 study based uncritically on Spanish sources.[40] The line between the two, however, is blurred. Spanish accounts were so strongly partisan, so driven to subjectivity by their format and purpose, that they virtually count as secondary. Conversely, the published histories are so overwhelmingly Hispanocentric, so incestuous in their use of each other and of the same Spanish sources, that they can be taken as primary—that is, primary sources on the European perspective.

For this reason, in both the primary sources and the histories (to 1948) the same two themes dominate the recounting of Conquest events. The first is a view of the Conquest as a herculean effort on the part of the Spaniards, requiring sacrifice and suffering. The second theme, which ennobles the motives of the conquistadors and provides a basis for justifying their methods, is that of conquest as the carrier of Christian civilization.

To some extent the nature of the primary sources—letters and *probanzas* to the Crown by conquistadors—determines the first of these themes. Such documents were written to convince the monarch and his councillors that the author had lost much and struggled much so that the king would gain much, thus justifying the rewards of royal patronage. Yet arguably this way of characterizing conquest enterprises strongly influenced conquistador culture and even the broader society's perspective. Few Spaniards would have been surprised or doubtful upon hearing Montejo speak of his campaigns as nothing but effort, as he did in a letter of 1529: "everything has been effort, such effort as has never been experienced in these parts."[41] Fifty years later Yucatan's governor at the time, don Guillén de las Casas, wrote to the king, "I have enquired whether the adelantado [Montejo] received any reward for the conquest of these provinces, and understand from those people from whom I have sought to know, that he was not given anything in recompense." Guillén's letter was in support of a petition by the conqueror's daughter, doña Catalina de Montejo, to receive various benefits on the strength of her father's many services, which were "worthy [*dignos*]" and "distinguished [*señalados*]."[42]

The priest Rodríguez de Caraveo wrote in 1533 that "from tremendous work and from illness" he had "suffered much over a period of about six years."[43] The sacrifices and services of the *adelantado* Montejo were such that he left his widow, doña Beatriz de Herrera, not only "old and sick" but "in extreme poverty."[44] Spanish reports, petitions, and histories repeat the same theme over and over, and subsequent generations invoked the sacrifices of their ancestors as the basis of requests for royal pensions.[45] It is no wonder that Chamberlain, reading nothing but these documents as the basis of his own account, concluded that the Conquest was made possible "only by the most sustained and persistent endeavor . . . one of the most prolonged military efforts the Spanish Indies witnessed."[46]

Similarly, Chamberlain began his study by declaring the story of the Conquest to be "a worthy part of the history of a great epoch" and "a great nation, Spain."[47] Such sentiments would have been applauded by the conquistadors, the later colonists, and their descendents, including Bishop Carrillo y Ancona. In what today seems a stunning denial, or, at best, ignorance, of decades of Spanish Conquest violence, late nineteenth-century Yucatec students were taught by Carrillo y Ancona that, following "the definitive triumph of the Spaniards" in 1541, "they treated the Indians peacefully and benevolently."[48] Accompanying the myth of colonial rule as benevolent was a characterization of its subjects as innately savage and childlike, yet amenable to being civilized. A fine example of the mental gymnastics the Spaniards went through to justify to themselves the entire brutal endeavor is this comment by Landa on his 1562 campaign: "Some of the Indians, out of grief, deluded by the devil, hanged themselves; but in general they all showed much repentance and willingness to be good Christians."[49]

Landa and other sixteenth-century Spaniards described and often praised aspects of what we would call Maya civilization.[50] Yet to them, Yucatan's pre-Conquest age was a dark era compared to that of colonial times. In most descriptions of the colony, the emphasis is on the buildings and inhabitants of Merida and the Spanish towns, with the Maya population reduced to the status of a material resource. One late sixteenth century report, drawn up for the archbishop in Mexico City, summarized Yucatan simply by listing its Spanish settlements. The entry for Merida remarked that the land around it contained "much cotton, which is sewn annually by the Indians, who pay tribute in cotton blankets, wax, and honey; there are very many indigenous people [*gente natural*], and cows, and mares sufficient for the land; there is much corn, as well as pigs and chickens. This city contains 100 houses and 190 Spaniards, 150 [African] slaves, 100 horses, twenty mestizos, and a very few mulattos, not even ten; there's a Franciscan monastery."[51]

It is striking how similar this report is to the comments of two British agents who visited the peninsula centuries later. "Beyond a few villages," one wrote in his diary of 1840, "we did not expect to fall in with any greater progress in civilization and were much surprised at finding Campeache [sic] so fine a Town; however, we were much more surprised at the extent and general appearance of Merida, [which had] every necessary thing to form an opulent and well populated city." Despite the fact that the expedition's purpose had been to explore and detail the ruins of Palenque and possibly other Maya sites, the official report to the British government ignored Yucatan's Maya face and detailed instead the architectural "beauty and splendour" of Merida. For these European visitors, as for Yucatan's European inhabitants, the peninsula's history began in 1542 and its vitality was rooted in Merida.[52]

CHICHEN ITZA: PRECEDENT WITH A TWIST

For the Mayas, of course, the peninsula's history began long before 1542. In fact, indigenous accounts of the Conquest suggest that for the Mayas the many centuries of pre-Conquest Maya history overshadowed the Conquest and colonial periods. As briefly discussed in the following pages, the Yucatec Mayas had a long history of outside influence, interference, and interaction, as well as a deep-rooted set of responses and accommodations to such experiences; the Mayas were fully aware of the significance and utility of historical memory.

The Nahua auxiliaries that Montejo brought with him to Calkini and other parts of Yucatan were not entirely unknown to the Mayas, whose name for these fellow Mesoamericans—Culhuas—had central Mexican origins. Furthermore, the presence of Nahuas in the Yucatan peninsula in the sixteenth century was paralleled by similar interventions to the south. As recorded in the Title of Acalan-Tixchel (Chapter 3), at the end of the Conquest era Chontal Mayas from the southwest end of the peninsula engaged in military campaigns, in conjunction with local Spanish settlers, against Yucatec Mayas to their east. Both of these intrusions, by Nahuas and Chontal Mayas, seem to have had precedents of some kind centuries before any Spaniard set foot on Yucatan.

Until fairly recently most archaeologists believed that in the ninth or tenth centuries Yucatan was invaded by Toltecs, warriors from the central Mexican city of Tula, who supposedly conquered the Mayas and ruled them for two or three centuries from a new capital at Chichen Itza. The so-called Mexican Period introduced a morally corrupt and highly militarized culture to a people previously more concerned with time and the planets than human sacrifice; Thompson, in his now outdated classic *The Rise and Fall of Maya Civilization*, used the analogy, drawn from a Kipling tale, of the wax moth getting into the beehive, bringing disorder and ultimately inviting destruction—the wax moth in the Maya hive being "a morally weaker culture which originated in central Mexico."[53] Other scenarios were proposed, but they were all variations on this same theme of bipolar civilizational opposites, with "sweeping changes of a debased nature" being introduced by crude Toltecs or Mexicans, in whose "bloody orgies" of human sacrifice defeated Maya warriors were executed on the Great Ball Court and Maya maidens hurled into the Sacred Well.[54]

This interpretation was based largely on two sources. One was archaeological evidence at Chichen Itza of a rapid rebuilding and expansion of the city in the tenth through twelfth centuries, featuring the same architectural and iconographic innovations found in Tula, which dominated central Mexico at the time. The other source was passages from the colonial-era Maya-language Books of Chilam Balam (see Chapter 7), which were taken as claims of the Mexican origin of Yucatec ruling dynasties and the moral disruption caused by the foreign invaders. The fact that the evidence was open to interpretation, to say the least, resulted in a confusing proliferation of creative constructions and re-constructions of the putative waves of migrations and invasions. The peoples starring in this drama were Toltecs and Mexicans (either the same or distinct), Itzas (either Mayas or Mexicans), Chontal (or Putun) Mayas (either Toltecized or Itzas or both), and Yucatec Mayas—who usually remained untainted culturally and/or ethnically during the time of their domination.[55]

Recent archaeological discoveries, however, have undermined the notion of a Toltec invasion of Yucatan. There is no doubt that during these centuries Maya culture was linked in profound ways to the Toltec city of Tula in central Mexico, and that this connection was expressed politically in Yucatan by an influential and powerful Chichen Itza. But the origins of this culture and the means by which it expanded appear increasingly complex. It is now evident, for example, that cultural ele-ments from central Mexico were in Yucatan before this period, and that Chichen Itza was a better-built and more architecturally innovative city than Tula—suggesting that expansion and influence may have gone in the reverse direction, westward from Yucatan.[56] Architectural reliefs at the central Mexican site of Xochicalco had long been viewed as some-what mysteriously Maya in style; a couple of decades ago another site in the area, Cacaxtla, produced a set of murals in which a battle be-tween warriors clad in Mexican-Maya military dress is depicted. Mean-while evidence of what might still be called a "Mexicanized" Maya cul-ture has been surfacing at archaeological sites up and down what is today Guatemala.[57]

A closer reading of ethnohistorical sources such as the Books of Chi-lam Balam also casts doubt upon the traditional Toltec invasion inter-pretation. As we shall see in Chapter 7, there is nothing in the Itza references in the Maya-language texts that clearly asserts that they were Mexican, let alone Toltec.[58] As has been the case in many other his-torical times and places, the ruling families in Yucatan claimed long into the colonial period to have a dual legitimacy deriving somewhat paradoxically both from their external origins and their long-term oc-cupation and rule of the region they eventually settled. However, the precise location of the pre-migration site of origin—like the historicity of the founding patriarch—is seldom clear. Nor, I would suggest, is it important.

What is clear is that it was prestigious for noble lineages to have alleged foreign origins—a probable legacy of centuries of multiple contacts and exchanges between central Mexico and Yucatan and an idea that must have been reinforced after the Conquest by the status of the foreigners from Spain. Thus what mattered to Mesoamericans was the symbolic value of these origin stories, their toponyms, and their protagonists. The best-known example of a Maya origin myth is that of Zuyua, or West Zuyua, from where nobles of the Canul, Xiu, and other lineages claimed to have come; accompanying the Maya myth is a historiographical myth asserting that Zuyua is a word of Nahuatl origins and was thus a place somewhere in central Mexico. In fact, there is no evidence of this at all. On the contrary, the significance to the Mayas of Zuyua was that it represented otherness and distance, a possibly sacred site that was not supposed to be identifiable as either a Yucatec Maya or Nahuatl toponym.[59]

Linguistic evidence, in fact, suggests one solution to the increasingly complex array of information on Yucatan's five centuries before the Conquest. It has long been apparent that Yucatec Maya contains a number of Nahuatl loan words, or words originally borrowed from the central Mexican language, while Nahuatl contains few if any Maya loan words—seemingly supporting the notion of central Mexican domination over Yucatan. But the discovery in the last two decades of large numbers of colonial-era documents written in Nahuatl and Maya[60] has enabled detailed linguistic comparisons to be made, one of which concluded that the heavy exchange of material culture between central Mexico and Yucatan lacked a substantial linguistic parallel; the evidence "strongly supports indirect and mediated contact" between the two areas before the Spanish invasion, not "direct and sustained contact."[61]

This view nicely complements one of the most convincing current interpretations based on archaeological evidence, which holds that Chontal (or Putun) Mayas (ancestors of the Chontals of Chapter 3) became Mesoamerica's "new power brokers" in the ninth century.[62] The Chontal Mayas were apparently not politically unified but they were to some extent culturally homogeneous and shared a common language. Whether or not it is accurate to say that the Chontal elite were "Mexicanized," that some Chontal groups were allied to the Toltecs, or that the Chontal and Itza Mayas were one and the same people, it seems likely that Chontal Maya expansion effectively spread and developed a culture most typically associated with the Toltecs in central Mexico and with Chichen Itza in Yucatan.

The Chontal Mayas or their influence expanded in all directions, taking advantage of (and thereby probably facilitating) the decline of the great cities of the Classic period such as Teotihuacan and Tikal— what was viewed until recently as "the Collapse."[63] One notable ninth-century Chontal (or Chontal-influenced) city was Seibal, down on the Pasión river to the southeast of the Acalan region; other Chontal groups established themselves (or became heavily influential) in the Guatemalan highlands, descended to the Pacific coast, or penetrated west into central Mexico. Chontal Mayas also moved northeast along the Yucatec coastline, using large seagoing canoes for economic and military purposes and establishing or taking over a series of trading ports, running from Xicalango to Champoton to Cozumel; one of these, at Isla Cerritos on the northern coast of the peninsula, served Chichen Itza, the city renamed after the Chontal group that seized it (or became highly influential there) in the ninth century and rebuilt it into a powerful regional center over the succeeding two to three hundred years. Seemingly politically dominant over northern Yucatan, Chichen Itza was also one of the centers of a vast Maya trading network that brought to the city pottery from central Mexico, gold from Panama, and many other goods from numerous points in between. In its heyday, Chichen Itza was probably the greatest metropolis in Mesoamerica.[64]

The sophistication, variety, and frequently the efficacy of Yucatec Maya responses to outside influence, interference, and interaction can be seen in the Maya reaction to the many Spanish intrusions into the peninsula during the sixteenth century. Although many of the long-term effects and implications of those intrusions may have been unprecedented, the experience was not.

How far this precedent can be pushed is another question. It is certainly tempting to seize upon the well-worn notion that "Chichen Itza was the host, or perhaps the consequence, of a momentous meeting between two radically different pre-Columbian people"[65] and to promote that story as a precedent and analogy for the Spanish-Maya encounter. The elision in the Chilam Balam literature (see Chapter 7) of events relating to the Itza and to the Spaniards would seem to support the idea. But therein lies the twist. The Books of Chilam Balam tell us of the colonial-era Mayas' *perception* of these past periods; they are not the direct historical evidence that early Mayanists took them to be. The Books do indeed draw parallels between Itza and Spanish arrivals, but not as momentous meetings. The emphasis instead is on similarities between periods of warfare and crisis, whatever the century and whomever the protagonists; indeed, the authors of such calamities are identified with considerable ambiguity, if at all.

From subsequent Maya points of view, the creation of Chichen Itza was not the watershed that archaeologists took it to be, nor (as we shall see) was the creation of a Spanish colony centered on Merida the watershed that historians took it to be. But the experience and memory of Chichen Itza did provide clues as to how such events could be understood in the present and incorporated into a perspective rooted in community continuities.

MAYAPAN: MYTHIC ARRANGEMENT

If Chichen Itza offers us, as it offered the Mayas, a way of accommodating the notion of foreigners in Yucatan, then the century of Yucatec history that preceded the Spanish invasion illuminates the Maya experience of internal dissension and prolonged civil conflict. This dimension of the Maya past also shaped Conquest-era events and is important to understanding Maya responses and perspectives. For example, there was a contrast between Maya images of Chichen Itza and Mayapan. The Chichen Itza tale internalized external relations; the Mayapan story externalized internal ones. In other words, Mayas interpreted interactions with outsiders during the Chichen Itza period from a highly local viewpoint, to the extent that the identity of the outsiders was blurred and the details of conflict were lost amidst a generalized lament on calamitous times. On the other hand, the civil war that appears to have violently destroyed Mayapan is viewed more as a positive moment of genesis, separating the narrators' lineages and communities from all others. Rather than a distant time of troubles, the period of Mayapan's fall was seen as the foundation of the present era in Maya history.

The city of Mayapan rose in the thirteenth century to a position of prominence in the peninsula; it collapsed in the fifteenth, almost exactly a century before Merida was founded. It has gone down in the historical record as the anchor of "an era of general prosperity" and political peace, or at the very least the capital of a loose federation of regional dynastic powers.[66] Situated about sixty miles west of Chichen Itza, Mayapan imitated (albeit on a less impressive scale) much of the architectural style of the city it replaced as the dominant city in the region. Its layout appears to have been a novel attempt to control internecine conflict; Mayapan was a walled city, large and densely inhabited with some fifteen thousand people, and divided into neighborhoods that may have housed noble representatives from the surrounding districts of the peninsula. The Cocom *chibal* (lineage), who had been important in Chichen Itza, were powerful in Mayapan but not totally dominant.[67] Thus the Mayapan arrangement appears to have been both a solution to the twelfth-century violence and disorder that followed Chichen Itza's downfall and a mechanism for sharing power among Maya dynasties for generations.[68] Office and authority were accessible to the male representatives of a number of noble families, whose rivalries were further controlled through marital alliances. This political system may have had precedence at Chichen Itza; it certainly continued, loosely within the format of Spanish-imposed *cabildo* government, throughout the colonial period.[69]

There is, however, a twist here too. Maya politics at the community level during the colonial period may look fairly peaceful, but that was largely because colonial rule prevented political factions within and between communities from resorting to violence and offered a litigation-friendly legal system as an outlet for hostility. No doubt Mayapan's secret was a similar mechanism or outlet for factional feuding; to think of the city as the site of harmonious Maya coexistence is to fall into the trap of the old-school Mayanists who romanticized the Mayas as peace-loving star-gazers corrupted by the brutal Mexicans—whose influence disappeared with Chichen Itza's fall and Mayapan's rise. The Mayapan arrangement, as told by scholars, is a myth. But, like all myths, it has some basis in reality: there was a deep-rooted tradition both of internecine conflict, and of various attempts to control such hostilities.

Of particular interest here is how later generations of Mayas perceived Mayapan's reality.

The arrangement at Mayapan lasted over two centuries until, in the 1440s, Xiu nobles massacred members of the rival Cocom *chibal*. Archaeological evidence shows that in the subsequent civil war Mayapan was destroyed and gradually abandoned. No city rose to replace the fallen capital (not until Merida was created to dominate the region a century later). Instead the noble families of the peninsula withdrew to its various districts and settled into an uneasy peace—the Chel a tad to the north, the Pech further to the north, the Cocom a little to the east, the Xiu to the south, the Canul and Canche to the southwest, and so on.[70] The impression given in Maya sources such as the Title of Calkini (Chapter 5) is one of migration to new and open lands.[71] The implication is that a dozen phoenixes rose from the ashes of Mayapan, and that this moment of genesis, not the Spanish Conquest, produced the world as it was when such accounts were composed. Such an interpretation of the past, intended to assert the legitimacy of settlement, occupation, and rule, was made necessary by several circumstances, both before and after the Conquest.

First, these districts were probably well inhabited before the post-Mayapan dispersal—by these same noble families as well as others. Thus in order to preclude prior settlement claims and at the same time seize the legitimating political legacy of participation in the Mayapan arrangement, the slate had to be wiped clean. Second, the regional powers of the century between Mayapan's fall and Merida's founding were little more than petty federations of small *cahob* (municipal communities) loosely bound by the domination of one local dynasty or oligarchy of noble families. The lack of centralized authority and the limited territorial control of each province is reflected in the absence of monumental architecture dating from this period; there was construction, to be sure (at the southeastern site of Santa Rita Corozal, for example), but it hardly compared in scale and scope to Mayapan, let alone to earlier sites such as Chichen Itza. The lack of a sixteenth-century equivalent to Mayapan meant the Spaniards were forced to proceed in a piecemeal manner in their campaign of Conquest, although, paradoxically, the highly localized nature of politics and community identity facilitated the eventual transition to a colonial system that relied on indigenous self-rule at the community level.

The colonial system was the third reason why the Mayas viewed the Mayapan collapse, not the Conquest, as their history's great watershed. For a small number of Spanish settlers and administrators to live off and govern a far greater number of native subjects, the colonial system of taxation and government had to some extent to be indirect. This in turn made two factors crucial: political stability and the partial cooptation of the indigenous elite. Spanish officials were thus concerned with confirming the pre-existing social status, local political position, and territorial arrangements of the established Maya nobility—particularly those who had collaborated early on in the Conquest. This coincided with native noble interests (see Chapters 5 and 6) and encouraged an emphasis on sixteenth-century continuities and the promotion of legitimating factors that were decidedly pre-Conquest; Mayapan (and the power shake-down following its collapse) conveniently fit the bill.

The significance of Mayapan, then, was not so much its past glory as a peaceful and prosperous Maya metropolis—the mythic arrangement of scholarly tradition—but the role played by the fall of the city in the creation of a new era in Maya history. What was important was not what one's ancestors had done in Mayapan, but that they were present at its collapse, and thus contributed to the post-Mayapan arrangement, in which political and territorial claims were asserted, consolidated, and validated. That was the myth that mattered to the Mayas, the one that helped determine how they dealt with the Spaniards and the Spaniards' own myth—Merida.

Upon the founding of the city of Merida, the Montejo family built their main residence on the central plaza. It took up half of one side of the plaza and was maintained by Montejos until 1828. Its doorway, commissioned in 1549 by the elder Montejo and still standing (see Figure 1.1), consists of a spectacular Plateresque façade featuring the two Montejos, father and son, standing on open-mouthed Maya heads. The work appears to have been carved by Maya masons from Mani working under Spanish masons brought from Mexico City or Cuba.[72] The Maya heads are usually taken to represent anguish in defeat, their mouths

Figure 1.1. *The portal façade to the Montejo House, Merida. Photograph by the author.*

open in pain and lament; or, as the heads appear to be severed, the faces are seen as death-masks. Either way, the image is one of subjugation, the literal embodiment in stone of Montejo's assertion that in the 1540s the Conquest was completed.

However, if Maya masons did work on the façade, they may well have seen these faces differently; perhaps, for the workers who helped carve the stone, the open mouths were a permanent but inaudible scream of protest, a symbol not of death but of vitality despite being underfoot. It seems plausible, in fact, that the image of conquest was read differently by Mayas than it was by Spaniards, not only by the stonemasons but also by the Maya men and women who, put to service in Merida's Spanish houses, walked by the Montejo house year after year, century and century. There was certainly the notion in Maya culture that ancestors retained some semblance of vitality through their connection to the living. The head played an important iconographic role in that ideology, as carved or drawn images of heads represented the ongoing significance and presence of revered ancestors.[73] Furthermore, we know now that the Conquest was indeed viewed differently by the Mayas, from texts which, copied and nurtured in native communities from generation to generation, gave voice to those open Maya mouths.

Alonso Canche recounts in one such text how, as a boy, he had seen a party of Spaniards and Nahuas led by one of the Montejos enter his home *cah* of Calkini. The scene that ensued would have been viewed by those Spaniards, as it was later recorded in their histories, as a simple act of submission—an acceptance, after years of warfare, of Spanish domination. But, like the façade of Montejo's house, the story can be read differently. Surely, for Alonso Canche, the scene symbolized the dignity of the defeated Maya lords, whose submission was made ignominious only by the undignified behavior of the crude and avaricious foreigners. This interpretation of submission as a symbol of Spanish greed was, like the stone heads screaming silently through the centuries, a subtle protest that proved to be permanently relevant to the Mayas of Yucatan.[74]

RECONTEXTUALIZING CALAMITY

CHAPTER 2

The trumpeting of the Spanish Conquest in a 1948 study as "a worthy part of the history of a great epoch, the sixteenth century, and of the history of a great nation, Spain" may be too insensitive to indigenous perspectives for modern tastes.[1] But an overly zealous sympathy for the conquered can be equally pernicious. One recent writer, for example, has characterized the Conquest period as "a monstrous project" that left in its wake a "silence [that] was immense, terrifying. It engulfed the Indian world from 1492 to 1550, and reduced it to a void. Those indigenous cultures, living, diverse, heirs to knowledge and myths as ancient as the history of man, in the span of one generation were sentenced and reduced to dust, to ashes."[2]

While the spirit of such rhetoric may be laudable, it ironically does a great disservice to the indigenous survivors of this period. As the Maya texts presented in Chapters 3 through 10 demonstrate, native culture was neither silenced nor reduced to a void. In fact, the body of literature presented here reflects so much of the complexity and vitality of Maya culture during and after the Conquest that the material can seem overwhelming.

Indeed, these texts are seldom simple narrations of past events. Drawn from a variety of genres, or types of historical document, and from a variety of communities across the Yucatan peninsula, the sources presented in these chapters often prompt more questions than they answer; the stories they tell can seem contradictory and the perspectives they represent can appear elusive. The Title of Acalan-Tixchel (Chapter 3) is almost a Conquest account without a conquest; the community histories known to scholars as primordial titles (Chapters 3, 5, and 6) are at times confusingly preoccupied with the names of people and places; the language used in the Books of Chilam Balam (Chapter 7), volumes which compiled a great variety of cultural information as though they were community libraries, is frequently opaque; the sound-bite histories known as annals (Chapters 4 to 6) can seem frustratingly restrained in their descriptions; and the examples of letters and petitions written in the early colonial period (Chapters 9 and 10) might at first seem too remote and stylized to qualify as accounts of the Conquest.

Yet at the same time these documents are deep reservoirs of cultural and historical information, overflowing with the kinds of fascinating insights and conundrums that the book's title is intended to evoke. These texts tell us a great deal about the Spanish Conquest, Maya views of it, and much more. In the present chapter I offer some comparative, analytical observations on three themes: calamity (demographic disaster, military encounter, and personal violence); continuity (from pre-Conquest to colonial times); and corporatism (as a framework that helps explain Maya reactions to the Spanish presence as well as their interpretation of subsequent events). Further comments on the nature of each text then begin each of the chapters.

Maya accounts of the Conquest thus demonstrate cultural survival —but not in a purist sense. They do not offer a monolithic Maya response to the Conquest or a homogeneous Maya counterpart to the Hispanocentric perspective offered in Chapter 1. Maya-language texts represent a multiplicity of Maya memories and interpretations; at the same time they reflect the profound impact of Spanish colonial settlement and rule. Colonial Maya perceptions of the past are just that— both colonial and Maya. This is symbolized by the fact that the Maya accounts were written down in the Yucatec language by indigenous notaries using a slightly modified version of the Spanish alphabet. Franciscan friars taught Maya nobles how to write alphabetically, probably beginning in the 1550s. Meanwhile, colonial administrators required each Maya community, or *cah*, to adopt the governmental format of the municipal council, or *cabildo*. The Mayas easily adapted the *cabildo* to their own system of local politics, granting, for example, particular importance to the post of notary.[3]

It was Maya nobles and notaries who wrote down these accounts of Conquest times, but they were written decades after the events described and, in some cases, then copied out over centuries.[4] We are given glimpses of the responses of Conquest-era contemporaries, but by and large we are viewing events through the eyes of generations of colonial-era Maya Christians who could not so easily identify with ancestors whose patterns of dress, nomenclature, worship, conflict resolution, and so on were somewhat different from their own. These texts are thus products of the Conquest as much as accounts of it, while at the same time being repositories of authentic (colonial) Maya voices.

CALAMITY

Accounts by Spaniards of the conquest of Yucatan did not lack for descriptions of violence and bloodshed. There was often considerable tension in the new Spanish American colonies between the clergy on the one hand, and settlers and civil officials on the other. Friars commonly accused conquerors and colonists of committing various atrocities against the indigenous population. Both the Dominican friar Bartolomé de las Casas and the Franciscan Diego de Landa wrote general denunciations of what the conquistadors had done in Yucatan. "The Spaniards massacred countless numbers," alleged Las Casas in 1552, and they devoted seven years to "despoiling and exterminating the inhabitants of this land." According to Landa, the first colonists "inflicted upon the Indians unheard-of cruelties."[5]

Both friars also recorded individual incidents of brutality. Las Casas' anecdotes focus on children. One baby, the friar alleged, was taken from its mother and cut up for dog food by the elder Francisco de Montejo; a boy, "the son of a chieftain of a certain village," had his ears and nose cut off because he was unwilling to leave with and serve the Spaniards.[6] Landa's list of atrocities is similar, with a particular emphasis on the mutilation, torture, and killing of women and children; he comments on the callousness of the conquistadors, describing them as "laughing" as they committed their crimes. Unlike Las Casas, Landa spent most of his career in Yucatan, and can thus claim to have been an eye-witness to —for example—one conquistador having "hanged from the branches of a great tree near one village many Indian women, and hanged their infant children from the mothers' feet."[7]

This catalogue of horrors could go on for pages—as indeed it does in several of the works of Las Casas. But our concern is the perspective of the indigenous population, so many of whom were the victims of these "wicked Spaniards" and their "outrages." Do Maya accounts record similar, or even the same, incidents? Is there a comparable emphasis on Spanish, as opposed to Maya, deeds? Is there likewise an accompanying tone of moral judgement and a characterization of Spanish actions as—to use a modern term—war crimes, as suggested by the attitude of the perpetrators, the civilian status of the victims, and the non-military context of the incidents?

Let me begin to address these questions by briefly turning to one of the Nahua accounts of the Conquest of the Valley of Mexico—the account from Tlatelolco. This text includes a summary of conquest violence so adroit and evocative that it was made the symbolic and titular passage of the best-known edition of "the Aztec account of the Conquest."[8] Even in a more literal translation, in which the phrase "the broken spears" is lost, the passage still conjures up much of the horror of battles fought in streets and homes: "And on the roads lay shattered bones and scattered hair; the houses were unroofed, red [with blood]; worms crawled on the roads; and the walls of the houses were slippery with brains. And the water seemed red, as though it were dyed, and thus we drank it."[9]

Yet as representational of the Conquest as these phrases might be, they include no clear statement to confirm our assumption that all the blood, hair, and bones being described are those of the Mexica inhabitants. Language and style aside, the passage could almost depict events in Bosnia or central Africa in the 1990s as much as Tenochtitlan in 1521; its focus is the calamity of war, expressed through images of material dislocation (both of homes and humans), rather than specific atrocities committed by Spaniards against indigenous defenders of the Mexica city.

Likewise, Maya accounts of Conquest-era violence seldom portray bloodshed and calamity as Spanish atrocity, either in general or anecdotal terms. Had Conquest-era Mayas been given the opportunity they could no doubt have corroborated the details of incidents such as those recorded by friars Las Casas and Landa. It is thus highly ironic that one of the few inklings we have of such testimony comes in a letter of complaint against the activities of that same Diego de Landa. The petition, signed in 1567 by two *batabob* (Maya municipal governors) of the Xiu *chibal* (lineage), and two of the Pacab, lamented that 1562 brought to them "a persecution of the worst that can be imagined [from] the religious of San Francisco, who had taken us to indoctrinate us, but instead of doing that, they began to torture us, [from which] many of us died or were maimed."[10] As discussed in Chapter 1, the toll of death and mutilation from Landa's inquisition of 1562 was considerable; the cruelty and context of the campaign underscore the notion that this was an episode of the Conquest, rather than a post-Conquest event. Still, the 1567 Xiu-Pacab letter describes the events of only one brutal summer and provides no first-hand, detailed account of the preceding half-century of violence.

Furthermore, when we turn to Maya sources that look back on the full sweep of the Conquest period, and which appear to have been generated for an entirely native audience, there is little sign of the specificity and context that characterize the Xiu-Pacab petition. For example, in the Books of Chilam Balam (Chapter 7), in particular that of Chumayel, the arrival of "true Christians" and "the true God" marks the introduction of various miseries: the seizing of tribute, church fees, purses, and corn cobs, a mass robbery the Spaniards accomplish by hair-pulling, torture, lies, and the firing of guns. Another passage in the Chumayel text, although explicitly referring to the pre-Columbian arrival of the Itza in Yucatan, makes a clear connection between sickness and foreigners in general, and provides a description of disease which seems to depict the sixteenth-century epidemics that decimated the Maya population—aching bones, high fever, pustule fever (probably smallpox, the main killer), burning chests, stomach pains, consumption, and headaches.[11]

The European invaders, however, are listed *among* the calamities of the era, rather than as the cause of them all. Christianity itself is not blamed for the afflictions that accompanied its introduction (most in fact preceded it). On the contrary, Maya accounts are post-conversion, written in an alphabet introduced by the Franciscans and reflecting a Christianized Maya perspective. The evidence is scattered throughout the Maya texts: pagan images are called "devils," for example; community leaders write to the king of Spain requesting that more Franciscans be sent to the province; and one Chilam Balam account of Conquest-related calamity ends with exhortations to the Maya audience to accept the word of "Dios."[12]

The Spaniards, too, are neither directly nor frequently blamed. Passages in the Book of Chilam Balam of Mani similar to those from Chumayel and Tizimin do not refer specifically to the Spaniards but to an invasion of foreigners who establish themselves as the new rulers. Although these invaders "do harm," they are not directly blamed for most of the disorder and calamitous events of the period—such as children disrespecting parents, people going barefoot, trees bearing little fruit, madness and adultery. The purpose of the passage seems ahistorical; it aims to provide an anatomy of calamity, not a contextual analysis of it, rather like "The Orphan's Mournful Song" in the Songs of Dzitbalche, a lament on the loss of family and friends that never states how they died.[13] By recounting the Conquest in the form of pre-Conquest prophesies that could refer to the Itza as well as Spanish invasions, and by merely implying that the foreigners caused a series of "misfortunes," the Chilam Balam text doubly mutes the link between Spanish Conquest and Conquest-era calamity.[14]

The conqueror-calamity link is also muted in the primordial titles, but in a different way. Primordial titles, or *títulos*, were municipal histories whose purpose was to promote the political and territorial interests of the community (*cah*) and the lineage (*chibal*) that dominated it. To this end, such titles typically included accounts of the pre-Conquest founding of the community by that *chibal*, the latter's role in the Conquest, and the subsequent confirmation by Spanish colonial officials of community land boundaries and the ruling lineage's social and political status.[15]

The purpose of the Pech primordial titles (Chapter 6) was to portray the Pech as allies of the Spanish conquerors (a topic to which I shall return shortly). These documents thus do give some account of Conquest-period violence, but in the context of civil war as much as ethnic conflict. "When the foreigners came here to the land of these districts," the Pech accounts explain, "there were no Maya people who wished to pay tribute to these first foreigners." It is thus the uncooperative Mayas who are blamed for the general misfortunes of the Conquest period, as well as for specific incidents such as the war of 1546, caused by Maya leaders who "came west to deceive the people and organize the war."[16] The context of most of the violence described in the Title of Acalan-Tixchel (Chapter 3) is also conflict among Mayas—in particular the late sixteenth-century campaigns by Chontal Maya Christians to bring other Maya communities into the colonial system.

Similarly, the Title of Calkiní (Chapter 5) cites Spanish abuses— mostly the violent seizure of people to be unpaid servants and porters[17] —but the impression given is that what was offensive to Mayas was not the taking of captives per se, but the choice of captives (nobles and community leaders) and their treatment (being carried on poles like animals, for example, and forced to strip). And while the title often mentions the slaves of Maya lords, there is no direct suggestion that the treatment of captive Mayas by Spaniards amounted to slavery. With respect to violence, there is ambiguity in the description of who was responsible (apparently Mayas as well as Spaniards) and of the specific nature of the violence (a theme of sexualized violence is introduced but not clarified).

All in all, the grievances expressed by Mayas parallel many of the abuses cited by Las Casas and Landa but lack any details or elements of tone and perspective that would provide a basis for comparison and contrast. This is because in Maya-language documents Spaniards are often incidental to Conquest-era encounters between rival Maya groups; references to Spaniards tend to be either neutral or intended merely to validate a claim or account (as discussed below). This is no doubt a reflection of colonial realities and, in the case of documents intended for Spanish eyes, a question of political, diplomatic, and legal expediency. But it also relates to the broader fact that in Maya accounts of the Conquest depictions of violence tend to lack moral judgement.

In accounts such as the Pech titles, both Maya and Spanish groups gather their forces, engage in attacks, murder named individuals, and commit large-scale killings, but these incidents are not described in any of the kind of gory detail found in the Mexica accounts,[18] nor is there any indication of judgment on the part of the author.[19] For example, the Pech account of the fighting in Saci-Valladolid in 1546 is summarized in the phrase "then the killing began." The term used for "killing," *cimsabal*, is simply descriptive (it does not mean "massacre" or "slaughter") and conveys reciprocity; Mayas and Spaniards killed each other.[20]

The failure of the Pech authors to denounce Spanish violence and to defend Maya aggression on the grounds of ethnic solidarity is paralleled in the Chontal account of the 1525 Cuauhtemoc affair. In this incident, the Chontal leader Paxbolonacha chooses to betray the captive Mexica leader Cuauhtemoc rather than join him in an anti-Cortés conspiracy. As a result, instead of the Spaniards being killed by allied native forces, Cuauhtemoc is bound, baptized, and beheaded.[21] Although there is a hint in the Chontal account of an apologia for Paxbolonacha's actions (that is, that he acted on moral principle), the matter-of-fact narration of the incident fails to portray any of the three protagonists, Cortés, Cuauhtemoc, or Paxbolonacha, in either a clearly positive or strongly negative light; each acted quite reasonably according to the imperatives of self-interest and the interests of his subjects. For Paxbolonacha, as for the Pech rulers to the peninsula's north, it was entirely rational for Maya leaders in the early sixteenth century to view the Spaniards as a temporary blight whose best remedy was an expedient alliance; by the time the permanence of the Spanish presence was clear, the playing up of that alliance arguably remained the most prudent course of action.

The Cuauhtemoc affair symbolizes in many ways the depiction of violence in the Maya primordial titles; even where the acts of violence or the calamitous ramifications of the Conquest are more substantial, as in passages in the Pech titles, neither the Spaniards nor their native allies (the authors of the accounts) are to blame. Nor are the collaborators in any way portrayed as betrayers of their fellow Mayas; the roots of conflict lie rather with those leaders committed to resistance and determined to deceive others into following them. Thus an historical memory of violence and calamity has been maintained, but it has been partially recontextualized as a result of Maya disunity and the localization of self-identity, and of the decision by some Maya nobles to pursue Spanish favor as a means of resisting complete subordination.

CONTINUITY

Another dimension to this recontextualization of Conquest-era calamities is the emphasis in Maya accounts on the continuity of indigenous life through the period of the Spaniards' arrival and settlement, which, in effect, relegates the Spaniards to secondary protagonists. This perspective complements well the promotion of the Pech and others to the status of conquerors. I would like to highlight three themes of the Maya emphasis on Conquest-era continuities: the persistence of everyday hardship, especially that derived from social inequality; continuities in local rulership; and the role played by Maya perceptions of time.

The evidence for the first of these three themes is contained mostly within the Books of Chilam Balam (Chapter 7), in which certain passages appear to reflect a Maya perception of the Conquest as a perpetuation of life's daily hardships, rather than a disruption or primary cause of them. Most of these hardships are depicted as stemming from social inequality. The list of Conquest-era woes contained in the Chumayel text is a standard lament,[22] comparable in some ways to the tone of lament and the declarations of misery that are fundamental to the style of address used in colonial-era petitions (Chapters 9 and 10). In such documents Maya municipal councillors (*cabildo* officers) use many of the terms also used in the Chumayel text to protest their poverty (*otzil*) and the misery (*numya*, which also means "poverty") inflicted by the abuse or excessive demands of particular Spanish officials or priests. From the Chumayel perspective, these officials abuse "the children of the *cah*" (*u palil cahob*), a common euphemism in petitions for humble or subject people; indeed these officials are also "the *cah* leeches that suck on the poor commoners (*mazehualob*)."[23] This is surely a class perspective that cuts across ethnic boundaries, a wry commentary on the nasty nature of everyday life among the unprivileged.

From the viewpoint of Maya commoners, class inequities persisted through the Conquest period as a result of efforts by the Maya elite to maintain their political and social positions (the second continuity theme).[24] From the other side of the social coin, the perpetuation of local political authority was, as might be expected, positively perceived and tenaciously promoted. This is reflected in various ways in Maya accounts of the Conquest. One of these is the treatment of baptism; the acquisition of Christian names, a potentially momentous break with the past that is frequently seen in the documentation, appears symbolic, almost superficial. In early-colonial legal records we find baptized Maya individuals referring to their parents by all-Maya names, but there is often little other indication that the Conquest has occurred during this person's lifetime.[25] Likewise, in the Title of Chicxulub, Nakuk Pech describes how he was a *batab* (municipal governor) when the Spaniards came, then he "entered the water" and became don Pablo Pech, an *indio hidalgo* (a special category of native nobility), after which he carried on being a *batab*.[26] Thus baptism is presented without any reference to Christianity or conversion, but as a symbol of continuity in office or in landholding, of a successful transition from pre-Conquest to post-Conquest rule and possession.

Literally illustrative of this portrait of the Conquest as name-changing is the Xiu family tree, in which the transition to colonial times is indicated by the acquisition of Christian names (Chapter 8; Figure 8.1). There are numerous such examples from elsewhere in colonial Mesoamerica. In the pictorial genealogy of the lords of Texcoco, the Conquest is likewise visible only in the change in naming patterns from one generation of rulers to another, as is the case in the Codex Muro and in many of the pictorial-textual manuscripts from central and southern Mexico known as *lienzos*.[27] Comparable textual examples can be found in passages of genealogical chronology in the Chontal Title of Acalan-Tixchel and the Quiché Title of Yax; in both texts, the Conquest is indicated by an unremarked shift from pre-Conquest to Christian nomenclature. A few Conquest details are briefly mentioned,[28] but in the text from Yax the full impact of the Conquest is illustrated by the names of the next generation of Quiché lords—"don Juan de Rojas and don Juan Cortés . . . the offspring of Tecum Q'uikab, grandson of Quik'ab."[29]

That the Nahua and Maya accounts refer to the Spaniards in more or less neutral terms also indirectly emphasizes the continuity of indigenous rulership. Just as Spaniards are not strongly condemned for their role in the violent confrontations of the Conquest, so are they named quite dispassionately as beneficiaries of indigenous labor and tribute; this is true of the Cuauhtinchan account and of Nahua titles, as it is of the Maya titles.[30] Spaniards are even portrayed in a somewhat positive light when performing official tasks that legitimated the status of local nobles, validated boundary agreements, or reduced tribute burdens. The *oidor* Tomás López, for example, who in 1552–53 reformed colonial administration in Yucatan under authority from the *audiencia* of Guatemala,[31] is credited in the Pech primordial titles with having succeeded in a mission given him by the Castilian king to protect the Yucatec natives from Spanish abuses, to confirm in office the *batabob* of each *cah*, and to lower tribute rates.[32]

In the highland Guatemalan primordial title known as the Annals of the Cakchiquels, two Spaniards are presented as saviors of the Cakchiquel Mayas, both of them governors of the Guatemalan colony.[33] The thoroughly negative portrayal in this text of the conqueror Pedro de Alvarado does little to offset the impact of the hagiographic treatment of two of his successors. On the contrary, the depiction of individual Spaniards as good guys or bad guys, combined with the lack of any blanket condemnations or demonizations of the Spaniards, effectively humanizes the invaders. In other words, the Mayas saw the Spaniards as fellow human beings, not as gods to be admired, demons to be feared, or dogs to be disdained; the invaders, like the natives, earned admiration, fear, or disdain on an individual basis.

There is no Yucatec equivalent (in the primordial titles or Chilam Balam literature) to Alvarado, no one Spaniard who is blamed by the Mayas for the horrors of the Conquest, but there are some minor exceptions in the Yucatec texts to the otherwise neutral or respectful representation of Spaniards. One is a hint of mockery in the characterization of Spaniards in both the Pech titles and the Chilam Balam of

Chumayel as "custard-apple eaters, custard-apple suckers."[34] Both texts give the same innocent explanation for the nickname—"never before had custard-apples been eaten"—but this does not convincingly dispel one's suspicion that the foreigners were being laughed at. Another hint of disrespect is found in the Calkini account of the presentation of tribute to Montejo.[35] The dignity of the Maya nobles is contrasted with the crude rapacity of the foreigners, who rush to grab the proffered tribute goods. Even so, the tone of disdain is fairly mild, and the Nahua auxiliaries come across as equally responsible for the breakdown in decorum.

The final aspect of this second theme of continuity is the Maya experience of the Spanish invasion. Like the constructed Maya memory of the Conquest, the actual experience of it for many Mayas was one of continuity and predictability as much as disruption and change. A corollary to the absence of moral condemnation of the Spaniards as evil or reprehensible in Maya texts is their depiction as a group seeking predictable goals (tribute, servants, deference) by predictable means—ritualized diplomatic encounters involving the exchange of goods and assurances of friendship behind which lay unmistakeable threats of military violence. That the Mayas understood the tension between diplomacy and violent hostility is well illustrated by a massacre in the late 1530s by Cocom nobles of a delegation of Xiu nobles who had been granted safe passage across Cocom territory to make a pilgrimage to Chichen Itza (see Chapters 4 and 8). Throughout the Conquest period in Yucatan the standard tactic of both Spanish expeditions and the regional ruling dynasties of the Mayas was to establish (and if necessary betray) one temporary alliance after another.

Thus Maya factions perceived the Spaniards as new political players in the peninsula that might be of use in the pursuit of long-standing rivalries;[36] they could not possibly have predicted the long-term effects of European disease and centuries of migration from Spain. Certainly Nahuas and Mayas were correct in the short run in assuming that the Spaniards' presence and the accompanying violence and disruptions were temporary, and that their purpose was to do what indigenous lords would do—establish a system of indirect rule and tribute exaction, which was more or less what the *encomienda* system was.[37] Again, if this was true in central Mexico, it was even more so in the Yucatan peninsula, where two generations of Mayas witnessed Spaniards coming and going numerous times. Not only did few Yucatec Mayas experience dramatic, large-scale violent confrontations with Spaniards such as those in central Mexico and highland Guatemala, but many became subjects of Spanish rule after little experience of military hostilities with Spaniards.[38]

If dramatic and violent episodes in the Conquest punctuated what was otherwise a gradual process that may have been perceived by Mayas as characterized more by continuity than change, there are hints in the Maya accounts that Mesoamerican conceptions of time may have bolstered the impression of continuity (the third and final continuity theme). Indeed, the treatment of chronology in the Maya accounts of the Conquest seems highly suggestive of Maya concepts of temporal cyclicity.

Indigenous *katun*-round dates are more dominant than linear chronologies (using sixteenth-century Christian-calendar dates) in the Books of Chilam Balam; the *katun* cycle is also present in the primordial titles. The conceptual and temporal linking of Itza and Spanish invasions in the Chilam Balam accounts is paralleled in the titles by an interspersing of events surrounding the Spanish Conquest and the fifteenth-century Mayapan wars (following the collapse of Mayapan hegemony) in such a way as to suggest patterns of repetition and continuity. The story of the Canul elite leaving Mayapan and founding *cahob* in the Calkini region is inserted between accounts of first, Canul and allied *batabob* presenting tribute to Montejo and welcoming their new *encomendero*, and second, a regional boundary agreement forged in the wake of the Spanish Conquest (Chapter 5). The Pech titles likewise fold fifteenth-century events into accounts of sixteenth-century ones, with a similar tale of post-Mayapan migration and *cah* foundation inserted into a description of the Pech role as Spanish allies in the Conquest (Chapter 6).

The use of nonlinear chronology was of course unique neither to this time period nor solely to the Mayas; as a Mesoamerican culture trait the topic has been well explored.[39] The Nahuas, for example, also used notions of temporal cyclicity, of the past's prediction of the present, and of meaningful continuities from pre-Conquest times to de-emphasize change and to counter the potential trauma of disjuncture with the prehispanic past. Mexica accounts of the Conquest invented or recontextualized tales of omens that foretold and helped to explain the disaster of military defeat;[40] the earliest extant text of a Nahuatl play, an adapted Christian drama titled "Holy Wednesday," depicts the coming of Christ as a well-prophesied event that served to "recapitulate ancestral patterns of penance and world renewal";[41] Nahua primordial titles integrated Spaniards and Christianity into the pre-Conquest past as well as the present.[42]

Just as Nahua concepts of time have been used extensively by scholars to explain Nahua understandings of history before and after the Conquest, so have students of the Mayas been quick to pick up on the theme. One historian has suggested that the Maya memory of periodic invasion from the west may have contributed to their "never perceiving or acknowledging the full significance of the Spanish Conquest," while "under the circumstances their cyclical view of time must have been a great source of comfort."[43] The Maya association of the Spaniards with previous foreign invaders, the Itza, has also been emphasized, with sixteenth-century Mayas imagined searching the Books of Chilam Balam to find, through an understanding of the past, a meaning in "circumstances of social and psychological disruption." The implication of these interpretations is that the Maya may have viewed the Spanish Conquest as a calendrically determined inevitability.[44]

While such a perspective is certainly one part of the picture, there is also a risk in emphasizing the contrasts between Maya and Western concepts of time—that the Mayas thereby become exoticized as the Other, romanticized along the lines of the early Mayanists' vision of a peace-loving people ruled by star-gazing time-priests. There are certainly differences between Maya and Western views of time and the past—indeed the contrast between Maya and Spanish perceptions of the Conquest era is a central theme of this book—but the fact remains that both Mayas and non-Mayas saw time as both linear and cyclical, rather like a multidimensional corkscrew. Depending on how the corkscrew is viewed, different perceptions of time become dominant; thus the differences are ones of emphasis.

The Mayas themselves perceived the parallels between their temporal corkscrew and that of the Spaniards. The Annals of Oxkutzcab, for example, reveal an interest in correlating native and Spanish linear chronologies, and the Books of Chilam Balam, particularly that of Tizimin, demonstrate a Maya appreciation of the multiple cycles of the Christian calendar.[45] Maya notions of temporal cyclicity were not only not unique, they were also not absolute; as argued earlier, the descriptions in the Chilam Balam of Chumayel of the misery inflicted by the Itza/Spaniards do not reflect the Maya acceptance of conquest as ordained by the cyclical calendar so much as the perception of regrettable continuities in Maya life.[46]

It is thus very possible that the appearance of Maya concepts of time in Conquest accounts is more than a reflection of indigenous discourse elements in the texts, but represents a post-Conquest response specifically to the Spanish invasion—not so much in the sense that past catastrophes were reinterpreted as harbingers of later ones and thus provided the reassurance of predictability, but more in the sense that historical repetition was used to mollify and mute the memory of conquest calamity. Not surprisingly, this response to the Conquest reflects something of the cultural impact of colonial rule (as was clearly the case with the Nahua examples above). For example, in the Xiu perspective on the Conquest, as told by Gaspar Antonio Chi, the prophet Chilam Balam anticipates the arrival of Spaniards and Christianity, predicting that "a white and bearded people . . . would become lords of the land, doing no harm to anyone who received them in peace"; furthermore, a cross symbol is introduced by Chilam Balam "a few years before the Spaniards came" in order to prepare them for imminent change.[47] The Chi account does more than simply make the Conquest predicted and palatable; its purpose is to explain how the people of Mani so willingly accepted Spanish rule and the Christian faith.

The depiction of the invasion as anticipated and positive turns the Conquest into an anti-conquest, an event anticipated by its own impact. Elements of temporal cyclicity play an important role, but they are part of a broader emphasis on aspects of continuity. The trick of turning calamity into continuity effectively weakens the impact of the Conquest by denying its uniqueness and its inexplicability; more than this, it also serves to deny that the Conquest, as the Spaniards saw it, ever occurred.

CORPORATISM

Maya perspectives on calamity and continuity were two sides of a Bermuda triangle that served to make the Conquest disappear; the third side was corporate opportunity. This is most strikingly illustrated by the phrase that inspired the title of this book; in their narratives from Chicxulub and Yaxkukul, Nakuk Pech and Macan Pech each introduce themselves as *yax hidalgos concixtador en*, "I, the first of the *hidalgo* conquistadors."[48] The Pech, as a lineage (*chibal*) negotiating political and social status during Conquest and colonial times, are exemplary corporate opportunists.

In their primordial titles, the Pech seek to identify themselves so closely with the Spaniards that they themselves become conquerors. The violence of the Conquest is perpetrated not by Spaniards against Mayas, but by other *chibalob* against the Pech and the Spaniards; the Conquest thereby becomes "the history . . . of how much suffering we went through with the Spaniards because of the Maya people who were not willing to deliver themselves to Dios."[49] Here the Maya people are those from outside Pech-controlled areas, but later in the title the phrase seems to refer to commoners, with the Pech denying their Mayaness, making themselves a lordly Us in opposition to a Maya Them. Thus both regional rivalries and a strong sense of class identity intrude into and complicate what might otherwise be a tidy distinction between the Spanish conquerors and the Maya conquered.

The Pech were not, of course, the only Maya conquistadors. In the late sixteenth century, don Pablo Paxbolon led a series of Chontal Maya campaigns into uncolonized territory to round up Mayas to be relocated, converted or reconverted, and otherwise incorporated into the Spanish colonial system. The Xiu collaboration in the Conquest's military campaigns stretched from the early sixteenth century to the seventeenth, when Mayas from Oxkutzcab avenged the killing of Spaniards in the same uncolonized region where the Chontals had campaigned. When, in the 1660s, don Juan Xiu called upon this legacy to support his claims to privileges of *indio hidalgo* status, he too was effectively asserting his identity as a Maya conquistador.[50]

For Maya nobles, the word "conquistador" was understood not only as a military term but, more significantly, as a designator of status. When the Spaniards granted their Conquest-era allies—the Canul, Pech, Xiu, and other nobles—the status of *indio hidalgo*, "Indian nobleman," the "Indian" part denied any possibility of equality with Spaniards, even though the *"hidalgo"* part granted Spanish-style privileges such as exemption from tribute. However, Mayas usually dropped the word *"indio"* (a term generally ignored by colonial-era Mayas), thus allowing *"hidalgo"* to become an assertion of equality. The use of *"conquistador"* in conjunction with *"hidalgo"* fortified that assertion. The Pech use of *"conquistador"* was thus somewhat paradoxical, simultaneously marking a claim to be leading participants in the Conquest and denying the Conquest's existence as the Spaniards conceived of it.

To identify a perspective that denies the Conquest is not to suggest that the Maya nobility were in a state of denial regarding the colonial implications and ethnic dimensions of the Conquest; indeed it is the harsh structural realities of colonial rule that necessitated Pech attempts to mask their subordination to Spanish authority by associating themselves with that authority, by emphasizing a nonethnic dividing line between commoners and nobles and thus reconfiguring the Spaniards' binary view of colonial society. As we have seen, stressing continuities from precolonial times had the effect of weakening what was from the indigenous noble perspective the negative impact of the Conquest; associating one's class or dynasty with the Conquest had a similar effect.[51]

The Pech position is further illustrated by similar examples from elsewhere in colonial southern Mesoamerica. For example, the Pech assertion of equality with the Spaniards as fellow conquerors is equaled and then bettered in a primordial title from Oaxaca. In this Nahuatl-language narrative, Oaxacan Nahuas not only defeated their local enemy (the Mixtecs) but also the Spaniards themselves, capturing two of the symbols of Spanish power, their African slaves, and forcing Cortés himself to request peace. In an inverted version of the same story, told by the Mixtec community allegedly vanquished by the local Nahuas, these Mixtecs ally with Cortés to crush the troublesome Nahuas.[52]

In reinterpreting effective defeat as historic victory, Yucatec Maya nobles were joined not only by Mixtecs and Oaxacan Nahuas but also by Cakchiquel Mayas. In the *Fiesta del Volcán*, held annually in the central plaza of the Guatemalan provincial capital, Cakchiquels and descendents of Tlaxcalan Nahuas played out an elaborate Conquest drama. While the Spanish audience enjoyed the performance as a ritual reconstruction of Maya defeat at the hands of the founders of the colony, for the indigenous participants, the most meaningful elements of the ritual celebrated the incompleteness of the Conquest and Cakchiquel political survival. In other words, in their interpretation of this Conquest enactment, it was the Cakchiquels who were triumphant.[53]

The Cakchiquel and Oaxacan examples would seem to differ significantly from the Yucatec perspectives by including an ethnic dimension. This was not necessarily the case. The participants in the *Fiesta del Volcán* were not from the entire Cakchiquel region, but from the indigenous communities, or *chinamit*, of Antigua; the pyramid-like volcano symbolized *chinamit*, not ethnic, pride. Likewise, while ethnicity undoubtedly played a role in the Oaxacan Nahua and Mixtec rivalry, it tended to be secondary to a more narrowly defined sense of corporate identity, that of the municipal community.[54]

These two Oaxacan titles and the Pech titles were written for the same purposes, all having survived in the files of legal proceedings over land disputes between indigenous nobles and communities. The self-promotion of the Pech accounts certainly represents the corporate perspective of the *chibal* (patronym-group or lineage), and reflects a sense of identity so oriented towards *chibal* as to give the Spanish invasion a more opportunistic than tragic spin. Yet a parallel corporatism is also at work here; in promoting the Pech *chibal*, the authors of the titles also repeatedly state their provenance, the *cahob* (Maya municipal communities) of Chicxulub and Yaxkukul, and reaffirm the authors' positions as *batabob* (governors) of these communities. Likewise, the Chontal title, while structured around the dynastic sequence of Paxbolon's ancestors and sons, is anchored to the fortune and fate of the region's *cahob*. The Calkini title, featuring pre-Conquest and Conquest-era roles by leaders of various *chibalob*, is even more overt in promoting the importance of the *cah*, for it is Calkini that ties together the subordinate *cahob* of the region and their various elite *chibalob*.

Just as we are given perspectives based not on ethnicity, but on kinship and class, so are we given the views not of nations or provinces, but of individual *cahob*—and where regionalism or patriotism does play a part, it is the micropatriotism of Acalan, or the superficial regionalism of the Pech, where communities are linked only by the *chibal* of their ruling lords, after whom the region is named (Ceh Pech), although even the name is seldom cited. In this sense, Maya views of the Conquest parallel not only the views of a Oaxacan Nahua community, but Nahua views from central Mexico, which also reflect the continued centrality of the *altepetl* as the focus of social and political activity, identity, and loyalty.[55] For both Mayas and Nahuas, the arrival and demands of the Spaniards were understood in the context of the Mesoamerican corporate perspective; these were not "Spaniards" as opposed to "Indians," as was the Spanish view, but a group of outsiders from a foreign *cah* or *altepetl* with whom the community had to deal as it would with any other such group.

Two additional, interrelated dimensions to this corporate perspective tie together the roles played by *cah* and *chibal*, by community identity and loyalty to lineage. These dimensions are geopolitical organization; and land. In both cases, the Conquest was seen by Maya leaders as a chance to consolidate the territorial claims of *cah* and *chibal*.

Geopolitically, early sixteenth-century Yucatan was divided into a couple of dozen loosely defined districts. The identification by one venerable Mayanist of sixteen "native states" or "provinces" has long been taken as gospel.[56] However, there is little evidence of the territorial integrity and centralized nature of many of these entities; attempts to categorize these "provinces" into three types contribute to our understanding of the complexity of Maya politics in the century after Mayapan's collapse, but they are not enough to support the idea that "the province was the most stable political unit through time."[57]

I suggest instead that the two most consistently stable political units before as well as after the Conquest were the municipal community, the *cah*, and the dynastic patronym-group or lineage, the *chibal*. "Provinces" or political districts were thus defined and made possible by the domination of a cluster of *cahob* by one *chibal* or an oligarchy of *chibalob*. In most areas one *chibal* was predominant, often represented by a *halach uinic* (a regional ruler who was typically the *batab* or governor of the dominant *cah* of the district). But the taboo on marriage within a *chibal* (which also lasted the colonial period) and the incipient nature of "state" organization, meant that each district was effectively ruled by an oligarchy of inter-married elite families.

The Canche, for example, were junior partners with the Pech in the Motul (or Ceh Pech) district to the northwest and with the Canul in the Calkini (or Ah Canul) district to the southwest, and the Pacab were similarly allied to the Xiu in the Mani (or Tutul Xiu) district. The Cupul were the most prominent *chibal* in their district, but there was no *halach uinic* in the area, nor even consistent amity between Cupul-ruled *cahob*. The regional political alignment of a particular *cah* was thus determined by the identity of its elite families and their relationship to the dominant dynasty or dynasties in the area.[58]

Spanish sources indicate that those *chibalob* most consistently hostile to the invaders were the Cocom (of the small central district centered on Sotuta), and the Cupul (of the larger Cupul district to Sotuta's east). Those most willing to ally with the Spaniards were the Pech, Chel, Canul, and Xiu, as well as the Chontal elite headed by the Paxbolon dynasty.[59] The Maya sources presented in this book confirm this, offering evidence (albeit often inflated) of the collaborative role played by these various *chibalob*.[60] These surviving Maya accounts do not include, for obvious reasons, the kind of anti-Spanish narratives that Mayas from Sotuta and the Cupul districts might have told.

The only hint that we do have of the eastern view is from the Book of Chilam Balam of Tizimin; that *cah* is located in the Cupul area, whereas Chumayel and Mani, the origin communities of the other Chilam Balam texts containing Conquest accounts, are in the Xiu district. The contrasts between the Chilam Balam accounts are not as strong as might be expected (see Chapter 7), but they do suggest some east-west antagonism that helps to explain these districts' different responses to the Spaniards. The idea that the coastal districts more readily appeased the Spaniards because these *chibalob* were relatively recent Mexican immigrants, unlike the Itza descendents who led the interior districts, is not convincing; it seems more likely that the ancient Xiu-Cocom rivalry simply helped push each *chibal* into opposing positions vis-à-vis the Spaniards—who colonized the peninsula from the west, where they concentrated their efforts and founded their city.[61]

In short, the geographical division between Spanish allies and opponents is more east-west than coastal-interior; the Xiu-Cocom feud provided a sharper boundary than would otherwise be expected between a west that was throughout the colonial period more thoroughly colonized than the east. The western elite *chibalob*, coming to terms with the persistence and subsequent permanent presence of the Spaniards, attempted to turn it into an opportunity to bolster their local territorial, political, and social positions.

Both *cah* and *chibal* were built upon territorial control and access to cultivable lands. It is significant that although Mayas resisted the imposition of the *encomienda* in the late 1520s and early 1530s, its implementation in the late 1540s was no doubt facilitated by its emphasis upon taxes, rather than land. The incessant Spanish demands for the payment of tribute and the provision of labor were clearly a cruel burden, especially at a time of massive mortality from epidemic disease. But, at least in the early colonial period, the Spaniards did not seriously threaten native landholdings. On the contrary, in implementing the system of colonial exploitation centered on the *encomienda* and *repartimiento*,[62] the Spaniards took pains to settle boundary disputes and confirm territorial rights. For Spaniards, this meant conducting and recording on paper legally valid land surveys and agreements. For Mayas, this meant taking the opportunity to consolidate the territorial underpinnings of community and lineage. Stability of land tenure was thus in the interests both of the Spaniards and the Maya elite.

This is the origin of the land-survey sections in some of the primordial titles (Chapters 5 and 6). Although such surveys date from the 1550s, it was not until the eighteenth century that increased competition for land between and among Mayas as well as Spaniards obliged communities to produce documentation proving ownership. For Mayas, this proof not only involved records of past border agreements but also the deep-rooted history of the community and its ruling families. As the accounts below show, land not only sustained *cah* and *chibal*, but it acted as a mnemonic for collective memory; the toponyms of the countryside surrounding the community prompted remembrances of past events and present realities. Into the fabric of that landscape the Conquest was woven.

The Maya view of the Conquest and of colonization in Yucatan was by no means homogenous. Just as the mundane documentation reveals the Mayas to be skillful political actors on the colonial stage, especially in the form of the Spanish legal system, so do we find the Mayas actively engaging their own history with self-interest, with irony, and with a view to manipulating the present. The Mayas were very much aware of the ethnic conflict that lay at the heart of Conquest, but their interpretation of it also reflected the centrality of *cah*, *chibal*, and class to post-Conquest Maya society. The violence of the Spanish Conquest could be cyclical calamity as well as a metaphor for class relations as well as an expression of inter-*chibal* rivalries; colonial rule could offer confirmation of social inequality or confirmation of social privilege; the reduction of the Conquest to "the time of the arrival of the Spaniards" or to "this change of rulers" could be a neutral temporal reference or a lament.[63] The Yucatec sources certainly offer drama, bloodshed, and expressions of great anguish, but they also offer so much more—challenging us to think of the Conquest and its colonial aftermath from multiple and complex indigenous perspectives.

PART II

The Maya Accounts of the Spanish Conquest of Yucatan

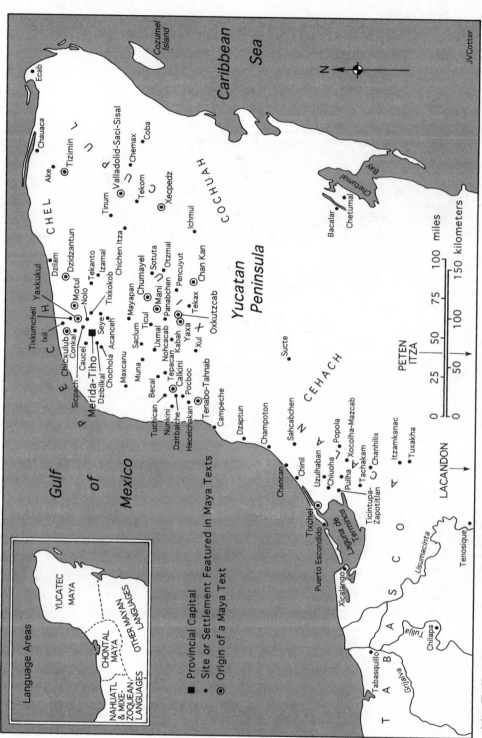

Language Areas

NAHUATL & MIXE-ZOQUEAN LANGUAGES

YUCATEC MAYA

CHONTAL MAYA

OTHER MAYAN LANGUAGES

■ Provincial Capital
• Site or Settlement Featured in Maya Texts
⊙ Origin of a Maya Text

Gulf of Mexico

Caribbean Sea

Cozumel Island

Ecab

Chauaca

Tizimin

Ake

Valladolid-Saci-Sisal

Chemax

Coba

CHEL

Dzilam

Dzidzantun

Xecpedz

Tekom

Tinum

Motul

Nolo

Tekanto

Izamal

Chichen Itza

COCHUAH

Tixkumcheil Yaxkukul

Conkal

Tixkokob

Ichmul

Ixil

Seye

Acanceh

Mayapan

Chumayel

Sotuta

Otzmal

Bacalar

Chetumal

Chetumal Bay

Chicxulub

Caucel

Chochola

Saclum

Mani

Panabchen

Pencuyut

Merida-Tiho

Sicpach

Dzibilkal

Ticul

Tekax

Chan Kan

E

Maxcanu

Muna

Uxmal

Kabah

Yaxa

Oxkutzcab

P

Becal

Tepacan

Nohcacab

Xul

Yucatan Peninsula

Tuchican

Nunkini

Calkini

Pocboc

Dzitbalche

Hecelchakan

Tenabo-Tahnab

Sucte

Campeche

CEHACH

Dzaptun

Champoton

Sahcabchen

N

PETEN ITZA

Chencan

Chinil

Uzulhaban

Chiuoha

Popola

Xocolha-Mazcab

Itzamkanac

Tixchel

Ticintupa-Zapotitlan

Pulha

Tachakam

Chanhilix

Tuxakha

Puerto Escondido

Laguna de Terminos

LACANDON

Xicalango

T A B A S C O

Tabasquillo

Chilapa

Tulija

Tenosique

Grijalva

Usumacinta

N

0   25   50   75   100 miles

0   50   100   150 kilometers

JVCotter

Map II. *Yucatan*

THE INSINUATED CONQUEST
The Chontal Account from Acalan-Tixchel

Some readers may be surprised that the series of Maya accounts of the Spanish Conquest presented here does not begin in the colonial heartland of the peninsula, the area that
has become the modern state of Yucatan. Instead the account
below describes events on the very margins of the peninsula, down at
the southern end of what is today Campeche state (see Map II). There
are a number of good reasons, however, for beginning with the Chontal perspective.

First of all, this was where the Spaniards began. Certainly, as discussed in Chapter 1, there were Spanish landings at various points along
the Yucatec coast even before the central Mexican campaign of 1519–21.
But the first significant moment of permanent accommodation to the
Spanish presence in Yucatan took place during—and in the wake of—
Cortés's 1525 trip through the Acalan region. As we shall see, the decision by the Acalan ruler, Paxbolonacha, to side with Cortés rather than
the defeated Mexica ruler, Cuauhtemoc, initiated a gradual but profound incorporation of the Chontal Mayas and their ruling family into
the process of colonial expansion and consolidation. Paxbolonacha's
namesake and grandson (who was christened don Pablo Paxbolon)
ruled his people into the early seventeenth century with considerable
autonomy—while also acting as a tributary and agent of colonial rule,
even to the extent of rounding up unconverted Mayas beyond Acalan's
borders as late as 1604.

Furthermore, it was Cortés's descriptions of abundant Acalan that
partly inspired one of his protegés, Francisco de Montejo, to obtain a li-

cense in 1526 to conquer the Yucatan peninsula. Having acquired the dual posts of *alcalde mayor* of the province of Tabasco and governor of Yucatan—largely symbolic titles as Spanish Tabasco barely existed and Yucatan was as yet unconquered—Montejo conceived of a conquest strategy that would use Acalan as a base for expansion into the peninsula, and to that end his lieutenant Alonso de Ávila entered Acalan in 1530, where he received Chontal allegiance and material support. But before long the Spaniards decided that Acalan was too isolated to be an effective springboard of conquest (Montejo had also lost control of Tabasco to a rival), so Campeche, further north up the coast from Acalan, became base for the protracted conquest during the 1530s and '40s. The rest—told above in Chapter 1 and in the Maya accounts of subsequent chapters—is history.

One can argue, therefore, that chronologically and geographically it was in the southwest corner of the Yucatan peninsula that the Conquest story really began. In terms of the content of the Chontal account—the events of the conquest of Acalan and the viewpoint of the conquered—the narrative below also conveniently introduces some of the key aspects of the multifaceted Maya perspective.

For example, although the Chontal story offers some dramatic moments—imagine the Cortés-Cuauhtemoc-Paxbolonacha encounter as the opening scene to a movie, with the protagonists recalling the conquest of Mexico in a series of flashbacks!—the tale of the conquest of Acalan is lacking in great battles, sudden reversals of fortune, or defining moments of triumph and tragedy. Rather this is an insinuated conquest, consisting of the gradual introduction of elements of Spanish colonial rule, whose full implications are only apparent to us in hindsight, as indeed must have been the case for the Chontal Mayas themselves. Accordingly, violence plays a secondary role, the Spaniards are not depicted in negative ways, and the most notable conquistador in the narrative is don Pablo Paxbolon himself, the heir to a deep-rooted legacy of conquest, settlement, and legitimated rule. Ethnic identity is obscured by micropatriotism and the promotion of community—the *cahob* (Maya settlements) of the Acalan region centered on their capitals of Itzamkanac and Tixchel. It is further obscured by the expression of community identity in the form of representation by the dominant dynasty—from the semi-mythologized founder to the two Paxbolona-chas of the Conquest era to the Spanish son-in-law seeking to secure familial rights in the colonial law courts.

That Spanish son-in-law was Francisco Maldonado, a settler in Campeche who had married don Pablo Paxbolon's daughter Catalina in 1591.[1] It is thanks to Maldonado that the Conquest account from Acalan-Tixchel has survived. Between 1612 and 1615 Maldonado put together his *probanza de mérito* (literally "proof of merit"). A *probanza* was a document, or in this case a series of documents, that Spanish officials submitted to the Crown as a routine record of service. Most *probanzas* also were intended to support accompanying petitions for royal support, in the form of a pension, *encomienda*, or particular office (as discussed in Chapter 1). Maldonado's hope was that his *probanza* would win him an *encomienda*, specifically the right to the labor and tribute from the indigenous communities he and Paxbolon had conquered in 1604. Therefore central to the way in which the Spaniard presented himself to the Crown was an emphasis upon his connection to the noble and conquering legacy of the Paxbolon family. This connection had present and future implications, as Maldonado's son Martín was don Pablo Paxbolon's grandson and heir to his rights as regional ruler and nobleman. It also had roots in the past—hence Martín Maldonado's request that his grandfather don Pablo Paxbolon allow a copy to be made of the Chontal-language papers translated below (see the opening lines of the text). This 1614 copy of the papers ended up archived in Seville, where it remains to this day; Paxbolon's originals have long since disappeared.[2]

The Chontal text begins with the Maya version of a sixteenth-century Nahuatl chronicle that is no longer extant. This document charts the ruling dynasty of the Acalan region from its founding father to don Pablo Paxbolon, and then lists the *cahob* of the region. The chronicle is updated to 1612, when it was verified by the *cabildo* of Tixchel. An account of the arrival and gradual invasion of the Spaniards then follows. This opens with a notably neutral description of Cortés's 1525 visit and closes with a wry comment on the implied indolence of a new priest assigned to the region in 1603.[3] Of the substance, perspective, and tone of this account something has been said in Chapter 2, and indeed the reader will glean much more from a careful reading of it. It may be useful, however, to comment here on its genre, especially as some of the accounts of subsequent chapters can be similarly categorized.

The Chontal text is not a *probanza*—it was merely used by a Spaniard as part of such a report—but its genre, that of the primordial title or *título*, does have something in common with a *probanza*. As a colonial Mesoamerican genre, the primordial title by definition contains some elements of format and style that are Spanish in origin, others that are indigenous, and others that so reflect the regionally varied intermingling of cultural influences that they can only be deemed, for example, colonial Maya. Although *títulos* in Nahuatl have been studied for decades, it is only very recently that the full scope and nature of the genre has become apparent. Primordial titles are now being found embedded in testaments and in land litigation records, while it is becoming clear that other documents for long considered unique—such as the Popol Vuh[4]—are also primordial titles. Nor are titles limited to examples in Nahuatl and various Maya languages; they were written in perhaps a dozen different Mesoamerican tongues.[5]

All this variation makes summarizing the genre a hazardous business, but some characteristics can be described as common to most titles. The essence of a primordial title is self-promotion. Like the *probanzas* of Spaniards, Mesoamerican titles presented a particularly partisan and self-interested view of the past and present, albeit in a manner that was often deadpan and ostensibly objective. But *probanzas* and titles are very different in one crucial respect. The former always promote the interests of an individual Spaniard (and perhaps, by extension, his or her descendents). The latter always promote the interests of a native community; even if an individual appears to be the author and focus of a title, or the document revolves around the achievements and status of a dynasty or family, ultimately it is always their community that is being protected and promoted. Furthermore, while in both genres the self-promotion is intended to win a specific benefit from the Crown, Mesoamerican *títulos* are also intended as repositories of community memory; they are a collective effort at recording—and reworking—the past for the benefit of future community members.

This emphasis on community shapes each of the four constituent sections of a typical primordial title. These are, first, an account of the

Conquest, centered on a declaration of who first received the Spaniards; as discussed in Chapter 2, the depiction of conflict with the Spaniards is often muted in these accounts, in favor of an emphasis upon
putative alliances between Spanish and Mesoamerican conquistadors.
Second, these passages often give rise to (or follow) a description of the
origins of the community and a genealogy of the ancestors of these
Conquest-era leaders. Third, this narration then leads to an assertion
that the Conquest resulted in a confirmation by colonial authorities of
the social status and political position of the same Conquest-era leaders.

Fourth, the dominant theme of continuity and confirmation tends
to culminate in a ratification of territorial boundaries. In fact, the older
texts narrating precolonial and Conquest-era history were often added
to land records in the late colonial period; these compilation documents were inspired by the need for more binding legal proof of land
tenure as competition for land increased between and among indigenous communities and Spaniards. Their mix of land treaty and Conquest narrative make the Title of Calkini (Chapter 5) and the Pech
accounts (Chapter 6) typical in this respect. Significantly, the Title of
Acalan-Tixchel differs from these other texts in two closely related ways:
it is an original early colonial document (featuring copying and compilation only as far as 1612); and it lacks a final land-treaty or border-
survey section.

What the Chontal text therefore offers us is a possible example of
what a primordial title, at least a Maya one, might have looked like before colonial circumstances obliged native communities to add records
of land agreements—records that were by necessity strongly influenced by Spanish genres and legal formats. Although the cultural impact of colonial rule is still highly visible in the Chontal document, the
text also bears the legacy of a tradition of political propaganda, dynastic promotion, and community-centrism that can be seen in precon-
quest hieroglyphic texts, primarily those in stone.[6] It also carries traces
of a related oral tradition, as do the other Maya titles in this volume.
This is reflected both in the content of the texts (such as references to
tales being told and heard, and testimonies being spoken, written
down, and read out) and in their style (in reported speech, for example).[7] The many dimensions of the Title of Acalan-Tixchel's genre are

certainly a complex reflection of its cultural context. But the title is also a simple story—a compelling historical narrative told much as such stories would have been told back through the generations to the time when Auxaual came from Cozumel.

The Title of Acalan-Tixchel

Don Pablo hereby ratifies this petition [*petimiento*] [TAT:69v],[8] stating that he gave the original to the notary of the *cah* and asked him to copy the document, which he gave to Martín Maldonado. This was done with the authority of the *cabildo* of the *cah* [the municipal council], who affirmed that it is a valid statement and that this is his true signature: don Pablo Paxbolon.

I, [Pablo] Paxbolon, public notary[9] here in the *cah* of Tixchel, translate here [*acahoche dzibil*] what was written in the Mexican language[10] by Juan Bautista, a notary long deceased. This is how it begins:

Here in the *cah* named Santa María Tixchel, in the jurisdiction and territory of the town [*villa*] of San Francisco Campeche, of the province [*provinziail*] of Yucatan, on the tenth day of the month of January of the year 1567, appeared Francisco Felipe and also Luis García, *alcaldes*, and also appeared Alonso Martín, Pedro Naua, Hernando Kanan, and Antón Quiuit, *regidores*, on behalf of our great ruler [*ca no ahau la*], his Majesty [*su mag^d*]. I, Juan Bautista, notary of this *cah*, was also present. Don Pablo Paxbolon, governor here in this *cah*, appeared and announced that it was necessary to collect the statements of the elders, because he wished to hear of, and wished to know of, his origins and those of his grandfathers and fathers, lords a long time ago. The elders named Alonso Chacbalam and Luis Tutzin explained and declared that which begins here below:

In the beginning Auxaual came from Cozumel [*cuçumil*];[11] he came to conquer[12] the territories here; he arrived in order to gather together at the *cah* of Tenosique [*tanodzic*] his principal men—Huncha and Paxoc and Chacbalam; four counting Paxmulu—whom he brought with him when he conquered the territories.

The second ruler who came was named Pachimal,[13] the son of Auxaual, whose name was just written.

Then came the third of the rulers, named Chanpel, the son of Pachimal, spoken of above. This Chanpel was ruler when he went to conquer the Tatenam territories, there on the other side of Bolonlamat, called Términos [today]; some reached Dzabibkan [TAT:70r], next to Boca Nueva, others arrived in Holtun—Puerto Escondido [*puertos contito*] as it is called.[14]

Then came the fourth ruler, named Paxua, son of the aforementioned Chanpel. He was the ruler who brought people to Tixchel; for sixty or eighty[15] years they were settled at Tixchel. When wars broke out with the many people of Champoton and Cactam[16] and those of Popomena and also of Acucyah—[now] called Tabasquillo—they therefore left Tixchel and went to Tamactun—[which they called] Acalan.[17] Tayel, the *cah* of the Cehach [*ciach*] people, was there, and the people of Cihuatecpan [*çiuatecpanob*] were settled at the junction of the rivers. This was the region and the people of Iztapa [*ytztapan*], which were conquered by the ruler Paxua, along with the territory of the Cehach—[also called] the Mazateca—and also the foreigners,[18] whose territory came under the domination of Acalan.

The fifth ruler was named Pachimalahix; he and Macuaabin, his younger brother, were sons of Paxua. This was the ruler when they went to Chetumal [*chactemal*], which is beyond Bacalar [*bakhalal*]; having arrived, they were there five or six years, during which time began the payment of tribute to them. Then the foreigners arrived to seize Balancal.[19] Tzitzimit was their captain's name, and he asked the ruler Pachimalahix to share the tribute from the region; and because he did not wish to give it to him, he gathered together all the communities of the region and waged war for eighty days. After they had come back from this war and arrived in Acalan, they took over the lands of the people of Chakam. Then began the rulership of Macuaabin, younger brother of Pachimalahix, of whom we have spoken.

The sixth ruler was named Paxbolonacha, son of Pachimalahix. He was the ruler who settled Itzamkanac Acalan. While they were living there the Castilian man [*castillan uinic*] came, the captain Marqués del Valle.[20] This ruler, the aforementioned Paxbolonacha, had three sons, [the first] named Pachimalahix; he had a son named don Luis Paxua, who went away. The second son was named Alamatazel, who was the father of don Pablo. The third son was don Pedro Paxtun; he was baptized [TAT:70v]. He had no child.

The seventh one was don Pablo Paxbolonacha, now governor, son of the Alamatazel written above.

Here ended and concluded what was asked of and stated by the two elders, Alonso Chacbalam and Luis Tutzin. These were the only rulers, they declared, and these were the ones who protected the *cahob*; and thus did they declare before Hernando Kanan, Antón Quiuit, Alonso May, witnesses, residents.[21] I have faithfully put down the signatures of the *alcaldes* and my signature as notary: Francisco Felipe, Luis García, Alonso Martín, Pedro Naua, Hernando Kanan, Antón Quiuit. Executed in the presence of myself, Juan Bautista, notary.

This don Pablo Paxbolon, now governor, married doña Isabel. They had a daughter named doña Catalina, who married Francisco Maldonado, a Castilian man.

Francisco Maldonado and doña Catalina, whom we mentioned, had a son, Martín Maldonado, who is still alive.[22]

Then doña Isabel, of whom we spoke, died; and the governor don Pablo Paxbolon married doña Mencía, daughter of Diego de Orduña. They had a child named María, who is still alive.

On the twenty-first day of July of the year 1612, I, Pablo Paxbolon, notary of this *cah*, in the presence of the principal men named Marcos Chacbalam, *alcalde*, Juan Chacchan, Francisco Tutzin, *regidores*, and the other [officers], Agustín Paxbolon, Alonso Patzinbolon, Baltasar Paptucun, read it before them so that they heard of the origin, region, and people of the governor don Pablo Paxbolon. They said it was correct and that there was nothing in it that was not true; this was their statement. Therefore I set down their names and signatures here with [TAT:71r] my own signature as notary: Marcos Chacbalam, Juan Chacchan, Francisco Tutzin, Agustín Paxbolon, Alonso Patzinbolon, Baltasar Paptucun. In my presence, Pablo Paxbolon, notary.

On the fifth day of July of the year 1612, I copied the list of the names of the *cahob* of the people of Tamactun Acalan, written by the principal men, our fathers, who lived and died long ago. First of all I write down the *cah* where the ruler Paxbolonacha lives, whose name I write thus:

Acalan Itzamkanac *cah*

Tahobo *cah*

Tapib *cah*

Tacacau *cah*

Cacmucnal *cah*

Tanauibcab *cah*

Tauchcabal *cah*

Tahkakalaez *cah*

Tapacauichcab *cah*

Tixkanculim *cah*

Tanacomchutte *cah*

Tahcehxuch *cah*

Takunchelal *cah*

Tatok *cah*

Tamauitz *cah*

Petenmax *cah*

Tachakam *cah*

Tayel *cah*

Temax *cah*

Tahaalkantelal *cah*

Tahmalin *cah*

Tahkomtilal *cah*

Tahaazcab *cah*

Petenaku *cah*

Uxpeten *cah*

Uatunhobonnixtte *cah*

Takoolku *cah*

[TAT:71v]

Tachimaytun *cah*

Panuitzcab *cah*

Tahcacab *cah*

Tixmalindzunum *cah*

Tahbidzcabal *cah*

Tancut *cah*

Chanhilix *cah*

Tachantoppoltun *cah*

Homolna *cah*

Taocabal *cah*

Tahuli *cah*

Çacchutte *cah*

Taniuitz *cah*

Tappottelal *cah*

Tapaxtoh *cah*

Tahchacchauac *cah*

Takucaycab *cah*

Palibpetette *cah*

Tachiciua *cah*

Tayaxttelal *cah*

Tayaxakcab *cah*

Tuxakha, where the Captain remained for some days[23] and decapitated the Mexican, Cuauhtemoc

Taynpilal *cah*

Tahbudzil *cah*

Hoknadzic *cah*

Tabidzcabal *cah*

Tanohun *cah*

Kanlum *cah*

Tapaxua *cah*

Yaxhopat *cah*

Tapob *cah*

Tabolay *cah*

Tapom *cah*

Tapulemttelal *cah*

Tuholham *cah*

Tacachilal *cah*

Boteac *cah*

Tahmomoncab *cah*   Tadzumuycab *cah*
Tachilcabal *cah*   Tahchimal *cah*
Tuholham *cah*   Yaxahintun *cah*
Taykbalam *cah*   Tahkomcab *cah*
Tanochich *cah*   Temoch *cah*
Tamultun *cah*   Taychilak *cah*

Sixty-seven *Pueblos*[24]

At the beginning all the Mactun people were settled in the lands of Tamactun, as it is called in the language here [Chontal Maya], or Acalan, as it is called in the Mexican language [*mexithan*]; all the Mactun people were in the subject communities [*u tzucul cah*]; the end [of which list] is written on the back [of the page]. The name of their city [*no cah*, great *cah*] was Itzamkanac [*ytzankanaac*], from where governed the ruler, who was named Paxbolonacha. To assist him in his realm [*y ahaulel*] were his principal men [*u nuc uincilob*]; these were the rulers Mututzin, Kintzucti, Padzayato, and Tamalyaxun, as they were named. The Castilian men arrived in the year 1527. Their captain was named don Martín Cortés.[25] They entered near Tenosique [*tanodzic*] and passed by Tachix, emerging at the border of the lands of Çacchutte, and stopping for a while in the *cah* of Tuxakha. While staying there with their followers, they called for the summoning of Paxbolonacha, the aforementioned ruler. He assembled all his officers and rulers of his lands—the ruler of Tadzunum, the ruler of Atapan, and the ruler of Taçacto—because nothing could be done without informing these rulers of the aforementioned four subject communities. Thus they listened to what he began to tell them, to the statement by their principal ruler; [TAT:72r] he discussed with them what would be best for them under his rule, considering that he had been summoned by the Capitán del Valle,[26] the Castilian man, who was in the *cah* of Tuxakha. They said it was not appropriate for their ruler to go, as they did not know what the Castilian man wanted. Then one of the rulers, one named Ruler Palocem, stood [and said], "Stay in your realm and in your *cah*!" And he went before the Captain [Cortés] with some principal men named Patzinchiciua, Tamalbinyan, Paxuanapuk, and Paxhochacchan, companions of the ruler Palocem. When they appeared before the Castilian man, the Capitán del Valle, some of the Castilian men would not accept them, for someone must have told the Castilian men that the ruler [i.e. Paxbolonacha] was not there. Therefore the Captain said to them, "Let the ruler come, for I wish to see him. I do not come to make war; I wish only to go and see the whole country. I will be good to him if he receives me well." This he said to the men who had come on behalf of their ruler, who returned to tell their ruler Paxbolonacha, who was in the *cah* of Itzamkanac. All the rulers of the province's *cahob* were thus gathered together— this was for the second time—and he said to them, "Fine! I shall go and see and hear what he wants, the Castilian man who has come." And so the ruler Paxbolonacha went. And the Capitán del Valle went out to meet him with many gifts—honey, turkeys, maize, copal, and a great quantity of fruit. Then he said to Ruler Paxbolon, "I have come here to your lands, for I am sent by the lord of the earth [*u yum cab*], the emperor [*enperador*] seated on his throne in Castile; he sends me to see the land and those who live in it, not for the purpose of wars. I wish only to ask for the way to Ulua, to the land where gold and plumage and cacao come from, as I have heard." Then he [Paxbolo-nacha] replied that it would be good if he left, but that he should come first to his land, to his home, to his *cah*, where they would dis-cuss what would be best. "Let us rest first," the Capitán del Valle then told him; therefore they rested for twenty days. The ruler [*ahau*] Cuauhtemoc was there, having come with him [Cortés] from Mexico. And it happened that he said to the aforementioned ruler Paxbolo-nacha, "My lord ruler, these Castilian [TAT:72v] men will one day give you much misery and kill your people. In my opinion we should kill them, for I bring many officers and you also are many." This is what Cuauhtemoc said to Paxbolonacha, ruler of the people of Tamactun, who, upon hearing this speech of Cuauhtemoc's, replied that he would first think about what he wished to do about his speech. And, in considering his speech fully, he observed that the Castilian men behaved well, that they neither killed a single man nor beat a single man, and that they wished only to be given honey, turkey hens, maize, and various fruits, day after day. Thus he concluded, "I cannot therefore display two faces, two hearts,[27] to the Castilian men." But

Cuauhtemoc, the aforementioned ruler from Mexico, continued to press him about it, for he wished to kill the Castilian men. Because of this, the ruler Paxbolonacha told the Capitán del Valle, "My lord Capitán del Valle, this ruler Cuauhtemoc who is with you, observe him so that he does not revolt and betray you, for three or four times he talked to me about killing you." Upon hearing these words the Capitán del Valle seized him [Cuauhtemoc] and had him bound in chains. He was in chains for three days. Then they baptized him. It is not known what his baptismal name was; some say he was named don Juan and some say he was named don Hernando. After he was named, his head was cut off,[28] and it was impaled on a ceiba tree in front of the pagan temple [otot ciçin, devil's home] at Yaxdzan. Then the Capitán del Valle came with the ruler Paxbolonacha and all the Castilian men and all the indigenous men [macehual uinicob], and they arrived at the city [no cah] of Itzamkanac. While they were there they determined where a bridge could be made in order to cross our river, which was one league [humppel legua] wide. And thus they filled up the swampland in order to cross the river. It was finished in four days because they were very many men. They also cleared the way as far as Cehach, and two officers [nucba uinicob] [TAT:73r]—named Çelutapech and Macuaaua—were sent to organize things. Çelutapech died—he was killed by the Cehach men—but Macuaaua, his aforementioned companion, escaped and returned to the cah of Itzamkanac. For this reason, the Castilian men went on with trepidation in their hearts, but as they killed five or six of the [Cehach] soldiers upon arriving in Cehach, it was Cehach men who cleared the way through to Tayasal [ta ytza]. Thus the Castilian men reached the entrance to the island, but when they saw that they could not cross [the lake], they came back and took the route that emerged at Champoton.[29]

A year after the Castilian man, the Capitán del Valle, passed through here, the ruler Paxbolonacha went to a certain cah named Tachakam, where he died. Having died, he was placed in a canoe by his people, who brought him to their city [u noh cahil] of Itzamkanac, where they buried him. This ruler had been dead three years when other Castilian men came, passing through the same way the Capitán del Valle had passed through, entering at Tachiix and emerging at the *cah* of Çacchutte. It was not known which of those who came was their captain, but Francisco Gil, Lorenzo Godoy, and Julián Doncel were the principals and leaders [*u nucalob u chun u thanob*] of the Castilian men. When they reached the *cah*, they asked for the ruler; they were told, "He is dead." So they asked for his sons, who were brought before them. The oldest of the sons was named Pachimala-hix, the second, Alamatazel, and the youngest, Paxtun. They placed the eldest of the aforementioned sons in prison for two days and told him that he should give them tribute. And thus turkeys and maize, honey, copal, beans, squash seeds, and many other things, countless things, were given to them. Then they crossed the bridge, just as the Captain [Cortés] had crossed the river.

The *adelantado* [Montejo] did not pass through Acalan, through Tamactun; only his deputy [*u than*] arrived and went on to Champoton, where they [the Mayas of Acalan] went to see them [the Spaniards], and they stayed there a long time. They brought tribute and many times returned to assist them there at the aforementioned Champoton. Then they [the Spaniards] went to Yucatan to conquer its lands.[30] Then Pachimalahix died [TAT:73v], at which time the ruler-ship went to Alamatazel. During the period of his governorship the padres [*padreob*] fray Luis de Villalpando, fray Juan de la Puerta, and fray Lorenzo de Bienvenida arrived. These padres came at a time when they [the Mayas] had not yet destroyed and finished with listening to the words of their priests [*yakinob*]. The Castilian men came with the padres to conquer the land; they came to bring the truly true god [*u to u tohal chu*] and his word. They taught the people that already our gods were destroyed and the day had already come when their worship would be ended: "You will never again see them worshipped, and he who does worship them lives a life of deceit; anyone who does worship them will be really punished. For they have had their time. Therefore nobody shall deceive the people, for that time has now passed." All the principal men [*nuc uinicob*] and the ruler and all the *cahob* under their jurisdiction heard what those priests [*akinobi*] said.

Then the ruler Alamatazel died, but only after he had assembled all the principal men together and declared to them that he was dying with sorrow in his heart, for he had not held [*uyili*, seen] the singular faith of Christianity. "As my life is ending, I entreat you to serve one god [*huntzuc chu*]. I have seen and heard the word of the priests; it will not be destroyed and ended. The truth and goodness of their statements is becoming realized. Therefore you should seek and bring the preaching padres to preach to you and teach you." After making this speech the ruler Alamatazel died.

Then the rulership went to Paxtun, his younger brother and the son of Paxbolonacha. He heard the news of the teaching and the baptizing by the padres. And having discussed it with all his rulers, he gathered the *cah* officers to go look for the padre in Campeche; and so the ruler Paxtun went with his lieutenants [*u cuchulob*] to seek the padre who was in Campeche. God [*Dios*] wished it [TAT:74r] that the day after they reached Chinil, padre fray Diego de Béjar arrived from Tabasco. They met him there and declared to him, "My lord and father [*ca yum ca pap*], we have come here to seek you for the sake of all our children; we have come, leaving behind our home, our land of Acalan—whose second name is Tamactun—to fetch you so that you will come and explain to our ears and teach us of the word of that god Dios [*u than chu diossi*], for we have already heard news that men are being baptized[31] by you padres. We wish this too and thus we have come to seek you." Thus spoke the ruler Paxtun and his companions.

Having heard what these men said, the padre fray Diego de Béjar replied, "My sons, it gives me much pleasure that you wish to take your souls out of the hands of the devils [*ciçinobi*] and that you wish to hear and understand the word of God [*diossi*], for such a duty and burden is mine and that of us padres. But I cannot come with you right away, as I have my duties with my fellow padres. Therefore you would be well advised to return, for I will soon come back, either to Campeche or to Champoton, where I will meet whomever you may send for me." This was what the padre said. Therefore they went back to their lands at Acalan Tamactun. When one month had come to pass, which was the time designated for the fetching of the padre by canoe, they reached Campeche, to the pleasure of the other padres. Thus fray Diego de Béjar came, arriving at Tamactun Acalan on the twentieth of April of the year 1550; and his arrival brought great pleasure to all the people. Immediately all the principal men were gathered together—Kintencab, Çelutholcan, Buluchatzi, Caltzin, Catanatz, Papcan[32]—the principal men were called together by the padre, [who said], "My sons, I am aware that in order to seek me and bring me you went a long way, a journey of ten or fifteen days. I am pleased to be with you, although I have endured the miseries of the road and the canoe. First of all I must tell you that you cannot [TAT:74v] worship two lords, two fathers; only one father [*pap*] is to be loved. I have come to tell you, to explain, that the one single God is three in one person [*huntuntul diossi uxtul tu uincilel*]—God the Father, God the Son, God the Holy Spirit—who created the invisible heaven."[33] And he told them other things about the word of God. "I wish you all to come and show me your devils."[34] Having heard what the padre told them, they began to bring and display their devils, including the idol of the ruler Cukulchan,[35] also the idol of Tadzunum, the idol of Tachabtte, the idol of Atapan, Taçacto,[36] and the other devils, all of which were brought before fray Diego de Béjar—who burned them. Then he began to teach them to recite and sing the Paternoster, the Ave Maria, the Credo, the Salve, and the articles of the faith [*articulos dzonoçaob*].

Then they were given their names. The ruler was named don Pedro Paxtun; Kintencab [or the priest Tencab] was named don Mateo; and Caltzin was named don Francisco. And thus they became Christians.

The devils which had been buried in secret places by the people—such as a devil called Ek Chuah, another called Tabay, also the idol Ix Chel, and Cabtanilcabtan,[37] and many other devils in these places—were sought out in all the *cahob* of the jurisdiction. The guardians of the devils went to fetch them to be burned, for those men who kept them were imprisoned and beaten before the eyes of all the people. In this way the idols disappeared. Some willingly caused them to disappear; others caused them to disappear out of fear.

As already written in the document [*hum*], beginning with the second time the Castilian men passed through Acalan Tamactun—when Francisco Gil, Lorenzo Godoy, and Julián Doncel passed through—from then on tribute was taken and paid in Tabasco every six months.

Also every two months there was another which was not a fixed assessment, but still they took as tribute canoes and paddles, honey, copal, hens, cotton blankets, beans, maize, squash seeds, chiles, cotton, calabashes. Whatever [TAT:75r] else they wanted to be given, of both food and drink, they took as tribute to Tabasco—to him, Palma. Then the *cah* was placed in the hands of Diego de Aranda. We do not know who placed the *cah* in the hands [i.e. jurisdiction] of Campeche, but Diego de Aranda ordered us to send the tribute there to Campeche. When Diego de Aranda died, Francisca de Velasco [his widow] married Antón García; Antón García ordered us to take and pay tribute at Chilapa [*chilapan*].[38]

During the time that tribute was being taken to Chilapa, the *oidor* Tomás López[39] came from Guatemala in the year 1552. He then arranged for the tribute to be paid every six months, along with the quantity of tribute that was to be paid every six months. And Tomás López thereby threw out [i.e. ended] the canoe tribute; he threw out the tribute of hens, mantas, maize, honey, copal, beans, squash seeds, chiles, cotton, calabashes, paddles, and other lesser tributes from the territories of Tamactun Acalan. He also issued decrees [*prouiciones*] to the rulers of the communities confirming the governorship of each *cah*, and he ordered that the tribute carriers and those who carried loads for the Castilian men from one *cah* to another be paid, according to distance, one or two *pesos*, and a *tostón* or two *tomines*,[40] according to the journey and if the *cahob* were still in Tamactun Acalan. During this time the padre of whom we spoke left—that fray Diego de Béjar. Then the second padre to come, fray Miguel de Vera, baptized people and administered the sacraments [*sacaramentosob*].

On this second occasion there also came fray Diego de Pesquera, who talked to them about moving the *cah* to Tixchel for the second time.[41] This was during the governorship of don Luis Paxua, son of Pachimalahix as written above. At the beginning of the year 1557, in January, people from Champoton and Campeche came to clear the lands of Tixchel in order that people could move down there—because Acalan Tamactun was a long way for the padres to come and so they seldom administered the sacraments to them; and because [Tixchel] was just a league from where the padres came through from

Mexico, those of St. Francis, St. Augustin, St. [TAT:75v] Dominic, and the [secular] clergy, who spoke of the word of God; and because the Castilian men, the Spaniards, often passed through that way; and also because they would be near the governor and principal magistrate [*nohal justizia*] sent by our lord the king [*ca yum la Rey*] in order to administer justice to the subject people [*chanbel uinicob*]. For these reasons they moved them here to Tixchel. It was also ordered by the *encomendero*, Antón García, who for a period of four years cancelled tribute payment until they had arrived at this site of Tixchel, which was settled in the year of 1557, on the tenth day of the month of July.[42] Don Luis fled on the day of the saint [*tu pixan chuil*, the godly spirit] Mary Magdalene, the twenty-second day of the said month of July; he fled to Chinil, and died in the *cah* named Chiuoha. It was in the next year, 1558, on the twenty-fifth day of the month of April, that the people of Chiuoha discovered it, and they then told don Pablo the news; thus it became well known that he had died of an illness.[43]

The years fifty-eight and fifty-nine passed and the people still did not completely abandon Tamactun Acalan. They were kept in Chanh[il]ix by don Tomás Macua. There they had great arguments with the people from here [Tixchel], who did not wish to give up their lands in Tamactun Acalan and went down there to bring back food; there they seized them, bound them, and beat them; they seized and destroyed the canoes of anyone who came from Tixchel to take food. There were also people [under Macua] at Tixbahumilha, where they worshipped the devil. It was about this time that all the people were going to flee. But God willed the arrival of the Castilian men, the Spaniards—Castrillo, Juan Vela, Tamayo; it is not certain which one was their captain, but these were the three principal men. Fifty soldiers came here into the *cah* of Tixchel. The *oidores* had sent them from Guatemala to seize the lands of Lacandon and the Poo people, but they stayed here in Tixchel because they learned that the captain Lic. Ramírez had seized the Poo territory and then returned. Furthermore, when they were there [in Tixchel] they were told by padre [TAT:76r] Pesquera that it would serve God and King [*dios yithoc rey*] for them to prevent any opposition down there [in Acalan]; "It will be good to pass that way, for you will thereby reach Lacandon."[44]

And thus what they heard was well received by the Castilian men.

And they moved down the *cah* of Bote,[45] the people of Çilba, the *cah* of Tutul, and the people of Pan; and they went to the site of Acalan and seized don Tomás Macua, Martín Acha, Jorge Laon, and Alonso Pacbac, and moved down the whole *cah* as well as those who were in Tixbahumilha. They brought them down to Tixchel in the year 1560, as a result of which there was a great famine, causing Francisco Acuz and Diego Paxcanan, and also Achachu and Gonzalo Pazcanan and Martín Pactum—they were innumerable—to flee with their people and their elderly. They were brought out by don Pablo Paxbolon, who found them at the site of Sucte, as is more clearly shown in the *probanza* of don Pablo Paxbolon, who went to seek them in the year he became governor. They fled again in the year 1568 and again he found them, along with those who had fled before being baptized and who were living in the *cah* of Chakam. The reason why these old inhabitants had fled was that their masters would come and abuse them, because they were slaves of the ruler and the other principal men. They were called Lamat, Chacantun, Paçimactun, Atoxpech, Apaxtucum, Paxbolon, Chancha, Palocem, and others, who numbered about six hundred, including their women and children.

As soon as he found them he informed don Luis Céspedes, who was governor in this province [Yucatan] and was in the city of Merida, called Tiho in the Yucatec language, while the bishop—the first in this bishopric—was fray Francisco [de] Toral of the Order of St. Francis. He sent fray Juan de Santa María of the Mercedarian Order, who went to baptize and teach the doctrine to those who had been located. Their *cah* was named Zapotitlan, because the name of that land was not known, as some of the principal men called it Tachumbay, and others, Tachalte, and others said it was Tanaboo, and others, Tamacuy. So for this reason it was given the name Zapotitlan.[46] This *cah* of Tixchel was given a great deal of work because of these people— because of the commission which don Pablo Paxbolon, our governor, held from the governor who was serving in the city of Merida, by dint of which he made us clear the roads and open the difficult rapids of the Acalan river where the padre passed, and carry him in a chair where he could not pass.[47] This was so the unconverted who were in

Zapotitlan might become Christians, as we have said, and in order to
carry ornaments from our church, such as chalice, missal, chasuble,
frontal, adornment for the mass and also the images. And our sons
went to teach them the Christian doctrine. Likewise he made others
of us go in the year 1570, when we went to Puilha, and also to Tah-
balam, to bring out the refugees.[48] In doing this we labored greatly
carrying the padre, who was called Gabriel de Rueda, clergyman, and
also padre Monserrate, who was our vicar in Tixchel. And because
they were far off, they were brought to settle in Hunlucho, where
they lived and where we brought them ornaments and a frontal and
often carried the minister. And thus the people of Zapotitlan and
Xocolha were settled.[49]

In the year 1574, on the twenty-fifth of April, don Pablo learned
that Luis Ceh of the *cah* of Xocolha had gone among the refugees
and that he knew their *cah*, so he ordered him and also Juan Chab to
be summoned to the said *cah* [Tixchel] in order to question them and
know the truth of what they had seen. And having come, don Pablo
asked them, "Is it true that you have been with the idolaters?" To
which they replied that it was true that they had seen their houses
and their *cah*, but that they did not know what it was called nor how
many people there were.

Upon learning this don Pablo wanted to go there at once by virtue
of the commissions he held from the governors who ruled this province for the purpose of bringing out such idolatrous refugees. He
summoned his Mactun[50] people and chose up to a hundred of them
from the *cah* of Tixchel, and we opened a road from Zapotitlan to
Xocolha, bringing our weapons of bows and arrows, shields and
spears, in case they were needed. And we left Xocolha and reached
Tachunyupi, where we spent the night, and in the morning we all
departed and at the hour of vespers we reached their *cah*. And we
caught them by surprise; some of the women fled and the men took
up their bows and arrows and came against us. Therefore don Pablo
said to them, "Don't shoot your arrows nor let there be any casualties,
because we do not come to kill you nor do we come for you. Rather
I come only to see you in order to tell you the word of God, and for
that which the great king, my lord, sends me, for he orders me to love

you." To some of them this explanation seemed good, to others it did not, and one of them, who was named Pazelu, went to let his arrow fly in order to shoot don Pablo, but his arms were held from behind by Juan Chab, aforementioned *maestro* of Xocolha. And the principal men of the idolatrous refugees—who were named Paxmulu, and the others, Paxtun—seeing that it was don Pablo, went to him and said, "Lord, whether you come to wage war or come for us or come to kill us, here we are. Do as you wish!" He replied to them, "Lords, I do not come to wage war nor do I come to seize you. I come only to preach to you the word of God and that which his Majesty orders me to tell you, in order that we may all love one another and have the same will in our hearts, so that we may love God and enjoy the justice of his Majesty—which is the good life. It is for this that I come, and to open roads, which is why so many of us have come. And if we bring weapons, it is to secure ourselves against whatever might happen to us, for we do not know what people we may encounter." And having heard these explanations, they were appeased. While this was going on all the people, women and children, had gone away, so that almost none were left or to be seen in the *cah*, save for a few. And when don Pablo saw that there were no people, he asked them where they were, and that they be called, assembled, and reassured; and thus he calmed their hearts and they therefore undertook to gather together the people, who were assembled within two or three days so that no one was missing. And in order to reassure them, he requested and called some of them to go to see the *cah* of Tixchel and see the padre and the Castilians.[51]

Having been brought to our *cah*, their hair was cut,[52] and they feasted them and took them to see the Franciscan padre who was ministering to us, who was named fray Bartolomé Garzón; this was in the year 1575. And he began to teach them the four prayers and the articles, commandments, and what the Holy Mother Church ordains, and having learned it, the padre baptized them. And from this church they carried ornaments and images, just as the adornment for divine office has always been taken [from Tixchel] from which we have always had much hardship. Our fathers received the very same [burden], as appears at the beginning of this document, at the time when

the Capitán del Valle came out to our land—and always paying tribute to the king, our lord, as is written in the year 1527. This *cah* mentioned above is now Chiuoha.

An account of how we the Mactun people, who live in Tixchel,
went and campaigned to make Christians of the unconverted:

In the year 1583 there came those who escaped death, one of
whom, named Pedro Chan, came out at Chencan,[53] and taking the
sea coast toward the south, he came to where don Pablo Paxbolon
was in his *estancia*, which is near Tixchel and is where he lives. And he
began to weep when he arrived with his emaciated children and he
with an arrow in the middle of his back. And he said, "Lord don Pablo
Paxbolon, I come here to tell you that we are the remainder who are
left and have escaped death, for my comrades were killed by the refugees of Chunuitzil, who are of the Keb name[54] and are many in number. We are from Hecelchakan; we had come to Chunuitzil but the
Keb refugees came to kill us. Some of them shot arrows, some of
them threw spears; they killed our old men and the principal men
who ruled us, as well as the *ah cuch cab* Tuyu—the *açitiache*, as we
would say.[55] And we killed five or six of them. Many of my comrades
died, and many fled, and I was shot in the middle of the back. Some
of my comrades went to the forest, some of them returning to Hecelchakan; some of them, women, children, and some men went in that
direction without knowing where." When don Pablo heard that those
people were wandering about scattered through the forest without
knowing where they were going and that it was to be feared that they
might perish of hunger and thirst, he went to Xocola and Zapotitlan,
which was of his jurisdiction and whose [people] he had brought out
of the forest, and he assembled them and sent them into the forest to
parts and places which they [Chan's comrades] might have reached,
sending out parties of men in all directions and charging them to
gather together those people of Hecelchakan who were wandering
lost and scattered by the [Keb] refugees. He sent those of Xocolha
to Puilha, near Chunhuitzil, where they had been dispersed, and it
served God that little by little they were found. It took about eight or
nine months to look for them, gather them together, and settle them
there in Xocolha near the others. Marcos Balam, Gonzalo Tzuc, the

old men of Xocolha, and Juan Cauich, who were the most senior of those found, seeing that about sixty had now been reunited, spoke to don Pablo and told him that they wanted to settle beside the jetty of Mamantel, because they had come far and labored much, and there they could attend mass. And so he assigned them land, which they call Popola, half-way on the road from Chiuoha, and there Cauich and his comrades settled.[56]

In the year 1586 Dr. Palacio [*palacios*] came to visit the land,[57] and we, the people of Tixchel, gave him canoes [and] paddles. We opened the roads so that the minister might go to visit these *cahob*, for whom we have always gone to a great deal of trouble to give them orna- ments so that the Holy Sacraments might be administered to them, and we have done all this in order to serve God and the king, our lord, even before it was ordered that through the tribute assessment all of us would support the minister, the church, and our governor.

I have already spoken in this account of the lineage of the Mactun people [*los indios magtunes chontales*] from when the Capitán del Valle came to their lands. And in order that our way of life be made known, from the year 1527 to the year 1610, which is the present one, it is nec- essary to write of their names and deeds in order to show who we are on our journeys and campaigns, even among the Yucatecans, people from all the *cahob*, like those who are in Popola, Mazcab, which was Xocolha, and the other *cahob* which are here.

In the year 1599[58] they began to gather together the Maya people [*maya uinicob*] who had escaped being killed by Pedro Tzakum May there in Holha and at the massacre in the savannahs of Chunal. There they were dispersed throughout the area and attacked those who came to hunt iguanas and collect wax from Campeche and the com- munities of the region. They also roamed the sea coast at Chencan, Uxkakaltok, and Tixcem, taking knives, machetes, clothing, and what- ever else was being carried by those who passed along the coastal road.[59] When don Pablo heard tales of all this from those arriving as refugees from Holha and the area around Uzulhaban, he asked for a commission from don Diego [Fernández] de Velasco, governor of this province of Yucatan, to go into the forests to seek and round up the refugees. He gave him the authority to go and round people up; we

residents of Tixchel, taking along some from Popola, Mazcab, Ticintupa, and Chiuoha to accompany us, went out by way of the *estancia*.
We were clearing a road towards Uzulhaban when we found a shelter
where the aforementioned refugees had passed through and made a
fire. I declare that it was the will of God [*yoli ix ti dios*] that at that
exact time the people of Champoton, having received news of them,
went out to look for the refugees and thereby scattered them at Kin-
acnal, forcing them in the direction of Uzulhaban. As that was where
we were, we were able to seize all of them; there were eighty [to] a
hundred, including their women and children. When they arrived
here in Tixchel, the padre guardian fray Diego Mejía [de Figueroa],
with his subordinate fray Joseph Bosque, baptized the children and
also the two or three adults who had not been baptized. Then they
were asked by don Pablo whether it was good land that they had traveled through, and they replied that it was suitable for homes and for
cultivation, and good for cacao. And therefore fray Joseph [TAT:76v]
Bosque was ordered to go and see the land. Entering [the area] at
Chiuoha, he passed Uzulhaban, where we had gone with them [the
refugees], and he then passed by the entrance to the *estancia* of Francisco Maldonado. Upon his return he gave an account to fray Diego
Mejía of how the land out there was good, how it had large cedars
and many other trees and an expanse of virgin lands, and that it
would be good for people from Popola, Mazcab, and Ticintupa to go
and make a home there. And they also told don Pablo that out there
a joint community [*ladzal cah*] should be established, so as to better
teach the catechism [*dotrina*] and preach the Holy Gospel [*santo eban-
gelio*]. Then they consulted the principal men, who listened and said,
"Good." Then we principal men wrote a letter to Mateo de Aguilar,
the *encomendero* for this *cah* of Tixchel. Then we turned to writing a
letter from everyone to the *defensor*,[60] Juan de Sanabria, so that he
might request on their behalf a decree and license [*u autoil u lissayl*] for
all the people to go to the *cah* at Uzulhaban. A license was then made
out to them at the word of the governor [of Yucatan], don Diego [Fer-
nández] de Velasco, in the *cah* of Calkini; there the license was given
to them to go to that site of Uzulhaban, for everyone together to go
to the *cah*. When the license came, don Pablo Paxbolon, the governor,

announced that the license for them to go to the *cah* at Uzulhaban
had arrived. Meanwhile there arrived word that they were going to
take the Franciscan padres away from the *cah* here at Tixchel. The
order came from our lord the king in Spain, that [secular] clergy had
to come; and thus the Franciscan padres left and clergymen came to
take care of the *cah* here at Tixchel.[61] And thus the reason that the
removal of the *cah* to Uzulhaban did not take place was because
nobody encouraged their going. Only a few went when the license
arrived; they are the following, whose names are written on the back
of this history book.[62]

Then arrived padre Juan Rodríguez to be vicar; he was sent by don
Juan Izquierdo, bishop of the province of Yucatan, on the sixth day of
the month of January of the year 1603. And it was because he said
that it was a long way out to Uzulhaban, and there were floods
[TAT:77r] during the rainy season, that Juan Rodríguez did not bless
the land and place the *cah* of Uzulhaban under the patronage of San
Felipe and San Diego until the twenty-third day of April of the year
1604.[63]

CONQUEST AS CHRONOLOGY
The Annals of Oxkutzcab

With the following brief document we move north to the heart of the Spanish colony in the peninsula—the region that roughly comprises the modern state of Yucatan—and encounter some of what were to the Mayas the central events of the 1530s and '40s. For the dozen years listed below, these events included the spread of epidemic disease, the Otzmal massacre, the founding of the colonial capital, the battle of Dzidzantun, and the implementation of a new tribute and a new religion—events which are explored in greater detail in the lengthier Maya accounts of subsequent chapters.

The document below is in the annals genre, a style of presenting historical information which occasionally creeps into the titles genre (see Chapter 3) and into the Books of Chilam Balam (see Chapter 7, in particular the annals section from the Book of Chilam Balam of Mani). Although annals were obviously not unique to Mesoamericans, the characteristics of Maya annals are similar to those of the Nahuas of central Mexico[1]—and markedly different from the equivalent Spanish genre of the chronicle. A chronicle chapter is given an event rather than a date for a heading and tends to be much longer than an annals entry, building upon narrative threads from previous chapters.

Three primary features of post-Conquest Mesoamerican annals are illustrated below. The first is the introduction of each entry with a combination of Spanish and indigenous calendar dates. The second is the straightforward manner in which information is offered, with minimal dramatization or judgement. The sole exception to this in the Annals of

Oxkutzcab—the exclamation "May it be remembered!"—could not be briefer; moreover, because it refers to an event not involving Spaniards, it makes the list of Conquest events seem even more flatly presented.[2]

The third feature is the centrality of the perspectives and concerns of the community in which the annals are maintained in the description of events, mostly disasters of some kind. These events usually have a broader regional significance (the introduction of Christianity, for example) but are considered in the annals for their impact upon the people of the local community (in this case, Mani and its neighbors, which included nearby Oxkutzcab),[3] especially their ruling dynasty or noble families (in this case, the Xiu, who dominated Mani, Oxkutzcab, and other *cahob* in the area, and allied noble *chibalob*). Outsiders, particularly Spaniards, are named according to the same criterion—their importance to community developments. The predominance of highly localized perspectives is of course characteristic of Maya views of the Conquest (as discussed in Chapter 2) and more generally of the post-Conquest culture of the Mayas—indeed of the Mesoamericans.[4]

The local angle of annals sometimes extends to personal comments by the annalist, usually the community notary or choirmaster (as in the Mani example in Chapter 7). While some Nahua annals feature biographical asides,[5] Maya annalists usually just declare themselves to be accurate copyists and entry-makers. What is unique about a comment made along these lines by don Juan Xiu is his assertion in 1685 that he was copying his annals from "an ancient book (or document; *uchben hun*) which is in characters (*calacteres*; a loan of the Spanish word *carácteres*)." It is tempting to jump to the conclusion that this page is thus a direct link to a lost codex; however, don Juan's phrase is ambiguous. Why not use a Maya term to refer to hieroglyphs, which were, after all, a decidedly prehispanic form of expression? Had such a term simply been forgotten by 1685? Or was Xiu copying from an older alphabetic manuscript, albeit a possible firsthand account? I suspect that, as some of the orthography in the text is characteristic of early colonial Maya writing (the locative preposition *te* for *ti*, for example, and *n* instead of *m*, as in *maya cinlal*), don Juan was indeed using a sixteenth-century alphabetic document, which we might reasonably speculate contained some hieroglyphs (probably the Maya calendar entries) and was itself

Figure 4.1. The Annals of Oxkutzcab (xc:54). Courtesy of Tozzer Library, Harvard University.

partly copied from pre-Conquest glyphic annals. He may even have borrowed the phrase "ancient book of characters" from an earlier copyist, and the way in which the Maya dates are described may be because an earlier text was a descriptive gloss accompanying glyphic dates.[6]

The systematic destruction of hieroglyphic materials by the Spaniards—most (in)famously by Diego de Landa in the mid-sixteenth century—made the survival of anything resembling a codex most unlikely (three of the four extant Maya codices were taken out of Yucatan at an early date). Thus the existence of a document copied from a codex—however indirect and tentative the link may in fact be—is most significant; with respect to the Annals of Oxkutzcab, there is an added twist of fortuity. By chance, the "original" annals came into the possession of don Juan Xiu, a nobleman of Oxkutzcab (the same don Juan Xiu featured in Chapter 10); by chance he copied them out on the back of a personal letter that was a decade old (paper was an expensive and rare commodity in a colonial *cah*); by chance, that letter was inserted into a collection of papers known as the Xiu Chronicle—which is not in fact a chronicle but a series of petitions by members of the Xiu *chibal* from Yaxakumche-Oxkutzcab requesting confirmation from colonial authorities of their noble status and privileges (see Chapter 10, which includes a couple of these petitions). There the page of annals lay hidden until the early twentieth century, when the Xiu papers came into the possession of Harvard University and to the attention of Mayanists; they remain unpublished.[7]

To such a series of chances,[8] then, do we owe this native-language snapshot of a dozen years of the Conquest era—this terse, truncated, but potentially rich insight into the Maya perspective on the past.

The Annals of Oxkutzcab

153[4].[9] The *cah* was devastated by the dying of the Maya [*maya cinlal*] in the year 1534, whose *tun*[10] was on 18 Yaxkin; 5 Kan was the year-bearer on 1 [Pop. In 11][11] Ahau the *tun* was on 7 Yaxkin.

153[5]. In the year 1535, 7 Muluc was the [year-bearer] on 1 Pop.

1536. This *tun* was on the year 11 Ceh; 7 Ix was the year-bearer on 1 Pop. In 3 Ahau the *tun* was on 7 Yaxkin.

1537. In the year 1537, when 8 Cauac fell on 1 Pop, the rain-bringers died at Otzmal; they were Ah Dzun Tutul Xiu and Ah Ziyah Napuc Chi and Namay Che and Namay Tun and Ah Men Euan, *halach uinicob*[12] there at Mani; they had been rain-bringers before at Chichen Itza.[13] Those who fled were Nahau Uech and Napot Couoh. It happened on 10 Zip, in 12 Ahau, when the *tun* was on 2 Yaxkin. May it be remembered!

In the year 1538, 9 Kan being the year-bearer on 1 Pop, there occurred a deadly hurricane. In 8 Ahau the *tun* was on 16 Xul.

In the year 1539, 10 Muluc was [the year-bearer] on 1 Pop. In 4 Ahau the *tun* was on 11 Xul.

In the year 1540, 11 Ix was [the year-bearer] on 1 Pop. In 13 Ahau the *tun* was on 7 [Xul].[14]

In the year 1541, 12 Cauac was [the year-bearer] on 1 Pop. In 9 Ahau the *tun* was on 2 Xul.

In the year 1542, 13 Kan being [the year-bearer] on 1 Pop, the Spaniards [*espayoresob*] founded a *cah* at Tiho [Merida]. There they settled, and for the first time tribute began to be paid by the people of Mani and its province. In 5 Ahau [the *tun*] was on 16 Tzec.

In the year 1543, 1 Muluc [being the year-bearer] on 1 Pop, the people of Dzidzantun were killed by an army of Spaniards whose captain was Alonso López. It was in 1 Ahau that [the *tun*] was on 11 Tzec.

2 Ix was [the year-bearer] on 1 Pop in the year 1544. In 10 Ahau [the *tun*] was on 6 Tzec.

In the year 1545, 13 Cauac being [the year-bearer] on 1 Pop, Christianity was started by the friars here in the *cah*. Here are the names of those padres—fray Luis Villa[l]pando, fray Diego de Béjar, fray Juan de la Puerta, fray Me[l]chor de Benavente, fray Juan de Herrera, fray Angel [Maldonado]; they established themselves at Pocobtok[15] there in the *cah* of Tiho. In 6 Ahau the *tun* was on 1 Tzec.

Today, the 29th of May of the year 1685, I copied out an ancient book [*uchben hun*] which is in characters [*calacteres*] and is called Annals [*Anares*].

I who am don Juan Xiu.

THE COMMUNITY VIEW
The Calkini Account

For several reasons the Conquest account from the *cah* of Calkini is a convenient link between the Chontal Maya account (Chapter 3) and the perspective the Pech manuscripts offer (Chapter 6). Calkini is located between the colonial centers of Campeche and Merida-Tiho, and the documents thus tell us of events in the southwestern portion of the colony, a region between the Chontal lands to the south and the Pech domain to the north (see Map II). Indeed, the Chontal account names the coastal *cah* of Champoton (about half way between Acalan and Campeche), as the Spaniards' stepping-stone to the rest of the peninsula, while the Calkini manuscript tells of envoys from Champoton arriving in the area to confer with the region's authorities—perhaps, one might speculate, in response to the presence of foreigners at the foot of the peninsula.[1]

In terms of style and substance the Calkini account also fits well between the Chontal and Pech documents. The emphasis in the Calkini is on the local rulers' peaceful reception of an invading Spanish force, an image of welcoming Maya nobles that is also central to the Chontal and Pech texts. The tone of the Calkini narration lies between the other texts, in that it lacks the detachment and neutrality of the Chontal account while also failing to muster any of the Pech nobles' professed enthusiasm for the Spaniards. Like the Pech accounts, the Calkini manuscript includes depictions of Spanish-Maya violence, which is largely lacking from the Chontal text. Yet the main thrust of the text is not about the Spaniards at all; the people of Calkini do not claim to be co-conquerors with the Spaniards or engage in campaigns against other

Mayas, as do the Pech and the Chontal Maya leaders. The concern of the Title of Calkini is more with the local, territorial impact of the Conquest.

A further point of comparison worth emphasizing is the fact that the Chontal and Pech accounts project the domination by one dynastic family over a series of communities—the Chontal account through its regionalist perspective and the Pech accounts through their intertextual parallels. The Calkini account, however, features and promotes more than one noble family from the region, with primacy given to two lineages or *chibalob*, the Canul and Canche (it is quite possible that earlier portions of the text were primarily about the Canul, and that Canche copyists altered and inserted passages to promote their own *chibal*). The effect is an emphasis on the community of principal men, past and present, and the community of communities—Calkini *cah* and its subordinate neighbors.[2]

These similarities and contrasts of tone are paralleled by those of genre. The Chontal, Calkini, and Pech manuscripts are all examples of the colonial Mesoamerican genre of the primordial title or *título*, discussed in Chapters 2 and 3. Suffice it to point out here that many of the features of the Calkini title (traditionally called a chronicle or codex) that are likely to strike the reader are characteristic of this genre. These include a complex and often contradictory attitude towards Spaniards, the use of a nonlinear chronology, a preoccupation with which prominent Mayas were where when, and, above all, the intermingling of three distinct but related narrative concerns—the original settling of the area's communities by their ruling families; the response to the Conquest by those families; and their consolidation of community territorial borders before and after the Conquest. As with the Pech titles to follow, much of the Calkini manuscript deals with land matters rather than Conquest events, but because these issues are ultimately bound up together from the Maya perspective (and to preserve the integrity of a text that is being published here in English for the first time), I have kept the title intact.

The original Calkini manuscript is currently owned by Princeton University. According to the early twentieth-century collector William Gates,[3] the manuscript became attached to the Book of Chilam Balam of Chumayel (see Chapter 7) possibly in the mid-nineteenth century when it came into the possession of Juan Pío Pérez. After retiring as a local government official in Yucatan, Pío Pérez had devoted himself to acquiring colonial-era dictionaries and Maya-language documents, and upon his death his manuscripts became part of the larger collection of Bishop Carrillo y Ancona—although according to a local historian's account of 1906, the bishop had acquired the Calkini manuscript from a man who had been given it in 1867 by the *batab* of Calkini.[4]

By the 1920s, the Carrillo y Ancona collection had been placed in Merida's Cepeda Library, from where it quickly, in bits and pieces, disappeared. The Calkini material was aquired by Gates and later by another collector; although it may still have been attached to the Chumayel when the latter was being offered for sale in Boston in 1938 for $7,000, by the 1950s it was in Princeton.[5] Part of the bishop's collection, including the Chumayel and Calkini manuscripts, was photographed in the late nineteenth century and again in 1910; in 1915 photostats were made of these photographs and it is in the form of these photostats that the Calkini manuscript is most accessible today.[6]

The first five folios of the manuscript were lost or fell apart even before it was photographed. The opening words of the text as we have it —the sentence that begins the eleventh page of the manuscript—tantalizingly suggest a link between missing details of the initial Spanish-Maya encounter and the description in the passages that follow. The surviving portion of the Title of Calkini is, as befits its categorization as a primordial title, a compilation of various post-Conquest documents. The compilation as we have it was made in 1821, the year the colonial period ended. Aside from the final entry, which provides the context for the drawing up of the title, its constituent parts all carry late sixteenth-century dates. Because we cannot be certain of the creative role that the notary of 1821 may have played in compiling the title, we must therefore take it to be simultaneously an account of the late sixteenth century and one from the very end of the colonial era.

In fact, it is more complicated than that. The fragmented nature of the text—the apparent incompleteness of some of the sections—suggest that much of it went through generations of copying and compilation between the sixteenth century and 1821. Furthermore, some of the material clearly predates the year to which it is attached in the title. For example, the 1579 document which comprises the first half of the title is itself a compilation of accounts that must have had oral antecedents and possibly written ones. The Mayapan-related events, for example, took place in the mid-fifteenth century, and their knowledge must therefore have been maintained in some fashion before the advent in Yucatan of alphabetic writing. Also, the story of the Spaniards' arrival in Calkini in 1541 comes across as a tale often told; note the dramatic codas of reported speech. In short, the title is a colonial-era document with surmised textual links to unknown precolonial narratives.

The Calkini document can be divided up a number of ways. Previous translators of the manuscript either left it as a single text or identified and numbered twenty-one subsections.[7] Both approaches are valid; part of the fascination of the title is the fact that it is both many documents and a single one. However, I have indicated with textual breaks original divisions between documents as suggested by closing and opening formulas (indented paragraphs have been entirely created by me). This produces six constituent parts. The multiple components of the long first part dated 1579 (Okoshi Harada finds thirteen of them) make it a primordial title in and of itself. The second part is closely related to the first, probably once carried the same date, and had the title evolved further may well have been subsumed by the first part. The third part, dated 1595, is also fairly lengthy and contains identifiable subsections (Okoshi Harada finds four). The fourth part is a fragment from a 1582 record. The fifth, a notation in Spanish, was probably written in 1821 along with the Maya-language entry that is the sixth part of the title.

The bulk of the title, therefore, lies in the first and third sections; although their dates of 1579 and 1595 must be taken with the caveats already mentioned, the two parts are sufficiently distinct to make for profitable comparison. In particular, the first part dramatically represents the Spanish invasion as a symbolic transfer of power with traumatic consequences; the authors have other concerns and topics to treat yet keep returning to the Conquest, so that the historical continuities stressed by the material on settlement and land are partially undermined by the disjunction of the Spanish invasion. By contrast, the third part neglects to mention the Conquest entirely, despite the fact that it is an account of the settlement of the region from precolonial times right through the Conquest period to 1595. The colonial era is reduced to a temporal reference—"the time of the foreigners"—and when the Spaniards are not being called "foreigners" they are ambiguously, and somewhat paradoxically, called "principal men, or officials." Even the subsequent entries (parts four and six), mundane notarial documents simply recording *cabildo* business, do little to dispel the impression that the Conquest was for Calkini an indirect affair. The impression is misleading but significant; the authors of the Title of Calkini have succeeded in taking us deep into the Maya world.

The Title of Calkini

. . . These then were the welcomers, those who went out into the middle of the road when the Spaniards came.[8]

Napuc Canul was in charge of the people of Chulilha—the *batabob* were established before the foreigners settled among them—and here in Calkini,[9] Nahau Canul was a *batab*, with his speakers.[10] Naun Canul was the *batab* in charge of the people of Tuchican;[11] Nahau Dzul was the deputy's name; Namay Canul was second speaker; Nabich Canul was the third of the speakers. Nahau Canul was *batab* in charge of the people of Maxcanu; Nakul Calam was the deputy's name; Ah Kul Cob was the second speaker; Ah Kul Chim was the third of the speakers.

Nachan Uluac was the *batab* in charge of the people of Nohcacab; Ah Kul Chan was the deputy; Ah Kul Yah was the second of the speakers. There was a very small break in the line of *batabob*[12] in charge of the people of Becal; Naum Canul was formerly the *batab* but he left and went to Tenabo; Ah Kul Yah was the deputy when Nachan Canul arrived from Tepakan[13] in order to assume the *batabil* [governorship], with Ah Kul Tucuch as deputy and Ah Kul Huh as second of the speakers.

Nabatun Canul was the *batab* in charge of the people of Tepakan, who in terms of tribute were united as one *cah* with the people of Calkini; Ah Kul Chi was the deputy and Ah Kul Dzib the second of the speakers. There were once many of them dispersed throughout

the *cah*. This then was their *batab* [TC:12] when he arrived here in Calkini with Napuc Chi as deputy; that Ah Kul Dzib later went to be with
his son at Tenabo.

Here ends my account of the names of the *batabob*, the deputies,
and the speakers to whom tribute was divided up on Napot Canche's
patio here in Calkini. Here each district's share of tribute was set: five
sacks of twenty turkeys each, one hundred altogether; likewise a hundred too of corn, but in small tied sacks, not in large loads; five jars of
honey; and ten large baskets of ginned cotton. Then they brought in
the breast plates made of sisal[14] and ten large baskets of warped cotton; however, they did not distribute the ginned and warped cotton,
whereas the turkeys, corn, and honey were for distribution. Then,
starting in the center, they began to line up behind one another.

And the Captain[15] said, "Give it up!" This was his statement, this
was how he declared himself to them. Then the Culhuas[16] and their
companions grabbed it all, some seizing much and some seizing a
little.

"Hey you, one at a time!"

Thus they quickly made their take before their Captain de Montejo, who oversaw the tribute distribution.

I was then just a boy, following my father, Napot Canche, who was
in office; meanwhile, it was all clearly observed, and I now relate it. It
took place here beside a well called Tixhalin where there stood a great
[TC:13] ceiba tree,[17] beneath which everything was well arranged, here
at Calkini. These are the *batabob*, as I have listed them, along with
their deputies; I have told their names above.

It was they who were present when the lordship was taken over
here; I have presented below the names of these deputies. It was [Gas-
par] Pacheco who was our foreign lord, he whom us people of Calkini first treated as lord. One slave girl, named Ixchan Uitzil, was delivered to him; she had been bought in common by the *cah* and at the
time that we delivered her, her value was two by two arm spans.[18] He
was not here long before he left. Then came the carpenter, as he who
works wood is called;[19] his hair was cut round in a bob, not sheared.
He had been treated as lord here for many days when he took Ixchan
as a wife, although she was not a Spanish lady.[20]

One male slave was delivered to him, named Nahau Tzel, the slave of Naun Canul, for whom he was purchased in common. However, they never made up the full payment of two arm spans, so his masters remained the elders,[21] those who were settled here when the foreigners arrived. Those who delivered him were Ah Kul Canche and Nachan Che; they did it.

There is also a digression here, the matter of what was done by the *chibal* [lineage] from which I come. They were not pretenders to *batabil*, nor were they trouble-makers, as has been said and told. My great grandfather was Namay Canche when they departed from within the walls of the *cah* of Mayapan[22] with the *batabob*. These were Ah Dzuum Canul, who came from this *chibal*, Ah Itzam Kauat, and those of the Canul, who were Itza settlers[23] when they departed at that time from Mayapan—Ah Tzab Canul, Ah Kin Canul, Ah Paal [TC:14] Canul, Ah Sulim Canul, Ah Chacah Canul, Ix Co Pacab Canul, and Nabich Canul. These *batabob* that I have listed, the nine of them, were told of by my great grandfather Namay Canche, who with the *batabob* began to take care of the *cahob* and in turn were taken care of by the *cahob*, just as my great grandfather took on the responsibility of rule.

But then the subjects gathered together and began to debate on the patio at the entrance to the town hall; then came their dispersal, their departure, and their coming to new settlements at Kalahcum.[24] Meanwhile, Nabich Canul and Naun Canul went to Tuchican, both of them as *batabob*. Thus began the scattering of that community. Chacah Canul went to Siho[25] with his subjects and with the wealthy men Naun Uicab and Chan, while Ah Tzab Canul established the *batabil* here at Calkini with himself as *batab* and as his deputy Ah Kul Canche—whose birth name was Namoo and who was from Namay Canche's *chibal*. The *chibal* of the *batab* Che had died at Mani with Ah Dzul Balam, who also had no *chibal*, it having been lost at Chakan;[26] therefore Ah Kin Canul settled by the well at Sacnicte, with Ah Kul Tinaal, Nacan Cauich, and Ah Kul Ceeh as his deputies.

Of the people of Dzitbalche there was Namay Canche, who recounted: "I then came into my *batabil* because the *batab* of the warriors[27] and *batab* of Dzitbalche died at Chunbilche near Hecelchakan, along with the priest [TC:15] Ah Kin Coyi—Chuen Coyi—and with

Ah Kin Tun, whose boyhood name was Ah Chac and whose second name was Ah Kin Chac. He was warrior *batab* when the soldiers of the people of Chakan rose up and killed him at the gallows, also killing countless men and their *batabob*. The *batab* of the warriors was seen dying where he had been hanged from the wooden beam of a Canche doorway,[28] wearing his necklace of precious stones that he had put on when he went to war, and with his shield on his arm and holding his spear; thus he died in the war, as I have told it." This is how the story is composed recording his valiant and *batab*-like death; for they revered his necklace of precious stones and flowers and his armor of precious stones, his spear and the lordly precious-stone armor of a Canche soldier, of a warrior officer.

This *chibal* ancestor of ours had three sons. His oldest son was Napot Canche,[29] the child of Ixikal; his younger brothers were Nachan Canche and Nabatun Canche, whose boyhood name was Siyah and whose mother was Ixchan Pan. It is also said that the three sons were also called Nachan; the boyhood name of Ixchan Pan's two sons was A.[30] When, as an adult, this Napot Canche took a wife, he took the daughter of Ah Kin Can, and thus were born Ah Col Che and Ah Itzam Canche; he conceived with his wife four sons [TC:16] and four daughters, born here in Calkini.

As Ah Tzab Canul had already died when the officers[31] arrived, Napot Canche received them with tribute—when they arrived on his patio where Nachanche Canul had gathered the *batabob* together. Napot Canche presented himself before the officers, so that the men might be served by slaves of his named Ah Cot Mas and Ix Cahum Kuk. He was then appointed to the *batabil* [governorship] by the foreigners, along with his son-in-law Nacouoh Mut and his younger brothers Nachan Canche and Nabatun Canche, to whom he was guardian. This Napot Canche held the *cah* governorship here in Calkini; it was on his patio that the tribute was delivered to the captain Montejo, when he and his soldiers arrived here in Calkini, when they arrived near the well at Sacnicte. Their swine and their Culhuas arrived first; the captain of the Culhuas was Gonzalo.[32] When the foreigners arrived, there was on the horizon a sliver of the sun as it dawned in the east. When they reached the entrance to this *cah* of

Calkini, they fired their guns once; when they arrived where the savannahs begin, they also fired their guns once; and when they arrived
at the houses, they then fired their guns a third time.[33] The people of
Calkini then gathered together to discuss the completion of the bringing of tribute from each district, which they then delivered to the
breast-plated Captain. That morning they delivered this tribute: one
hundred loads of corn all in all; one hundred turkeys also; fifty jars of
honey; [TC:17] twenty large baskets of ginned cotton; the sisal breast-
armor was brought in; also the white cotton yarn. These were the
tribute items received by Montejo under the ceiba in Halim. Then the
constables[34] began to distribute the corn among themselves—the
names of the assembled constables are not known—distributing not
just half of the turkeys, but all of them, as they did the cotton and the
yarn. Then, having become gluttonous, they began to break the line
and form a tightening circle.

And the Captain said: "Give it up!"

"Take all of it!" they replied.

Then they began to be suspicious of each other, holding piles of
things tightly in their arms; some were able to grab a great deal,
others grabbed a little; one and all, women and men alike. And thus
they did it in haste.

Then the following began to occur on Napot Canche's patio: the
district nobles, the residents, and their *batab* Nachan Canul, who were
not responsible for watching this splitting up of spoils that took place,
were hidden at the back of their homes; but those in front of Napot
Canche's home were tied up by the foreigners. They took all who
were there: Namay Tayu, and Nachan and Ah Kul Couoh; and the
speakers, the priests, those who interpret the cause of things; the
priests Kin May and Ah Kul Uh;[35] Nabatun Uc. One who was there
was Namay Tayu; Ah Dza Tiya was another one; Ah Chauil was one
more—Ah Dzuun Che was Ah Chauil's first slave, and his second
was Ah Chuen Chay.

These also were men of Calkini, elders living here in the *cah* [TC:18]
of Calkini, those who were the leaders of the *cah* residents: Nahau
Kumun, whose boyhood name was Ah Tzab, and who was the father
of Juan Kumun, as he was called when he was baptized; Nacahun

Che, whose son lived at that time and was called Juan when he was baptized; Nacahun May, whose nickname was Ah Xun May; Napuc Cime, nicknamed Ah Pach Uitz; Nadzul Cime; Nacouoh Mut, son-in-law of Napot Canche, whose son Nachan Couoh attained the *batabil* here in Calkini—his nickname was Naitza; Nahau Ku, whose *chibal* had no members as it had died out; Nachan Che, whose nickname was Ah Kan Tzohom; Napuc Uc, nicknamed Ah Tup Kabal; another Napuc Uc, with the nickname of Ah Xochil Ich.[36]

These were all living here when the official[37] arrived, he for whom they worked here in Calkini, making many bundles and carrying loads without pay day after day. The work burden of the highway was divided into two parts: from Pocboc to the patio of Napuc Canul (whose boyhood name was Ah Cen Canul) at Chulilha (Nacabal Batun was the slave on Ah Kul Canche's patio); from there it came up here to Calkini, to the patio of Ah Kin Canul, from where it arrived back at Pocboc. Armed men went out on the road to steal, coming together with the magistrates.[38] This Ah Kin Canul, with his slave porters and his men—of which there had previously been many— now went out to rob. They all fell on hard times: his sons, Ah Tok the eldest son and Ah Chim Canul his younger brother; the five slaves of the lords; and their five men too; Ah Kul Canche and those of his patio; all their porters. [TC:19]

"You nobles are greatly burdened; the story of your hardships is no joke. It is a tale of partings, of endless deprivations, and of people being left by the roadside because there they had been knifed—as it was at Balcab, where you runners were cut up while on foot on the road, and as it was in the scrub forest, where the runners went along afraid of being raped,[39] of being forced to assume a shameful burden by the foreigners, the abuse of all the foreign dogs together empowered by the possession of steel to lift skirts."

"You! Man! Your clothes to the dogs!"

The *cah* residents were lifted up and hung like pigs; they suspended them like swine.

"Your clothes, man!"

They had also abused the women in this same way: "Woman! Your clothes! Off with your petticoat!" This was the nature of the burden.

What has been told here happened not once, nor twice, but many times; on countless occasions these things were done to our lords here on the road to Calkini. It was not done to those of Pocboc, those on the road between the people of Pakmuch and those of Tenabo; but it was done to all those who were taken prisoner on that road to Tiho,[40] and also to the people of Chulilha, to those of Tuchican, and of Maxcanu, and of the Chakan area, and of Dzibilkal—whose *batab* was Nacouoh Canul (his birth name) and deputy was Namo Uc.

So then the *batabob* listed above dispersed into the other *cahob*; those which have been spoken of arrived together here in Calkini. Here Ah Tzab Canul elevated Copacab Canul to the *batabil* at Bacabchen, where he went with his subjects and his deputy Nachan Coyi. He was in the *batabil* at Bacabchen when the elders arrived from Champoton, when [TC:20] the *batabob* gathered together and he was sent by the *batabob* to Champoton.[41]

So too, when they had gathered together in conference here in Calkini *cah*, Ah Tzab Euan, the *batab* of the people of Mopila, arrived to speak; he spoke with Nachan Canul, the *batab* of the people of Calkini, and the *batabob* together came to an agreement as to where lay the borders between the fields of the people of their *cahob*. They also drank much chocolate[42] as the groups arrived from the *cahob*. This was the reason for the gathering of the people of Calkini with their *batab* Nachan Canul and their speakers, together at the home of Napot Canche. There they began to confer with Ah Tzab Euan, *batab* of Mopila, who had with him his speakers and his younger brother Ah Xoc Euan, whose birth name was Namay; Ah Kin Canche was his speaker, Ah Kub Xool was his second speaker, and Ah Kul Chi was the third of his speakers. They also drank much chocolate and wine while they were in discussion with the *batab* of Calkini. And at this conference they delineated their shoreline forests that were to the east of the *cah* of Calkini, including those on the lagoon at Dzalal and those on the lagoon of Lake Tzemes[43]—which until that point had not been the forests of [i.e. worked by] slaves but the fields of the people of Mopila.

Nachan Canul, *batab* of Calkini, and Napot Canche, now said, "Nobody shall sow discord among our children in the days [TC:21] that are now coming, nor in the future shall great quarrels be provoked, for just as we and you are brothers,[44] so too in the future will our children take possession [of the lands] together."

Thus spoke the *batab* of Calkini at the end of the conference with the *batab* of Mopila, and he added, "If the alliance of our other *cahob* here in the Calkini area falls apart and ends, their fields shall go to the section to the south that approaches the hills; and if they should ask you, you'll know whether to give them fields among your own fields, depending on the agreement that you make."

Ah Tzab Euan, the *batab* of Mopila, then asked, "Where are the forests given out to the north and also where do the forests of the people of Becal end?"

And the *batab* of Calkini, Nachan Canul, along with Napot Canche and Nachan Che, replied, "There at the lagoon of Lake Tzemes, at the end of the savannah of Matu that is to the north; because one of the elders, Namay Tayu, settled there at the lagoon of Lake Tzemes. And because this, the border of our territory, runs from Tzucxan[45] to the middle of the great savannah north of Lake Xicinchah, then to Kochyol, on to Calxub, and on to Calakya, where it reaches the edge of the forest of the people of Halacho to the north of the *cah* of Chochola."

This was known by *Batab* Nauat, Naun Canul, and Nachan Canul, *batabob* of the people of Becal—Nachan Canul had left Tepakan and arrived at Becal [TC:22] to become *batab* of Becal at that time[46]—and they knew the border of those forests, and Ah Tzab Euan, *batab* of Mopila, knew it too.

"These are the corners[47] of this forest; the forests of Halacho are at the edge of the *cah* of Chochola, and here too is the corner of the forests of the people of Mopila. For this reason, nobody shall say anything nor shout out about it. Let only good words be spoken, as lies would undermine the agreement on forest boundaries that we have now given to you. Nor shall anyone place stone mounds [marking borders], for these are the roots of discord and of killing one another. Wherever and whenever in the days to come stone mounds are placed on the forest boundary by wicked men, they shall be moved. From now on it shall not be possible to build stone mounds on the edge of those forests. This is the end of what we have been telling you. Let none of you see this altered in the coming days ahead, because a great many *cahob* have now come to be the responsibility of this little Calkini."[48] This is what Calkini's *batab*, Nachan Canul, said, along with Napot Canche, Nachan Che, Namay Tayu, and Nabatun Uc.

When he had finished conferring with the *batab* of Mopila, he listened to Napol Huchim and Ah Ceh Huchim, and went to Xicinchah with Naun Chi, Nabatun Tacu, Nachan Chi, and Ah Xoc Chi, [TC:23] as his three sons were called, Nabatun Che, and Na Canche. All of them were tanners, and therefore went up to their fields and came back down below from the Puuc [hills] to Sinab, Kochyol, Itzimte, Pacante, and Kumtun. Those of Mopila came with them to Lake Tzemes; on the lagoon began their conference, and our *batab* began to discuss matters with the *batab* of Mopila.

Thus it shall be seen that we told all our children of the trails and landmarks, the history and the names of the forest boundaries, lest these precious things be lost; it is said that formerly they were lost to us until we discovered them again. Nobody shall be able to insert a statement; no one can make a speech. Any suspicions are but minor grievances and petty jealousies. Nor shall any man be able to shout out because the property is not his.

This then is the reason that we now give the title[49] of our statement, we people of Calkini: so that it shall be seen by those children of the people of Mopila who shall come later. We do it now before the *batabob*, on this very day, the twenty-first of April of the year 1579. This is the truth. Our signatures are at the end there.

Don Francisco Chim, governor.[50]

Alonso Canche, Gonzalo Canul, Pablo Cauich, *alcaldes.*

Juan Canche; Agustin Ci, *batab*; Jorge Canul, *batab.*[51]

Juan Ku, Diego Uc, Juan Canche.

Pedro Kuk, notary.

[TC:24] I hereby place in order our testimony within the account, we Alonso Canche and Pablo Cauich, elder men of Nunkini, with Francisco Chable.

We have seen the conclusion of the conference, in which they debated, made agreements, and had the idea of the renovation of the roads by the people of Kalahcum; this was initiated at the conference in Xkalakya. On the north-east side they went to confer, beginning at Xkalakya, moving to the lagoon at Calxub, passing on to Lake Tixcum to the west of Calxub, coming out at the base of the mound of Kochyol,[52] passing to the north of the Tahpuc lake, emerging to the north of Lake Xicinchah, at the corner of the savannah at the foot of a calabash tree; on the rise a cross [*cruz*] was planted at the foot of an oak tree;[53] [the boundary] continued and came out next to the savannah of Chanap, then emerging at Xnob, some distance[54] from Matu.

This was the end of the speech, the end of the statement by don Miguel Canul, the senior *batab*, the *batab* of the people of Calkini. Thus did he join the *batabob* together in conference and thus ended the gathering here of the *cah*. This is Calkini's forest boundary, according to don Miguel Canul. This is the absolute truth and is also truly just; this is no false account. Nor are these separate adjacent forests, but they belong to us, to [TC:25] Calkini, to these three *cahob* alone. This is the truth that we speak; we now ratify [the document] before the *batab*, don Jorge Canul, governor here in the *cah* of Nunkini; before the *alcaldes* Pedro Ayil, Martín Cauich, and Pablo Cauich the elder, and Pablo Baalche of Mopila; and the *regidores*, the principal men, these the *ah cuch cabob*.[55] For this reason the nobleman and governor don Jorge Canul gave his name, for he knows how to write. And I wrote the names of the *alcaldes*; they did not see it done, for they do not know how to write documents; I am the notary [*ah dzibulob hun*].

Jorge Canul, Pedro Ayil, Martín Cauich, *alcalde*. The names of the principal men are written below:

Melchor Hau, *regidor*; Francisco Chable of Tepakan.

Juan Tacu of Mopila; Miguel Ake of Mopila.

Juan Canul, notary.

Luis Chan; Miguel Can, officer emeritus.[56]

This is the opening of the declaration by the senior *batab*, don Miguel Canul: "It begins at Calakya, [then goes] to the Becal road, to Calxub on Lake Che [or, the wooded lake], [going] east of Calakya, then to Lake Cum, [going] east of Calxub and east too of Kochyol, to the foot of Kochyol mound, passing by [TC:26] the edge of the savannah, by the curve of the savannah at Xicinchah, passing the milpa fields at Chanap, passing the end of the fields to reach Lake Tzemes and Matu; the declaration ends at the entrance to the forests of the people of Saclum." This is the end of the statement by don Miguel Canul, senior *batab*.

Here in the *cah* of Nunkini in the jurisdiction of San Luis Calkini, today on the fifth day of the month of May in the year 1595, are gathered together the *batab* don Jorge Canul, governor of the people of Nunkini, with the principal men, the speakers [*u chun than*], *alcaldes*, and the rest of the officers [*ah belnalob*].

Don Jorge Canul declares that the principal men have been summoned so as to know how they came to be settled here in Calkini. And thus Alonso Canche and Pedro Uc of Calkini have been called; they have come before the *batab* don Jorge Canul as true elders of Calkini. Likewise Juan Chinab of Dzitbalche is summoned; he is a former elder of Calkini, his father being truly of Calkini. Antón Che, a fellow Dzitbalche resident, is also called. They know how the people of Calkini came to be settled. Don Jorge Canul has therefore asked them to speak of it, and so they shall begin to tell it—to tell what they know.

[TC:27] This is their account from the beginning: They know that the *cah* where they had lived was Pacante, and they know the names of the men who were settled in Pacante and in Sinab, as well as in Itzimte and at Lake Tacpuc; they had also lived at Xicinchah and Lake Tzemes, and also at Matu. They all know about the time before the coming of the principal men [the Spaniards];[57] and they truthfully declare that which they know—that is, the names of those who were settled at Pacante, all of them residents of Calkini. This is clearly the reason why the elders were summoned, so that they could dictate their account, their true statement; so that they could make a true statement regarding the forests there. Because the fields of the men of three communities are defended by the *cah*—these are the men of Nunkini, those of Mopila, and our allies, those of Tepakan; and also those of Becal—and because it defends their fields and their forests, the men who work the fields have now gathered themselves together to defend their fields.[58] And they have asked their speakers [*chun u thanob*] to enquire into their condition.[59] They asked for it, and so now we are entering into and beginning our writing down of what is true and also what is just. This was before the time the principal men came here to the province, to the settlements of we people here.[60]

These are the names of those who are in the know; [TC:28] we shall write down the names of the men who know it. And thus have been written down the names of the men who settled on the lake, formerly people of Calkini; as they were announced, I, Alonso Cob, wrote down their names. They do not know how to write documents. Alonso Canche and Juan Chinab of Dzitbalche, declared as elders, are witnesses;[61] they state that they shall recount that which they know. They shall begin with their account of Tepakan, where up to the present there has been a *cah*.

This is the first of the men who are in the know—Alonso Canche of Calkini. This Alonso Canche, truly of Calkini, knows about these forests, [including] all of the forested land of those of Nunkini. Up to the present, people of Calkini have been resident in the *cah* of Tepakan, just as Calkini people lived in Tepakan in the past—before the time of the foreigners. So begins the recounting of the names of those of Calkini who lived in Tepakan: Nachan Canul, a true Calkini man, resided in Tepakan; his responsibility was in Tepakan while he was in the *batabil* at Becal; he had four sons; Nabatun Canul was his younger brother's name; his boyhood name was Ah Man Canul and his younger brother's name was Nabatun. [TC:29] His deputies were Ah Kul Che and Ah Tzom Chi, whose birth name was Napuc Chi. Nachi Tec was their priest when these true Calkini people settled in Tepakan, the ones who then went to live in Xicinchah; they were the first settlers of Xicinchah, where these true people of Calkini had fields and roofed houses.

Pacante—these are the names of the true people of Calkini who settled Pacante, from the beginning until the present: Nachan Dzul, the birth name of Ah Ceh Dzul; he is said to be a true Calkini man. Nachan Dzul's younger brothers were killed at Dzitbalche; there were two of them. The residents of Pacante have their fields at Sinab and Itzimte and Tahpuc; they took possession of these fields while living in the *cah* of Pacante before the time of the foreigners.

These are the names of those of Calkini living behind Lake Xicin-chah, where they were living when there arrived [TC:30] the *batabob* from Becal. The Calkini people who lived behind Lake Xicinchah were the ones related to those settled on Lake Halal. The wealthy Tayu lived at Hahal with his slaves. They joined with those who had settled at Xicinchah. Namay Tayu, whose boyhood name was Ah Dza-cab Tayu, was speaker [*chun than*] of those who had settled at Xicin-chah. Ah Kul Xool was the deputy [*kul*] of those Calkini people who had settled at Xicinchah. Nahau Cocom was ally to those who had set-tled on the lake, where there were the fields of Nachan Uc, brother-in-law of Napuc Dzib, whose birth name was Ah Xoc Dzib. Nachi Tec was the priest of the Tepakan residents who went to live at Xicinchah; with their subjects, there were very many of them settled at Xicin-chah. The wealthy [family] of Nachan Cocom, people of Calkini, lived at Xicinchah. This [TC:31] we know—we, Alonso Canche, and I too, Juan Chinab—we know their names because the people of Calkini were all together before the time of the coming of the princi-pal men [the Spaniards].

These are the names of the people of Calkini who settled on Lake Tzemes: Nacouoh Mut, ally to the people of Calkini; he was lord *batab* Mut, as he was made *batab* by those of Calkini; Nachi Yam—Ah Col Yam—was wealthy in slaves; one was called Ixcan Canul. Their allies were Nachan Uc, the son of Namay Uc and son-in-law of Antón Che, who lived in Dzitbalche and was son of *Batab* Che (previously [known as] Ah Chan Tunich). Their priest was Ah Kin Chan, father of Naun Chan who died at Kuxubche. This was when *Batab* Canul, *batab* of the people of Chulila, arrived to take a reckoning of them; his birth name was Napuc Canul, his boyhood name Ah Cen Canul. He lived at Lake Tzemes. He had slaves [TC:32]—Nacamal Batun and Ah Kauitz Hau; *Batab* Canul's other slave, in Matu, was Nacahum Uc; there were four of them. This one was the father of Pablo Uc, an elder settled to the north of the well of Ixocolbilchen inside the Calkini area. Pablo Uc lived there with his sons, his two boys. His ancestors and descendents [*u chibalob*] are people of Matu, people of Calkini.

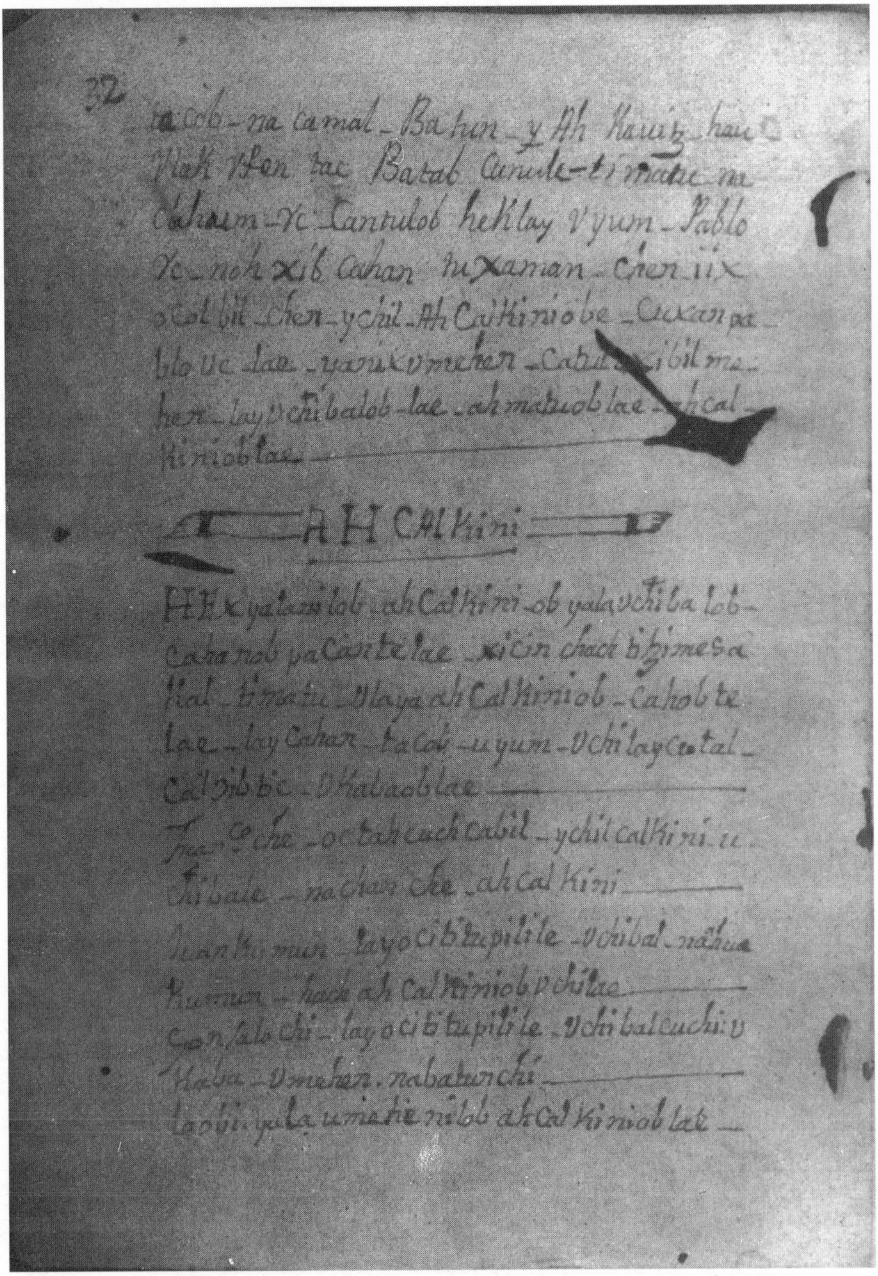

Figure 5.1. *A page from the Title of Calkini (TC:32). Courtesy of Tozzer Library, Harvard University.*

People of Calkini [*Ah Calkini*]

Here below are the descendents [*yala u chibalob*] of the people of Calkini who settled at Pacante, Xicinchah, Lake Tzemes, and Matu. These Calkini people live where their fathers lived before them. We hereby write down their names: Francisco Che, councilman [*ah cuch cab*] within Calkini, [a descendent] of the Calkini *chibal* of Nachan Che; Juan Kumun, constable [*tupil*]; of the *chibal* of Nahau Kumun, true Calkini ancestors; Gonzalo Chi, constable [*tupil*]; his ancestral *chibal* carries his name; the son of Nabatun Chi. These are the sons of the people of Calkini, [TC:33] truly natives of the *cah* of Calkini, whose fathers formerly settled Pacante, Xicinchah, and the area of Lake Tzemes.

This is a just statement: the lands and fields are all the property of the people of Calkini; they know what formerly belonged to their fathers, the names of those who had the fields and forests. We know, we who are those in the know: I, Alonso Canche; I too, Juan Chi—my father was one of the principal men [*u nucteil uinicob*] of Calkini.

I, Alonso Canche, state the real truth; my statement is well known, that which I have recounted before don Jorge Canul and the speakers [*u chun u thanob*] and *alcaldes*, gathered together on the patio of Pablo Cauich, the elder, who designated the speakers of Nunkini as witnesses to my statement—I, Alonso Canche; they are Juan Tacu, *ah cuch cab*, and a certain Francisco Chable, Juan Tut, Miguel Ake of Mopila. This is my account, I, Alonso Canche, homeowner of the *cah* of Calkini, San Luis's *cah*. Also I declare [TC:34] to the notary [*ah dzib hun*] to write my signature [*yn firma*] on my behalf, because I do not know how to write a document. And he has also given the signature of the *batab* and the signatures of the *alcaldes*; they do not know how to write.

And I give my signature at the end, I the notary [*ah dzibul*]; completed on the fifth day of May in the year 1595.

Don Jorge Canul, *batab*.

Alonso Canche of Calkini.

Miguel Cutz, Pablo Balche, Pablo Cauich, Pedro Ayil, *alcaldes*.

Alonso Cab, notary [*escribano*].

Juan Tut, *regidor*.

Here in the *cah* of Nunkini in the jurisdiction [*tu cuch baal*] of San Luis Calkini, today on the fifth day of May of the year 1595, appeared the principal men [*nucte uinicob*] to make their statement about the *batabob*, the senior *batabob*, the *batabob* of the *cahob*, when the foreigners arrived. The first ones were don [TC:35] Miguel Canul, *batab* of Calkini, and don Juan Canul, senior *batab*, a relative of don Miguel Canul —who is the father of don Jorge Canul, *batab* of Nunkini—and don Francisco Ci, *batab* of Kulcab, father of Agustín Ci. On this day.

Here in the *cah* of Calkini, today on the fifth day of the month of January of the year 159[5],[62] gathered together the nobles, the principal men, our ancestors [*ca kilacabil*], to pass on their memory and understanding before their *batab*, Ah Tzab Canul—Nachan Canul being his [birth] name.

When there were not many *cahob* here, these were the homeowners: Nachan Che, Namay Tayu, Napot Canche, Ah Kul Couoh ✝; with the Cupul and those of Ceh Pech they surrounded[63] the subjects of the Xiu. Their lands and forests were recorded when the *cah* of Mayapan broke up; they were remembered by us of the *chibal*, by whoever we are descended from. [TC:36] This is the reason that the lands and forests of us Canul descendents are intact. We also know how we came from the east, we Maya men,[64] and that we come from those people of West Zuyua.[65] At that time we did not defend ourselves individually; we Canul nobles[66] pulled together. Traveling along the road, they came to rest in the Itza region,[67] which is where those of the Canul name came from; uprooted, they first were sent along the road to rest at Thoncucsuuna and at Kaxek, and [going] to the east [they came] also to Cabchen, and to the east to Sucte, and to the east onto Lake Ixkalakche.

At the corner of that which belongs to Dzitbalche is the great stone mound, to the south of Dzitbalche property; here to the north is that which belongs to Calkini and Yiba, Uxmal and Ochil and Nohcacab, and also to Sacluum and Canxel—a *cah* that was taken and settled by Sacluum—[TC:37] and to Cumul and Haatzchen and Kanche.

These roads were shown to us by our *batab*, Ah Pa Canul, Ah Dzun Canul, of the *chibal* of Ah Itzam Canul and Ah Chuen Kauil—who settled where the Itza were and established order there. And [to the north lie] the lands of Chulul, of those who came from within the *cah* of Mayapan. They end at Copouatun; there they end and go back again; this is the land's end. There shall be no purchase later on; we know that here end the Canul lands. At present a portion of the Canul area that is for the people of Xamancab should rightly go to the edge of the lands of Acanceh, and not next to Chakan-Tiho.[68] It [the border] passes to the east of Ucu until it reaches the coast of the sea; there at the seaport of Kopte is the Canul shoreline. Likewise there is [on the coast] Sisal and Ninum and Tixpat [TC:38] and Kinchil. There is on the Canul sea a stone house, the Coba stone house, that of Kinchil Coba and Homonche. At Pachcaan[69] the Canul sea ends; there the Canul sea begins. Ah Kin Canul has his boats on the Canul sea; he has four which are used for fishing by his slaves—who were at Sacnicte well when the foreigners arrived at the entrance to the lands of Campeche [*canpech*], at the seaport. At Homtun the lands of Campeche end; it is not on those of the Canul area. The sea coast of Campeche ends at Dzaptun; at that point it [the coast] is taken by Champoton.

Today on the ninth day of December of 1582 ended the opening of the street [*u hol calla*] here in Calkini. Fray Pedro Peña Claros did it. Three years [TC:39] it took to make it. There were many *batabob* there when it was done; all the *batabob* were here.[70]

I saw this book [*quaderno*] [and] map of those of Calkini, and it has twenty useful folios, including this one. Crespo.
[3]9 pages.[71]

We who are men of Calkini, Juan de Dios Puc, Juan Ascención [*Acencio*] May, Basilio Che, José Tziu, Bernardino Chim and don Francisco Che, Manuel Roman May and Manuel Antonio Pan, we arrived at the great *cah*, the head-town [*noh cah cabesera*], of Mani, in order to uncover the map of the communities [*u mapail u cahalob*] that they have in the great archive [*Noh Archivo*] made for them by don Francisco de Montejo Xiu, governor here in Yucatan.[72] We have just been given the truth; [TC:40] and we truly saw where is the end of our lands and our forests, as stated in the map given to us and in our possession. This verifies this map which we uncover, on this day, the twentieth of November of 1821.

Juan de Dios Puc.

Ascención May.

Basilio [Che].

I, Simón Tzab wish that it be given to them by the foreign lord constitutional and municipal *alcalde*[73] here in Mani.

Simón Tzab, of Mani.

MAYA CONQUISTADORS
The Pech Accounts from Chicxulub and Yaxkukul

CHAPTER 6

The Maya manuscripts translated in this chapter are presented as a single document although they actually represent four community histories and Conquest accounts. As will be explained, these are the parallel texts from Chicxulub and Yaxkukul, communities (*cahob*) ruled by nobles of the Pech lineage (*chibal*), which incorporate an account from another Pech *cah*, Motul, and one from the Cupul region to the east.

The only extant version of the Chicxulub manuscript is a nineteenth-century copy made by Juan Pío Pérez. This copy later became the property of José Rafael Regil y Peón, until the Mexican Revolution exiled Regil from Yucatan in 1915, after which the manuscript disappeared from his house in Merida. It has never resurfaced. Fortunately, William Gates had photographed the document—how much we owe to Pío Pérez and Gates (see Chapter 5)!—making possible its translation below.[1]

An older and more legible copy of the Chicxulub's sibling manuscript, the Title of Yaxkukul, survives in Tulane University's Latin American Library. This document of 1769 had passed from the Maya *cabildo* of Yaxkukul into private hands by 1918, when it was presented as legal evidence in a land dispute between the Chan brothers and an *estanciero* named Castro Fortuny—this was according to Juan Martínez Hernández, who published a transcription and Spanish translation of the document in Merida in 1926.[2]

The two manuscripts—the Title of Chicxulub and the Title of Yaxkukul—are very nearly identical, and I have thus made of them a single translation.[3] The similarities between the two accounts strongly suggest either that one Pech community copied from another, or that various *cahob* made out their own written versions from a master Pech account whose origins were at least partly oral. Probably both patterns occurred. In the second half of the sixteenth century, Maya communities began to draw up a variety of written records, some under local impetus, others to meet colonial requirements. In this way oral accounts of the Conquest came to be recorded along with land treaties, thus generating Yucatec versions of the colonial Mesoamerican genre of the primordial title (one example of which was presented in the previous chapter). Over the decades and centuries these documents were copied and recopied, both from earlier versions in the same community and from versions maintained by neighbors.

No doubt other Pech *cahob*, such as Conkal and Ixil, once kept near-identical titles. Indeed, a portion of what I have dubbed the Title of Motul can be found embedded within the Title of Yaxkukul, presumably reflecting this text-borrowing pattern.[4] Furthermore, the Pech were apparently not the only Mayas in the north to maintain a community history of this sort. One section of the account presented below, embedded within the Chicxulub and Yaxkukul manuscripts and identical in both, appears to have originated in the Cupul region to the immediate east of Pech country (or Ceh Pech); I have called it the Title of Saci-Sisal, as those *cahob* (upon which the Spaniards founded Valladolid) feature strongly in the account. The Cupul title nevertheless includes people and places from Ceh Pech, possibly as a result of a Pech editorial hand during the copying stage; note in particular the rather propagandist assertion that the Pech were the principal *chibal* of the Cupul region.

The complex and protracted composition of the text of the Pech titles clearly complicates their dating. One portion of the Yaxkukul account is dated 1522; even if, as a couple of scholars suggested,[5] this is an "error" for 1544, the problem remains of the document's description of events up to 1552, let alone the unlikelihood of Mayas being this alphabetically literate by the early 1540s.[6] I suspect that the Yaxkukul notaries were going for 1542, a date of composition claimed by the Chicxulub version, because of its symbolic value to the Spaniards—who viewed

the founding of Merida as the colony's moment of genesis. The attempt to appeal to the Spanish sense of historical significance failed,
however; a colonial judge, presented with the Yaxkukul manuscript in
1769, read its date claim as 1522 and promptly pronounced it "without
validity." From the Western viewpoint, the Spanish judge, and the Yucatec historians just mentioned, are right; the Title of Yaxkukul, in its
1769 form, was not written in 1522—or, for that matter, even in the sixteenth century. But from the Maya viewpoint, the issue is entirely different. The very characteristics of the Pech titles that made them suspect
to non-Mayas—their compound chronology and compilation structure and their emphasis upon the symbolic meaning of dates—were
those which imbued them with value and validity for Maya notaries
and nobles.

The Pech titles are thus neither "authentic" Conquest-era accounts
nor "fraudulent" late colonial constructions (for a parallel discussion of
authenticity see Chapter 9). Rather they are a mixture of both, reflecting barely filtered eyewitness views as well as long-term perspectives
colored by colonial considerations. The most prominent of these considerations was as relevant to the Conquest era as it was to the end of
the colonial period—indeed as it was to the decades before the Spanish
invasion. I refer to the promotion and protection of the privileges of
each *cah* and its Pech nobles, with the interests of community and family so closely intertwined that the variations in author and *cah* names in
these titles barely alter their substance and significance at all. Accordingly, while I refer to Macan Pech and Nakuk Pech as the titles' authors,
they share responsibility for the manuscripts both with generations of
notaries and editors, and with generations of Pech nobles who used
Macan and Nakuk as representative, ancestral advocates for family and
community interests.

The Titles of Yaxkukul and Chicxulub (incorporating the Title of Saci-Sisal and the Title of Motul)

The Foreign Conquistadors [TY:1r; TCH:19][7]

Captain don Francisco [de] Montejo, the first to settle the *cah*, the senior magistrate, with Bernardino de Villagómez [Villagenes] and Francisco de Siesa, *alcaldes*, and Luis Diáz and Alonso de Arévalo [Arevarlo] and Francisco Lugones and Pedro Díaz de Monxibar and Alonso de Villanueva [and Gonzalo] Guerrero, *regidores*, Pedro de Molina, *procurador*, Juan de Cuenca, notary, Baltasar de Gallegos, majordomo, and Andrés González de Benavides.[8]

Juan de Azamar	Gaspar González
Juan López de Mena	Pedro Zurujano
The other Blas González	Francisco Hurtado [Hurado]
Marcos de Salazar	Pablo de Arriola
Alonso Baez	Pedro de Lugones
Francisco Hernández [Hernades] Calvillo	Mister [Miser] Esteban
Juan Núñez	Francisco Ronquillo
Alvaro Osorio	Pedro Costilla
Juan Enamorado	Santistevan [Santesteban?]
Toribio Sánchez	Antonio Ruiz [Rios]
Juan Gutiérrez Picón	Pedro Durán
Marcos de Ayala	Damian Dovalle
Martín Ruiz [Luis] Darce	Martín Recio
Diego de Ayala	Miguel de Tablada
Juan de Cárdenas [Cardenias]	Juan de Palacios
Juan de Contreras	Pedro de Valencia
Juan López de Recalde	Giraldo Díaz
Rodrigo de Cisneros	Alonso Parrado
Alonso González	Belez de Mendoza [Mondesa]
Francisco Martín	Martín de Velasco
Francisco Hernández [Hernades]	Juan Rodríguez
Esteban Xinobes	The names of the conquistadors who set-

Juan Bote
Juan de la Cruz
Juan de Morales
Martín Garrucho
Francisco de Palma

tled Tiho when Tiho was founded; and they settled the *cah* of Bacalar [*bakhalal*] but only until they returned [TCH:20] to live again in Tiho, at the end of the year 1545. Captain Francisco Montejo and his *cabildo* book recorded the settling of Ichcansiho[9] and the names of the conquistadors, all of whom founded this new *cah*.

Likewise, [TY:1V] this was when they gathered together in the second founding year; likewise,[10] having traveled and gathered and blessed this land here, in this way they settled in these two *cahob*, Ichcansiho and Bacalar [*bakhalal*]. The first one, then, to request the pleasure of being received as a resident was this don Francisco Montejo, the son of the *adelantado*, lieutenant to the chief ruler [*halach uinic*] and to the Captain General in these colonies [*u hedzlumob*]. Likewise, on this same day the authority [*hahal u than*] of the *cabildo* was established; so too were the first *alcaldes* and *regidores* established and settled. And I have written the names of those in power; therefore they are written down so that the truth be well known;[11] thus their true names are below.

Alonso de Reynoso
Alonso de Arévalo
Alonso de Molina
Alonso Pacheco
Alonso López Zarco
Alonso de Ojeda
Alonso Rosado
Alonso de Medina
Alonso Bohorques
Alonso Gallardo
Alonso Correa
Andrés Pacheco
Antonio de Yelves
Bartolomé Rojo
Blas Hernández [Hernades]

Francisco de Arceo
Francisco Tamayo
Francisco Sánchez
Francisco Manrique
Francisco López
Francisco de Quirós [Quiro]
Fernando de Bracamonte
[TCH:21] Gaspar Pacheco
Gonzalo Méndez
Gaspar González
García de Aguilar
García de Vargas
Gómez de Castrillo [Castillo]
Gerónimo de Campos
Hernando de Aguilar

Beltrán [Betran] de Zetina   Hernando Muñoz [Muño] Baquiano
The other Baltasar González, *cabildo* porter
Cristóbal de San Martín   Hernando Muñoz [Muño] Zapata
Diego de Briceño   Hernando de Castro
Diego de Medina   Hernando Sánchez de Castilla
Diego de Villarreal   Juan de Urrutia
Diego de Baldivieso   Juan de Aguilar
Diego Sánchez   Juan López de Mena
Esteban Serrano   Juan de Porras
Esteban Martín   Juan de Oliveros [Oriberos]
Esteban Yñigez [Yniague] de Castañeda   Juan de Sosa
Francisco de Bracamonte [Bracamote]   Juan Bote
Francisco de Siesa   Julián Doncel
Francisco de Lubones [Lobones] Juan de Salinas
[TY: 2r] Juan Cano   Juan Vela
Juan de Contreras   Juan Gómez de Sotomayor
Juan de Magaña   Juan Ortíz [Orti] de Guzmán
Juan Vizcaino   Juan de Escalona
Juan de Parajas   Juan de[l] Rey
Juan Ortes   Juan de Portillo
Jorge Hernández [Hernades]   Baltasar [Batasar] González[12]

[TY:2v; TCH:1][13] It was in the fifth part of Katun 11 Ahau when the Spaniards came and settled there in that city [*noh cah*] of Tiho. Then it was in 9 Ahau that Christianity began. This was the year that the Spaniards first came here to this land: the year 1511.

I who am Macan Pech, the first noble conquistador [*yax hidalgo concixtador*] here in this land, of the district of Chacnicte, I was given to the principal *cah*, Yaxkukul.[14] I now compose in good order the state and history [*u belil u kahlail*] of the *cah* here of Santa Cruz; my first governorship is this *cah*, with its chapel [*capilla*], of Yaxkukul.[15] My name was Ah Macan Pech before I was baptized [*ococ ha tu pol*]; I am the eldest son of Ah Tunal Pech who comes from the *cah* of Motul.[16] When I was promoted to guard the *cah* of Yaxkukul,[17] there was no sign of the coming of the Spaniards here to this land of Yucatan. Thus I was chief ruler [*halach uinic*] here in the land of Yaxkukul when our

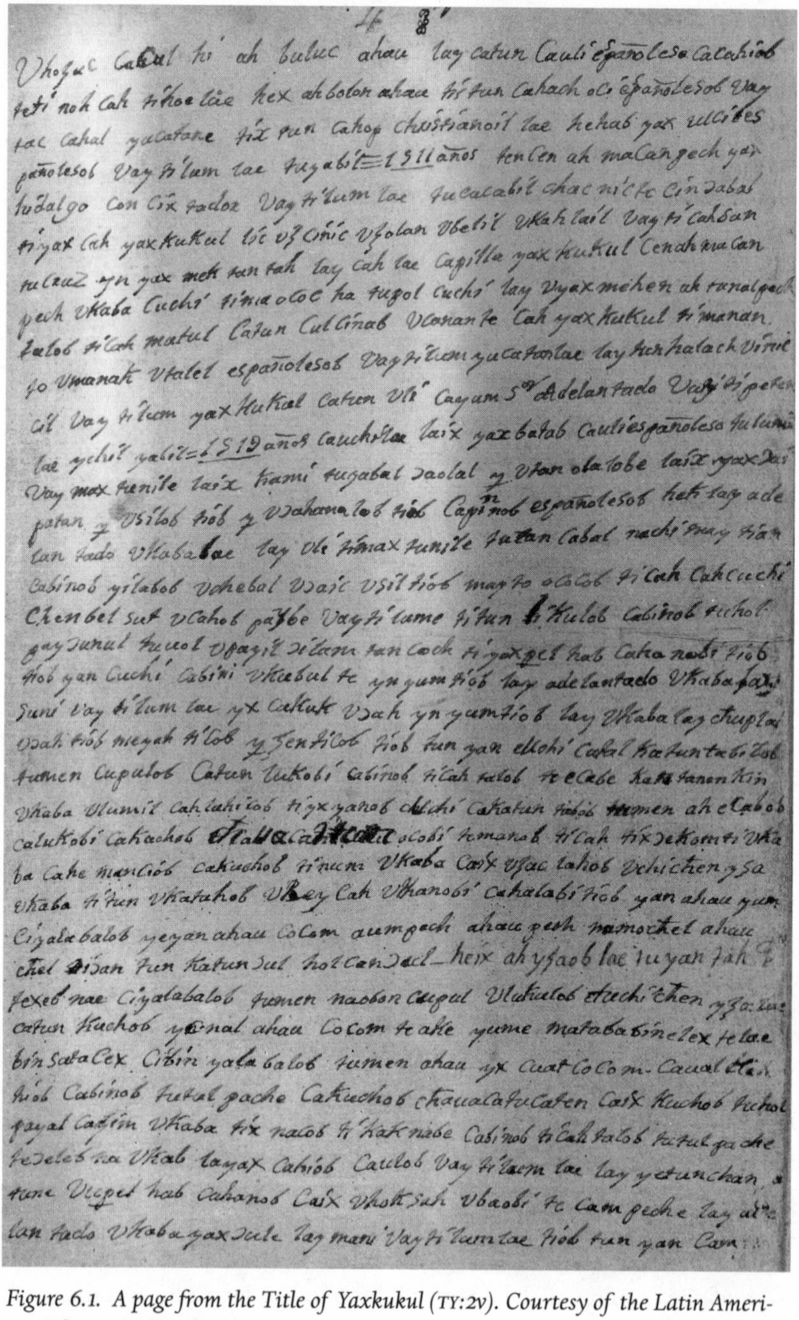

Figure 6.1. A page from the Title of Yaxkukul (TY:2v). Courtesy of the Latin American Library, Tulane University

lord the *señor adelantado* came here to this province during the year
1519.

I was also the principal governor [*yax batab*] at the time when the
Spaniards came here to the land of Maxtunil; I also received them
with abundant attention; I also first gave tribute and respect and gave
food to the Spanish captains. [TCH:2] He who was called *adelantado*
came to Maxtunil to the patio [*tancabal*] of Nachi May; they were
there when we went to see them in order to give them respect. They
did not enter the *cah* to settle at this time; they only traveled through
the *cahob* of this land.[18] Then from here they went to Dzunul seaport,
to the seaport of Dzilam, where they resided for three and a half
years. They were there when my father went to surrender [*u kubulte*]
to them. He who was called *adelantado* returned here to this land; my
father gave them Ix Cakuk, as the woman was named whom he gave
them to work for them and feed them. They were there when they
were attacked by the Cupul; then they left, and went to stay at Ecab—
the land where they settled is called Kantanenkin. They were there
when they were attacked by those of Ecab, so they left and arrived at
Chauaca, which they entered, moving on to the *cah* of Dzekom
[Tekom]—as the *cah* they passed through was called—[19]and they arrived at the *cah* named Tinum. They then went looking for Chichen
Itza, as it is called, where they asked for the king [*Rey*] of the *cah*.
They said and told them, "Lord, there is a ruler [*ahau*]"; and they told
them, "There is the Cocom ruler, [and] Naun Pech, the Pech ruler,
[and] Namo[20] Chel, the Chel ruler of Dzidzantun." "Foreign warrior,
foreign soldier, rest here in those stepped houses [*xebnae*] of the
Itza!"[21] they were told by Naobon Cupul. They departed from Chichen Itza and arrived with the Cocom ruler at Ake. "Lords, you cannot leave here, you will get lost," they were told by the ruler Ixcuat
Cocom, so they turned around and went back again until they arrived
at Chauaca, for the second time also arriving at the seaport called
Catzim, where they took to sea and went subsequently to reside at
Dzelebnae, as it is called, where they had first stayed when they came
here to this land. [TCH:3] They remained in Champoton [*chanpatun*]
for seven years,[22] until they went to Campeche. He who was called
adelantado, the first foreigner, passed here through this land. It was

while they were in Campeche [TY:3r] that they asked for tribute, and
so it was that at the orders of the *batabob* [governors] of all the *cahob*
tribute was brought to them; the tribute carriers traveled by sea. I
went there with my younger brother, Ixkil Itzam Pech, ruler of the
cah of Conkal [*cumkal*], and with Ah Dzulub Pech, of the district of
Ixil.[23] These were my companions when I went for the tribute; they
too saw it. Nachi May also accompanied us, because he knew their
language, for they first stayed in his house when they came here;[24] he
and the Spaniards were together when there was a delivery by the
captains. From them we had been given clothes—coats and cloaks;[25]
we were made very content by these captains, and we left when
the Spaniards stopped giving these gifts. Thus when we arrived we
already had our clothes—the coats and cloaks; Ixkil Itzam Pech of
Conkal, and also his companion Ah Dzulub Pech of Ixil, were my
companions.[26] I, Ah Macan Pech of Yaxkukul, as was my name, was
principal *batab* when they first delivered tribute, when we went to
Campeche to deliver tribute, and we came back while the Spaniards
were coming on the road from Campeche, coming from the *cahob* to
settle at Ichcansiho, the city [*noh cah*] of Tiho. When we heard that
the Spaniards were coming,[27] we went to give them gifts a second
time, and went a second time to deliver tribute.[28] I, Ah Macan Pech,
with Ixkil Itzam Pech, the senior *batab* of Conkal, with Nakuk Pech,
batab of the district of Ixil, there counted out the gifts for them; we
gathered together at Dzibilkal for the second time in order to deliver
gifts;[29] they received turkeys and honey and sweet foods. Finally they
left Dzibilkal [TCH:4] so as to come and live in Tiho. This don Francisco de Montejo, Captain General, was the first to come here to
this province of Tiho with Francisco de Bracamonte and Francisco
Tamayo and Juan de Pacheco and Pedro Alvarez [*perarberes*].[30]

These captains came in the year 1541; in that year they came to settle Tiho. These captains commanded the Spaniards that came to Tiho.
I, Ah Macan Pech, was *batab* when the Spaniards came to Tiho. They
were the first to receive tribute when the Spaniards arrived in Tiho. I
was the principal *batab* here in the *cah* of Yaxkukul.[31] Meanwhile, Rodrigo Alvarez was notary during the year 1542. When the *cahob* were
divided up among the conquistadors by the captains of the *adelantado*,

the first Spaniards, and the notary Rodrigo Alvarez, wrote down the
tribute evaluation pertaining to each of the *cahob*. And accordingly all
my companions, those of my *chibal* [i.e. fellow Pech], delivered tribute
—sufficient tribute according to the division of tribute to the Spaniards made by the captains of the *adelantado* and the notary Rodrigo
Alvarez. Each and every year Spaniards came to Tiho and began to
take over the lordship of the principal men of all the *cahob*.[32] And Ah
Macan Pech was also taken and given to Gonzalo Méndez; he was the
first to have the lordship [*yumil*] of Yaxkukul here; he was the first
encomendero, and he took him [Ah Macan Pech] by the hand and in the
presence of Captain don Francisco de Montejo, *adelantado*. And he
was placed in the *batabil* [governorship] by the hand of Gonzalo Méndez, and this principal man Ah Macan Pech began to serve the tribute
of the lordship. He bore the responsibility of governing the community[33] when Gaspar Suárez [*uares*][34] arrived as first *alcalde mayor* [Span-
ish district official] here in this province of Tiho, Yucatan; and also
when Alvara de Carvajal [*Cauayor*] was first *alcalde mayor*; and when
the *oidor* Tomás López came, he was *batab* there at that time. He used
to be called Ah Macan Pech until he was baptised [*oci ha tu pole*] and
he received baptism [*bautismo*]. Don Pedro Pech, the son of don
Alonso Pech, and his second son, don Miguel Pech, were given names
as rulers of the same [lineage] name [*u kaba*] as Ah Macan Pech—
[TY:3v] as *hidalgos* [*ydalgosob*], as principal *batabob*—by the captains
who first seized this province here.[35] These were the first to pay tribute to the foreigners, and this status [i.e. as *hidalgos*] was given to
them through God [*dios*] and the reigning king [*Rey ah tepal*], to all
of their descendents until their days are gone.[36] [TCH:5] These were
the principal *batabob* here in this land when there were no holy
churches [*santa yglesiasob*] in the districts, before the Spaniards began
to travel around the country or to congregate together in order to
worship Dios.[37]

For formerly the common people were not all Christians; all the
subject people[38] then received Christianity when Ah Macan Pech was
batab and likewise received the Holy Oils and the Holy Faith, so that
[I might teach][39] all my *cah* subjects. He was also the first to receive
the baton [*bara*] of justice, whereby he instituted the word of Dios

and our great lord, the ruling king [*ca noh ahau ti Rey ah tepal*]. Then
our lord the *oidor* Tomás López[40] became the first here to give out the
tribute measurement[41] to the *batabob* of all the *cahob*; he lightened the
tribute burden and then the *oidor* Tomás López finished his term of
office [*yahaulil*]. Then he [Ah Macan Pech] delivered his baton to his
son, don Alonso Pech,[42] during the year 1552.[43]

This was the number of the year; it was in this year that the service
began to my lord don Miguel Pech, governor here in Yaxkukul, thirty
years to my father, Ah Macan Pech, don Pedro Pech, the son of Ah
Tunal Pech. His four constables [*tupilob*] thus came to settle with their
lord Ah Kom Pech here in the *cah* of Ixil and also in the *cah* of Maxtunil. The principal *chibalob* there in Yaxkukul were those of Nakuk
Pech and Ah Macan Pech.[44] And the councillors came together when
they came here to reside,[45] and they came with their priests [*ah kinob*]
and their captains [*holpopob*] and their deputies [or officers; *ah kulelob*]
together with their chief rulers [*halach uinicob*], when they came here
to the *cah* of Yaxkukul and settled here.[46] Ah Macan Pech, don Pedro
Pech, was appointed by his father, Ah Tunal Pech, the son of Ah Kom
Pech—his son was also Nakuk Pech,[47] of the first [TCH:6] *chibal* of
Maxtunil—to govern the *cah*. When the foreigners came here to the
land of these districts there were no Maya people who wished to pay
tribute to these first foreigners. They were the first to converse with
the Spanish foreigners, after which Ah Macan Pech was given charge
of the *cah*, being the first to receive the *cah* of Yaxkukul when the
magistrates [*u chun u thanob*] came. They came together with their
deputies and their captains and their priests, whose names were Ah
Kul [deputy] Matu and Ah Kul Che; the priests were Ah Kin [the
priest] Cocom and Ah Kin Tacu; these were the priests who held
office when they came here to establish Yaxkukul with Ah Kul Kiix.
The captains who came with them were Nachan Cen and Captain
Xuluc; these were the captains when they settled the land here at
Yaxkukul.[48]

There also came the warriors [*holcanob*] and their officers [*nacomob*]: Officer Ku,[49] Officer Xuluc, Officer Poot, Officer May—his
name was Ah Cuy May, and Officer Ek; these were the names of the
officers under the authority of the *batab* Ah Macan Pech when they

came here to the *cah* of Yaxkukul. They were those selected to serve [*muk*] the *cah*. They were [TY:4r] brought out by the chief ruler and selected for the *cah* of Yaxkukul by its principal men. There were no others and they alone were selected for the *cah* here of Yaxkukul.[50] The Spaniards had just come to the city [*noh cah*] of Tiho, and Christianity was received by the people here of Ceh Pech; the *cah* had just been gathered together [TCH:7] by my father here in Yaxkukul *cah*,[51] when the war began between the Spaniards and those of Cochuah over the land and *cah* of Ichmul. My father, Ah Macan Pech, and Nakuk Pech, of the principal *chibal* of Maxtunil, and Ixkil Itzam Pech, of the principal *chibal* of Conkal [*cumkal*] went together to the war. Then began the Cochuah tribute; they were thus subject to the lordship of the principal men;[52] when they went to the war there was much misery because of the expenses of the principal men [i.e. the Spaniards]. For six months this suffering was endured by my lords accompanying the principal men. My father was then governing through his magistrates [*u chun thanob*]; these men really saw that it all happened just as I have related it in my report [*in informacion*], all of it, so that it may be known by my *chibal* members, by my sons, after me, after my death here on this earth. For my *título*, my *probanza*,[53] was given to me through our lord Dios and our great ruler, the reigning king; I have no tribute nor do I pay tribute, nor will my sons nor my daughters pay tribute. For our lord Dios released me from it in the fear of my heart; before I had yet to see the face of the Spaniards He gave me the will to deliver myself and all my *cah* residents of every *cah* into the hands of the Spaniards, of the captains of the *adelantado*, the first conquistadors who came here to this land of Yucatan.[54]

This is the year in which the foreigners first came here to this land of Cupul—the year 1511.[55] The Spanish foreigners had not previously been seen by anyone when Gerónimo de Aguilar was captured by the people of Cozumel [*ah cusamilob*]. [TCH:8] Thus the whole country [*peten*] became known, once they had walked all over it; previously all the lands [*lumob*] had not been touched by them—all the lands of the country. So I then related this before the ruler, when Ah Macan Pech, don Pedro Pech,[56] and his followers, and the principal men of his

chibal, and all his captains with him, went before the ruler; they all
went with him to honor the ruler, that he might see the faces of his
commoners [*u maseualob uinicob*]. And so thirty of the principal men
[*u nucil uinicob*] went afterwards with the captain don Francisco de
Montejo, *adelantado*,[57] to the ruler, the reigning king, to obey him at
his table [*messa*] far off in Spain. Those who remained also obeyed the
reigning king. Then the ruler said that everyone should pay tribute,
even all the nobles, even we who are the Pech, the first *chibal* here in
this land, and the first *chibal* therefore of the Cupul. When it was said
that there was a great province with many Maya people and things in
the land, our great ruler therefore [TY:4v] ordered that an account be
made of it for him, for which purpose they came to affirm the land
boundaries of the ruler's subjects. Thus the land was discovered by
Aguilar, who was taken as a son-in-law[58] by Ah Naum Ah Poot of
Cozumel [*cuzamile*]. In the year 1517, in this year, ended the catching
of the *katun*, ended the selecting of the community stone [*u tunil
balcah*]. For formerly the community stone had been selected every
twenty years [*tun*], when the Spanish foreigners had not yet come to
Cozumel and here to this province; because the Spaniards came, we
stopped doing it. In the year 1519 the Spaniards first came here to
Cozumel [*cuzamil*], for the first time [came] Hernando Cortés [*fer-
mado de cortes*] and Espoblaco Lara [*espobalco lama*]. Those who know
can testify that it is true that they came to Cozumel for the first time
on the twenty-eighth of February. In this year the custard-apple eaters
first arrived at Chichen, and then for the first time Chichen Itza
became known to [TCH:9] the great Spaniards, to Francisco Montejo,
adelantado, the chief ruler [*u halach uinicil*] when they gathered at
Chichen Itza. In the year 1521, on the thirteenth day of August, the
land of Mexico was conquered by the Spaniards. In the year 1528[59]
it happened that the Spaniards were attacked by the *cah*—by all the
Cupul residents here—when they went looking for Ah Ceh Pech,
upon the death of [i.e. having killed] Sulibna and his lord [*ahau*] Cen
Poot of Tixkochoh in the province of Tekanto, as well as Kinich
Kakmo of Izamal, the ally of Holtun Ake. This was the year in which
the Spaniards arrived in Chichen Itza for the second time—to settle
Chichen Itza—and it was when Captain don Francisco de Montejo ar-

rived, he who honorably captured [*yah tohil yah tocil*] Naobon Cupul. Twenty years had passed since they had first arrived in Chichen Itza and were called custard-apple eaters, custard-apple suckers.[60]

1542 was the year when the Spaniards founded Ichcansiho, on Chuncaan [mound]. All the discussions and the agreements began there at the place called Chuncaan.[61] The priest Kinich Kakmo and his ally Ah Tutul Xiu—the ruler of the head-town [*cabecera*] of Mani, the head of the land [*u pol luum*], the seat of the principal *chibal*—these were the first to begin paying tribute to them there. The third time they [the Spaniards] came to this land, they settled permanently and are thus settled here today. The first time they came to Chichen Itza was when they first ate custard-apples; never before had custard-apples been eaten, so when the Spaniards ate them they were called custard-apple eaters. The second time they came to Chichen they seized Naobon Cupul. The third time they came was when they settled permanently.

That was in the year 1542, when they thus settled permanently in the Ichcansiho region, where they are today—13 Kan being the year-bearer according to the Maya calendar [*ti maya xoc lae*].

1543 was the year that Ah Tzitz Mop was killed in the war with the Spaniards.[62] This was also the year that the Spaniards went north to the Chel region to procure Maya men to be servants [*maseualtobe*] because there were no commoner men [*maseual uinic*] to be servant boys [*u paliltob*] in Tiho; they came to procure men to be ordered about as servants. It was when they reached Popce that they increased the tribute payments to Tiho. Having reached Popce, they then went on to Tikom; they remained at that time [TY:5r] in Tikom; the Spaniards were there for more than twenty days before they left.

1544 was the year when foreigners descended on Cauaca; Asiesa was the captain when they descended on Cauaca. Thus it happened that the lords [*yumili*] came to begin paying them tribute. They gave them honey, turkeys, and maize. They were in Cauaca when they locked up Ah Kul [officer] Camal of Sisal in prison and demanded a census [*u xocan*] of the whole *cah*. He was locked up in prison by them for a year. [TCH:10] It was he who guided the Spaniards when they came to live in Saci [Valladolid]; this Ah Kul Camal of Sisal entered into the *batab*-ship [governorship] of Saci-Sisal, and became named don Juan de la Cruz Camal, because he spoke very truthfully and was the first to set up a cross [*cruz*] in Cauaca. The foreigners listened to what he said, and thus he entered into the *batab*-ship at Sisal. He was *batab* a long time before he died. He also guided the Spaniards when they went to wage war with those of Cochuah. These foreigners stayed in Cauaca for a year before leaving to come to Saci to settle permanently; they locked people in prison, as seen in [the case of] that *batab* Camal.

In the year 1545 the foreigners descended on Saci. This was the year Christianity was introduced by the padres of the order of San Francisco in the port of Champoton; there the padres first came, having in their hands the redeemer called Jesus Christ [*Jesuchristo*] with which to gesticulate to the common people. This was when they first came to the port of Champoton, to the west of this district—Ichcansiho, as they say here; Ichcansiho, as the *cah* of Tiho is called. These are the names of the fathers who began Christianity here in this province [*cah peten*] of Yucatan; these are their names: fray Juan de la Puerta, and fray Luis de Villalpando, and fray Diego de Béjar [*becal*], and fray Juan de Herrera,[63] and fray Melchor de Benavente. These were the ones who started Christianity here in the west of this province, before Christianity came here to our Cupul *cah*; afterwards Christianity came quickly to us here in Cupul, so they say.

In the year 1546 there occurred an uprising [*ah etzil*]. The country rose up on the ninth of November. Peace returned in four months, but following the ninth day of November of the year 1546, there were four months of war. When they had previously started it [war], the men were on the run for a year; when they came to gather a second time to put together the wax tribute, they initiated a war; brought together to confer, the insurgents [*ah etzob*] then came west to deceive the people and organize the war. The insurgent Canul and Ah Camal came west. The foreigners that they killed were two foreign boys, students of Mena; they died in Chemax, where they were left. Then this Mena[64] and all the foreigners came to Saci eager to wage war against them; then began the killing. The insurgent Camal of Pakam—he was from Pakam—killed Surujano [*surusana*] in Nicte. One night a foreigner was killed by the people of the *cah*, by the men, because they fell sick in their hands and feet; there was then war for a day and a night in all the *cahob*.

1547 was the year when a boatload of black people [*ek boxe*] was shipwrecked at Ecab and the Spaniards went to capture them; they waged war upon the blacks [TCH:11] at Ecab and brought out those black people tied together [*uak ek boxil lae*].

The year 1548; the hermit padre⁶⁵ came to Saci [Valladolid] to begin Christianity.

The year 1550; there was a gathering of all the *cahob* tied to Mani.

The year 1551; the padre guardian fray Fernando Guerrero came to Saci-Sisal and he baptized the people. He introduced Christianity here into the whole district of Saci: they came from Chikin Chel; they came from Ecab; they came from Cozumel; they came from the north; they also came from the south. He initiated the construction of the monastery that is at Sisal. 1552 was the year [TY:5v] the padres resided away from where they were before; in this year there arrived here at Sisal teachers and singers, who came from the west to teach and sing mass and vespers with the singing of the organ and flute, and the plain-chant, which we never knew here before.

1553 was the year the *oidor* Tomás López arrived here in this land of Yucatan; he came from Castile, a messenger sent by our great ruler, the king of Castile,⁶⁶ to protect us from the hands of the Spaniards here. He put a stop to our being robbed by the Spaniards, he put a stop to the dog bitings, and he introduced the appointing of *batabob* in each *cah* by the giving of the baton and of commissions for the *batab*-ships.⁶⁷ He also set the tribute rate for the third time, the tribute obligation to the Spaniards. Cotton blankets, wax, turkeys, maize, wooden buckets, salt, peppers, beans, pots, pans, and jars; these items above are the tribute paid to the lord foreigners before the *oidor* gave his attention to these things. At this time occurred the capture of Kul Chuc by Ah Macan Pech; and they left Sisal [to do it], because he asked to be the captor of Kul Chuc, who had eluded capture by Ah Ceh Pech here in Cupul.⁶⁸ He came here to the *cah*, coming with Ah Kin [the priest] Pech, Macan Pech, the first conquistador, the servants [*u palil*] and officers [*u nacomob*] of Macan Pech, here to Yaxkukul.⁶⁹

They did not pay tribute[70] because they were the first to be given the baton by the captains of the *adelantado* [Montejo] here in these our districts [*ca cabob*]; nobody may take from them their *probanzas* [proofs of status]. Power [*uchucil*] was given to them by the king reigning in Spain [*pañia*], for not all the subject people [*maseual uinic*] have to deliver tribute to the foreigners. They also went before the king, who is truly far away; the ruler, the reigning king, was far away, as don Pedro Pech, the governor, told his sons, don Alonso Pech, don Miguel Pech, don Lucas Pech, and don Francisco Pech. There was also Ursula Pech, who was called Cakuk Pech; she gave chocolate to the *adelantado*, the first of the captains; she was the elder sister of Ixkil Itzam Pech and the daughter of Tunal Pech, the conquistador of Motul, whose ancestors took possession of it in the past. These too were the councillors and officers—including Kom Pech and his son Nakuk Pech of the principal *chibal* of Maxtunil—who governed the principal *cah* here of Santa Cruz, as Yaxkukul here was named, of the jurisdiction of Ah Macan Pech, called don Pedro Pech, who was the first to receive the [governorship of the] *cah* from the Spaniards. These are the names of the priests, the officers who accompanied the captains; these are their names: Ah Kul [officer] Matu, Ah Kul Chel,[71] Kul Kiix, and Kul Che; and the priests were Ah Kin [priest] Cocom and Ah Kin Tacu. They governed when they came here to the land of Yaxkukul [TY:6r] from the district of Chacnicte, from the district of Cupul. And Ah Kin Chuc also came; he came from Ecab, for there he had been named Kul Chuc and was captured by Ah Ceh Pech there in Cupul. He had been named Kul Chuc because he was courageous.[72] He was then given to don Pedro Pech, Ah Macan Pech, by don Francisco de Montejo, the *adelantado*. These then were the others who descended here to this land, the principal *cah* here, from Cupul: the captains Chan, Cen, and Xuluc; the warriors Officer (*Nacom*) Kuob, Officer Xuluc, Officer Poot, Officer May, Officer Ek, Kul Chuc—the Kul Chuch who was the servant of Ah Macan Pech, and Officer Poot; and the deputies, the rest of the principal men, sons, and sons-in-law. Two or three years passed in which they were resident [here], while they were appointed to the *cahob* by our lord foreigners, while the *oidor* surveyed the *cahob* and the forests[73] of the *cahob*, and certificates [*sedulas*] were in his hands from our great ruler in order that the forests could be divided up among those who had settled them. Then the conquistador don Pedro Pech ordered it to be done by the councillors and captains with measuring rope[74] and the Itza priests. They and that don Pedro Pech did not pay tribute, because they delivered themselves to God [*Dios*] and to the great ruler [*noh ahau*], truly of their own free will; because they were afraid [i.e. feared God], they delivered themselves.

The Year 1541

[TY:7r][75] This is the declaration of how the Spaniards came here to this land, through the will of our lord, the ruler, Dios, here in this province. It is also the statement of our lord *señor* don Juan de Montejo, and don Francisco de Montejo [*monte*], who were the first to come here to this land and also to order the building of churches [*iglesia*] in the head-town and *cahob* of every district, a *cah* home, and a temple [*kuna*] for our lord, the great ruler, and also a *cah* guesthouse,[76] a home for travelers.

It is likewise the account of our great lord, Ah Naum Pech, don Francisco de Montejo Pech, and don Juan Pech, as were their names when they were baptized by the padres. And the *adelantado*, the first captain of those who came here to this land of Yocol Peten[77]—given the name of Yucatan by the first lord Spaniards—and our lord Spaniards likewise declare that this indeed is what was done. When they said that we are to live eternally with Dios, the Maya people [*maya uinic*], as they were called, heard them.

Naum Pech then spoke to his subjects of every district: "Know that one god[78] is coming to the *cah*, to the province; the true Dios; by the sign of the true Dios will you live! Welcome him! Do not wage war against him! Offer up your food or drink—maize, chickens,[79] turkeys, honey, and beans to eat—so that Christianity may enter the *cah* and that we may be servants of Dios." They then agreed that nobody would wage war but that they would commit themselves to going and helping the Spaniards in their conquests and to traveling together with the foreigners.

Likewise Nachi Cocom, of the *cah* that headed the district of

Sotuta [*sotupta*; *Sutuyta*] in the province of Chichen Itza, that which was called Chichen Itza, and Ah Cohuoh Cocom, assisted the word of Dios and our great ruler, raising up the standards and banners of our [TCH:13] great ruler and of the conquest. And so the *adelantado* and our lords the padres, the clergy assigned to the *cahob*, also did not make war, but refrained from evil, and laid out a church [*kuna*] and homes for their *cah* subjects.

Nadzi Mabun Chan also established in his district the understanding of how eternal life was coming to the *cah*, and wished that truly would be delivered to Dios the Catzin and Chul people of the district of Mani, as well as the Tutul Xiu, and here to the east those of Lakin Chel and Cupul, and Nadzaycab Canul in Campeche. Thus was this province here redeemed by its service to Dios.

[TY:7v] Here on the mound, the home, of Sacmutixtun of Sacuholpatal, here in this *cah*, Tunal Pech of Motul settled. And here Ah Naum Pech called the young men and said to them: "Know that One Imix is the name of the day when, at dawn, there will come from the eastern districts bearded men carrying the sign of one god [*hunab ku*] to the province! Go and receive them with your white pendants! Do not make war on them![80] Go and receive them with true joy!" Therefore they went and journeyed beneath the trees, beneath the branches, until they arrived at the patio of Nadzaycab Canul in Campeche. Then they told him: "Your guests are coming very soon, Ah Nadzaycab Canul; receive them promptly, O lord!" That is what they said. When the ships appeared at the entrance to the port of Campeche, and when they saw the waving of the banners and white pendants, they knelt down before the *adelantado*. Then they were asked by the Christians and the *adelantado*, in the Castilian language, "Where do you live?" As they did not understand the language, they could only reply, "We do not understand what you are saying [*matan cub a than*]." Because of these words, they said that this land here of the wild turkey, this land of the deer, was Yucatan.[81]

Therefore the captains and our lord the *adelantado* don Francisco de Montejo went on; and they made much cloth and thread to cut into clothing for the horses [*tzimin*], as they wished to go to the *cah* of Mani where Ah Tutul Xiu was. When they reached Yiba, they conferred in Yiba; leaving Becal, they arrived at Nohcacab; thus the Spaniards passed through and arrived at Mani, where Tutul Xiu was. And he then appointed Officer [*nacom*] Ikeb, Officer Caixicum, and Officer Chuc to go and invite Ah Cuat Cocom. As a result, they were put in a cave by his subordinates and their eyes were put out beneath a large sapote tree [*ya*]. Then they took one of them whose eyes had not been put out at the sapote, and in the cave of Sabin [or Weasel Cave] they put out his eyes. Then they set them on the road to go groping to where the *adelantado* was;[82] thus returned [TCH:14] those who were thrown out of the *cah* of Ah Cuat Cocom. Then Ah Naum Pech left with two of them and went to bring Ah Cuat Cocom. When they arrived, he said to Ah Naum Pech that he had neither seen nor heard of it; he said he had gone to Chichen Itza. Straightaway he was brought by the Pech and arrived at Mani to give up the prisoners; Ah Cocom quickly said that he had not seen what had happened in his *cah* and that he had given authorization for those who had [TY:8r] committed the crime to be seized. Then Ah Pech came to the *cahob* in order to see his subject people; there he had come when the foreigners also came, because it happened that a foreigner had been killed by his subordinates. Then they passed on and went to where Ah Batun Pech and Cay Chel were; having seen them, they went to Maxtunil, where Nachi May and Ah Macan Pech were. They then returned to their lands in their jurisdiction of Yaxkukul, so as not to abandon the deputies. In Tixkumcheil they did not give up building a palisade around the *cah* because they did not want foreigners in the *cah*. Therefore Ah Naum Pech stayed put in Yaxkukul, for he was not envious of them; those of the *cah* at Tixkumcheil had always been treated like dogs; their end was shown by the will of Dios in the *cahob*.[83]

From now on then this is the history [*ytoria*] of don Pedro Pech and don Martín Pech,[84] of all the places through which the lord *señor* Spaniards passed, and of the deliverence by the first padres, and of the names of the first foreigners; it shall be set down as it was heard, because it is composed in order that it may be known how the conquest [*concixta*] occurred, and what manner of suffering they went through, here beneath the trees, beneath the branches, beneath the foliage, in those years,[85] and of the rest of the principal men and their

sons and their sons-in-law. Two or three years passed in which they
were resident [here], while they were appointed to the *cahob* by our
lord foreigners, while the *oidor* Tomás López surveyed the *cahob* and
the forests of the *cahob*, and a certificate [*sedula*] was in his hands from
our great ruler in order that the forests could be divided up among
those who had settled them,[86] by those who previously had no *cahob*.
For we were all of us natives here, before, during the reign [*u halach
uinicil*] of Naum Pech, before, when the foreigners had not yet come
to establish Christianity in this land. But then the day came for their
arrival here in the province, and when the foreigners came here to this
land of Yucatan, we went to receive them with fear in our hearts, and
Christianity was introduced here to this land, and we were appointed
to guard the *cahob*; for when as yet there was no church, then there
really was no *cah*. Here now begins my [TCH:15] declaration of how
the conquest took place and of how much suffering we went through
with the *señor* Spaniards, because of the Maya people [*maya uinicob*]
who were not willing to deliver themselves to Dios; now then I, don
Pablo Pech, recount what I heard about the district of Maxtunil. We
did not settle until we descended to the district of Chicxulub; when
the holy church had just been built, then we measured its dimensions
and took possession of it so that our children should remain there
after their death on this earth, so that we should not be hindered by
the Maya people, subjected neither to their witchcraft nor their stone-
throwing; for we have entrusted ourselves to our lord Dios with fear-
ful hearts. Therefore power was given to us by our great ruler, the
reigning king; and thus the church was established in order to worship
our lord Dios; and the *cah* home to the east of the church [*iglesia*], the
temple [*kuna*] of our great ruler; and the guesthouse. I also built my
home, a house of stone, to the north of the church. The Maya people
may not say one day that it belongs to them; this is why I make it
clear that I did not build it for them. I, lord don Pablo Pech, and Ah
Macan Pech, and my father don Martín Pech, Ah Kom Pech, and my
lord don Ambrosio Pech, his Maya name also being Op Pech, and Ixkil
Itzam Pech, and don Esteban Pech, Ah Kulul Pech; we received the
great commissions to measure the forests, under license given by our
great ruler, the reigning king to our lord the first *oidor*, Tomás López,

so that we might be given to understand his word to us, so that we might measure the borders of the abandoned houses that exist here at the edge of the *cah*, so that we may know where the boundaries of our lands pass in order that our descendents may maintain them and give food to the *encomenderos*. Therefore I give an oath [*u juramentoil*] before all the people that this information is true, that they may see the abandoned houses and not enter another's abandoned house; I therefore give the truth. The first *encomendero* here in the district of Chicxulub was don Julián Doncel, *encomendero* here in this *cah*. He told the governors [*batab caxicob*] to have the markers of the bound-aries of their forest lands placed here around the jurisdiction's *cahob*; therefore they measured the boundaries of their lands and their for-ests to the east, to the south, and to the west, all of the places where there are residents. For Christianity was already established here in this land of Chicxulub and of our holy lord Santiago the patron who guards the *cah* of don Pablo Pech.

Then they measured,[87] section by section, from around the holy church here in the old *cah*, extending out to the forest landmarks of my sons. This is truly my signature, today, eighth of May of 1522.[88]

Don Pedro Pech; for don Alonso Pech and don Miguel Pech and don Francisco Pech and Ixkil Itzam Pech and Ah Dzulub Pech and Tunal Pech and all their descendents who shall live here afterwards. He who was the first *encomendero* here in the *cah* of Yaxkukul was Captain don Julián Doncel, *encomendero* here in this *cah*. When previ-ously there was no church here, he told the *batab* that he should pro-vide the landmarks of the forests and lands of the jurisdiction around here, that the borders of the forests to the north, to Cupul in the east, and also in the west, should be measured. Then the privileged nobles [*ah matanob hidalgosob*] and the councillors got themselves up and went out to place the stone mounds [*pictunilob*] around the *cahob*; thus they got up and went out to the forests. Straightaway they went to the district of Chacnicteil; for four or three days they labored in Chacnicteil so as to know where the borderline of the territory runs. And Ah Macan Pech said, "Today, we shall go to the west." And so all together they placed the first stone mound to the north of the edge of the Chacnicte well. Then they went west, passing inside the lands that reach the edge of the Dzadza well. There is a great corner [*noh sicina*] there; at the base of Dzadza mound is a cross ✝. Then they went towards the southwest, organizing the spaces between the stone mounds, going along so as to reach Kanpepen, where there is a stone mound at the edge of the well. Going along, organizing the spaces between the stone mounds, so as to reach Chuncatzim. There is a great corner there, and a cross ✝. Going along to the south, organizing the spaces between the stone mounds, until [TY:8v] passing Pacabtun; going along organizing the spaces between the stone mounds towards the south as far as Komsahcab. Then going southward until emerging on the highway [*noh be*], the road to Sicpach; in the middle of the highway there is a cross ✝, the end of the lands of the people of Sicpach. Going southward until reaching the great corner of Yokactun, there is cane [*halal*] and a great corner; at the cane of Yokactun there is a cross ✝. At the corner [*titz*] of the forests of the people of Nolo, going eastward, to the east of the cane, as far as Huhbilchen; there the stone mounds are organized; there is a stone mound at the entrance to Huhbilchen well. Going eastward to reach Chacabal; to the south of Chacabal there is a stone mound. The stone mounds are organized coming as far as Kanpepen, where there is a stone mound. Going as far as Uste, where there is a stone mound; going eastward, organizing the spaces between the stone mounds, emerging at the road to Nolo, where there is a cross ✝. Going eastward, to the west of the road to Tixkokob, there is a cross ✝. The other stone mound is at the foot of Cacablum, to the east of that road. Going as far as the great stone mound to the south of Chachil well; having organized the stone mounds and gone eastward as far as the entrance to Tahtzek well, there is a stone mound at the corner facing Kancab. Having gone east and organized the stone mounds as far as Ticinmul, there is a stone mound at the entrance to Ticinmul well; at the great corner there is a cross ✝. Then going northward, organizing the stone mounds and going along until reaching Yaxicim, where there is a great corner. The great corner turns to the northwest. Going along to Piste, the stone mounds are organized up to Tixualahtunich; the stone mounds are laid out towards the west until one emerges onto the road, the middle of the road which comes from Tixkumcheil. Then they walked along two corners and entered the west, where there is a stone mound [*multun*] to the west of the road. Having gone westward and organized the stone mounds [*pictunil*] until reaching Chenhaltun, they came eastward and then went to the northwest as far as the great corner of Euan Cauich; there is a cross there +. From the great corner going toward Yokmux there are stone mounds organized. The stone mounds go along to the west until reaching Sahcablum, where there is a stone mound. This line goes westward towards the arrangement of stone mounds coming from the east, to the east of the mound of Chacnicteil, which closes the line of the possessions of our *cah*; for this is where it began here in Yaxkukul.[89] Because they had just opened the roads between all the *cahob* and created the *cahob*,[90] all the Maya people were thereby brought together—from the west, from the east, and from the south where the Xiu ruler is. Thus were we settled by these foreigners. Here are those who first confirmed Ah Macan Pech in office: Captain don Francisco de Montejo, *adelantado*; and Julián Doncel. Here is the one who gave power to the ruler Tutul Xiu, the principal *batab* there in Mani: Captain Gonzalo Méndez [*menes*], who was also the first *encomendero* there. And the captain in Cupul was don Francisco de Bracamonte [*Bracanmote*]. And those empowered not to pay tribute were Na Tzuc, Na Chan, and Na Kuk Pech, daughters of the tribute-exempt Pech [*ah mapatan pechob*] here in this principal *cah* of Santa Cruz Yaxkukul. This is a valid forest title [*u tituloil kax*] pertaining [TY:9r] to the possessions of Yaxkukul, the property of don Pedro Pech, Ah Macan Pech, the principal *batab* here in the *cah* of Yaxkukul, granted by our lord don Francisco de Montejo, *adelantado*, and Captain Julián Doncel. This is the true origin of the title and map of the *cah* possessions. Today, the eighth of May, of the year 1522.[91]

Ah Macan Pech, resident member [*ah cahanal*] of the *cah* of Yaxkukul; don Lucas Pech, the son of don Pedro Pech; don Francisco Pech; don Miguel Pech; don Alonso Pech, the son of don Pedro Pech, Ah Macan Pech, descendent of Tunal Pech; here is that Alonso Pech, the son of don Pedro Pech; don Alonso Pech's son is don Juan Pech, the father of

Bartolome Pech; Bartolome Pech's sons are Diego Pech, whose son is Andrés Pech; here are the true conquistadors—don Francisco Bracamonte and Gonzalo Méndez, Julián Doncel, don Francisco de Montejo, Martín Méndez.

THE CRUEL CYCLE
The Accounts from the Books of Chilam Balam

The Books of Chilam Balam are compilation volumes written during the colonial period for Maya audiences. They consist of prophetic, calendrical, historical/mythological, ritual, satirical, and medicinal information. A number of examples have survived, each named after their *cah* of origin or maintenance and varying from community to community.[1] Although they appear to contain some material from pre-Conquest versions of these books, possibly a master book authored by a priest or prophet (*chilam*) named Balam (a Maya patronym), extant Chilam Balam books date from at least a century after the Conquest and probably no earlier than the eighteenth century.

In some respects the Books of Chilam Balam are like the primordial titles of the preceding chapters. Both genres are quasi-notarial, written by *cah* notaries and *maestros* (schoolteacher-choirmasters) who were approved in office by the Spaniards to perform duties that did not include maintaining these books. Both are also compilations whose copying and recopying over the centuries resulted in alterations, additions, and omissions—and thus extant examples cannot be specifically dated. Accordingly, the Conquest accounts in both types of document contain traces of Conquest-era perspectives while also reflecting the cultural impact of centuries of colonialism.

The excerpts selected below from the books of Tizimin,[2] Chumayel,[3] Mani,[4] and Chan Kan[5] feature prominent passages that are structured as annals; indeed they compare closely to the Annals of Oxkutzcab (Chapter 4), which could well have been copied from an

129

early version of a local Book of Chilam Balam. Potentially these excerpts could have run to dozens of pages, but I have kept them brief for several reasons. First, the Chilam Balam literature is, unlike the other texts in this volume, widely available in various English-language editions. Second, many passages are repeated in somewhat altered forms from book to book, complicating the selection process. Third, the majority of Conquest references in the books are ambiguous descriptions of periods of warfare, migration, upheaval, and various calamities, often couched in a discourse of riddles and metaphors that is less accessible than the other sources presented in this volume; a sample of such passages suffices to demonstrate their perspective on the past. Fourth, where Conquest references are more accessible in the Books of Chilam Balam, they tend to take the form of straightforward, dispassionate annals entries; again, a couple of examples are sufficient.

One example from those ambiguous Conquest passages is the final paragraph of the Chumayel excerpt below. The references to Mayapan and the Itza suggest that the precolonial period is being interpreted, yet the colonial period is evoked by other phrases: the description of what presumably are the diseases brought by Europeans to the Americas; the use of *dzul* ("foreigner"), a common colonial-era name for a Spaniard; and the reference to the tribute cut-off age introduced in the late sixteenth century. There is also a feeling of immediacy to the warning of the final sentence. It seems most likely therefore that both the precolonial and Conquest periods are being described here. The passage is intended as an indictment of foreign invasion and political change, the evils of which are considered endemic to the process, regardless of the who-and-when specifics.

This general condemnation of conquest thus offers considerable insight into Maya views of history and of the Spanish invasion. While the historical perspective of the Chilam Balam annals is clearly linear, there is also a parallel awareness of a lamentable repetition of the community's experiences—an awareness of the cruel cycles of Maya history.[6]

Although, as I commented above, these Chilam Balam examples are part of an intertextual series and thus feature many parallel passages, there is still a notable difference between the texts from the Xiu region —the Chumayel and Mani (both *cahob* are featured in the Mani map;

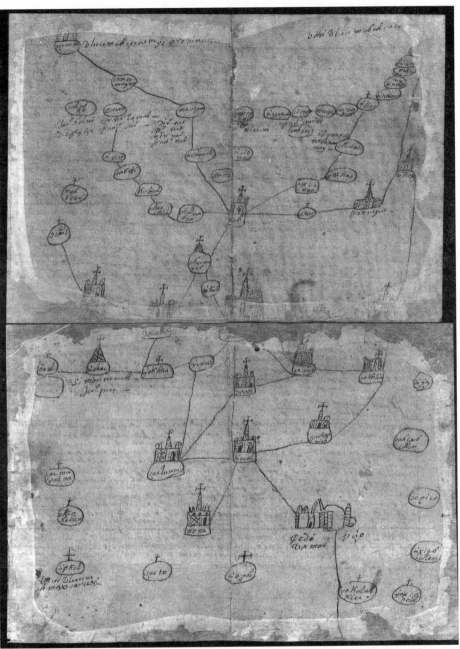

Figure 7.1. A sixteenth-century Maya map of the Mani region, from the Xiu Chronicle. Courtesy of Tozzer Library, Harvard University.

Figure 7.1)—and the Tizimin, a book from the Cupul district to the east
(see Map II). As one of the preeminent Chilam Balam scholars has
noted,[7] the impact of Spanish on the language of the Chumayel was
three times greater than its impact on the Tizimin's language, reflecting the more profound incorporation of the Xiu district than of the
eastern areas into the colony. Consequently the Xiu, relatively early allies
of the Spaniards and converts to Christianity, denigrate the easterners
(whom they call Itza in the Chumayel) for perpetuating conflict and being slow to accept "Dios." Correspondingly, from the Tizimin perspective, the Xiu are illegitimates; thus, argues Edmonson, in this book the
Xiu-Itza rivalry is seen as the real story of Maya history, from ancient
times through the Conquest and to the end of the colonial period.[8]
Without losing sight of the themes of long-term continuity and of rivalry between regions and *chibalob* (lineages), we might also note an
additional interpretation of the antagonism expressed in the Tizimin
text; the disdain expressed for the new rulers in times of turmoil (including, but not limited to, the Conquest era) could also be a class perspective, in which the ruled lament the poor quality of their rulers.
These rulers could be Xiu or Itza, Maya or Spanish (one is reminded of
Alonso Canche being appalled at the bad manners of the Spanish invaders, as told in the Title of Calkini); or all of the above.

Excerpt from the
Book of Chilam Balam of Tizimin

[CBT:54; f.16r] 11 Ahau was the first *katun*,[9] the start of the *katun* count.
In the first part of the *katun*, the white men [*sac uinicob*] arrived. Ichcansiho was the seat of the *katun*. How their beards were red, the
sons of the sun, [CBT:55] those white men! How we wept[10] when they
came! From the east they came until they arrived here, the bearded
ones, the carriers of the white god [*ku sac*] displayed up on a cross
[*uaom che*]. One league, one ear-shot before they came, you could see
them. They came to make piles of logs and piles of stones; with them
came the fathers [or lords] of our souls, to introduce the word of the
true god [*hahal ku*] to your hearts. That declaration, the word of god

raised up, will be planted among the whole *cah* membership [*bal cah tusinil*]. How we wept when they came! You younger brothers, you elder brothers, the word of god is no lie; the coming of the word of the lord of heaven and earth shall be fulfilled! Receive and welcome the coming to the *cah* of the people of those stone façades.[11]

[CBT:59] 9 Ahau was the second part of the *katun* whose count, whose *katun* seat, was at Ichcansiho [Tiho]. It was also the start and the rise of Christianity, which was taken up by the whole *cah* membership, here in the surrounding land. [CBT: 60] It was also the start of the building of the church [*ku na*] that is in the middle of the *cah* of Tiho. A great deal of work was the burden of the *katun*. It was also the start of hanging, and there began too the epidemic of stones under the arms, white lumps. They brought their diseases and their ropes with them to those districts, to all over the community, coming to infants and younger brothers with their forceful demands, their forced tribute. There was also a great initiation of tribute, and a great initiation of Christianity; and the transition to the seven sacraments, the word of the great Dios. Receive and welcome the coming to the *cah* of those older brothers of ours!

[CBT:63] 7 Ahau was the third part of the *katun* whose count, whose *katun* seat, was at Ichcansiho. Yaxal Chac was the one who went into the lordship, to organ music below and tambourine sounds above.[12] Plumeria [*nicte*] food and plumeria water were the burden of the *katun*. There was also the start of the meeting of the wise men, who rolled their eyes at us, the *cah* members; these lords of idiocy[13] were Kuk Yaxum and Amaite Uitz, who was the one whose words were deceitful and insane. The Jaguar Possum and Jaguar Fox[14] no longer issued the word of the *katun*. There was also the start of the anal boils *katun*. There was also [CBT:f.16v] the start of the quail branch plumeria [*bech kab nicte*]. Bring out a great reception for the coming into your communities, the coming to your *cah*, of the request that you be Christians on this very day!

[CBT:67] 5 Ahau was the fourth part of the *katun*; at Ichcansiho was the count, the *katun* seat, the rule, the shield of the *katunob*. There also took place the hangings of the principal men [*u nucul uinicob*]; this was the death of the great *chibal* [lineage(s)]. There was also the

start of illegitimate women's sons, illegitimate men's sons; insane
women's sons, insane men's sons. They came and went with the god
faces [i.e. masks], with the holy faces, of the four disguises of heaven,
the four disguises of the way. There was also the start of the demands
of the devil [*u tsa cisini*]; and the arrival of the season of rain and
witchcraft [*u esili*] too. [CBT:68] There was the start of famine that
affected the *cah* membership. It provided the means to the end of the
maintenance of the *chibal* [lineage(s)]; it provided the power over the
chibal of the rain lord [*chac ahau*] Can. There was the start of those of
the two-day throne, those of the two-day mat. The reputation of
Jaguar Possum and Jaguar Fox was that of dog and vulture. Two were
their hearts; there were many two-faced men,[15] their faces miserable,
day and night. The burden of the *katun* was that the word of god
above [*ku canal*] was now mocked.

Excerpt from the
Book of Chilam Balam of Chumayel

[CBC:20] 11 Ahau is the beginning of the count, because this was the
katun when the foreigners arrived. They came from the east when
they arrived. Then Christianity also began; in the east its word [proph-
ecy] was fulfilled. The *katun* was established at Ichcansiho [Tiho].

This is a record of the things which they did. After it had all passed,
they told it in their own words, but there is no clear meaning to it all.
Yet it passed directly as it is written. Although it can all be clearly
understood, they did not see it, they did not write so much then,
nor was very much written of the accusations of their conspiracies
against each another. Thus it was with the ruler of the Itza, with
those of Izamal, Ake, Uxmal, Ichcansiho; also the Couoh people of
Citab. The very many chief rulers [*halach uinicob*] did not make forced
sales of [i.e. did not force each other to reveal] their conspiracies with
one another. Nor are they revealed in what is [written] here; that
much cannot be told! For in fact that knowledge comes from our
chibal [lineage], we who are the Mayas. He will know the meaning of
the account that is here. When he sees it, then he will understand

how the *katun* was made covetous [i.e. turned out badly] by our priest, Ah Kin Xuluc; but Xuluc was not his name formerly.[16] It was only because it was the time of this wretched priest of ours, that misery was introduced, that Christianity was introduced by the real Christians, who arrived with the true god, the true Dios. Herein was the beginning of our misery. It was the beginning[17] of tribute, the beginning of tithes, the beginning of violent purse-snatching, the beginning of violent rape, the beginning of violent crushing of people,[18] the beginning of violent robbery, the beginning of forced debts, the beginning of debts from false testimony, the beginning of violent hair-pulling, the beginning of torture, the beginning of violent robbery. This was the origin of service to the Spaniards and to the priests, of service to the *batabob*, of service to the teachers, of service to the public prosecutors [*fiscalob*] by the boys, the youths of the *cah*, while the poor people were made to suffer greatly. These were the very poor people who did not depart despite the violence that was done to them. This was the Antichrist [*antachristoil*] here on earth, the kinkajous of the *cahob*, the foxes of the *cahob*, the human leeches of the *cahob*, the bloodsuckers of the poor commoners. But it shall still come to pass when tears shall come to the eyes of our lord Dios, the justice of our lord Dios shall descend everywhere in the world, straight from Dios upon Ah Kantenal [he who adulterates maize], and upon Ix Pucyola [she who destroys souls], the avaricious sorcerers of the world.

[CBC:21] In the year 1541; 181 [days, i.e. the middle point of the year, when] the foreigners were in Tiho was today, December 9, a year-bearer [*2nhele*]. The history which I have written of how the mounds were constructed by the heretics [*heregesob*]. They were built during a period of seventy-five *katunob*,[19] made by the great people; these people then went to Cartabona,[20] as the land was called at the time they were there. They were there when San Bernabé came to teach them, but he was killed by the people—the heretics, as the people were called.[21]

1[5]56 is today's count, fifteen years [later]. Today I have written of how the great mounds were built by the *chibalob* [lineages], and of the deeds of the rulers, who made these mounds in a thirteen-*katun* six-

year period. This was their construction burden, the origin of the
mounds that they built. Six thousand and fifty mounds was the total
tally of the mounds they built all over the land—the peninsula
between the sea and the base of the land. They also named them,
as well as the wells. Then a miracle was created for them by Dios;
they were burned by fire in the *cah* of Israel, with the timber that was
there.[22] This is the history of the *katunob* and the years [*haabob*] since
the *chibal* of the Tutul Xiu left Viroa Chacunescab.[23]

The count of the *katunob* and years when the province of Yucatan
was first seized by the foreigners, the white men. Their seizure of the
port of Ecab took place during *katun* 11 Ahau. They came from the
east when they arrived. They were the first to eat the custard-apple for
breakfast; this is the reason they were called the pond-apple foreigners; the foreigners who sucked custard-apples, they called them. This
is the name of the householder whom they seized there at Ecab:
Nacom Balam [Captain Jaguar] was his name. He was the first to be
seized at Ecab by the first captain, don Juan de Montejo, the first conqueror. It was here in the province of Yucatan. Their arrival at Ichcansiho took place during this same *katun*.

It was in the year 1513 in *katun* 13 Ahau when they seized Campeche. They were there for one *katun*. Ah Kin [the priest] Camal of
Campeche admitted the foreigners here into the province.

Today, on August twentieth in the year 1541, I have made known
the name of the years when Christianity began.

In the year 1519, after seven score and eleven years, occurred the
agreement with the foreigners,[24] according to which we paid for the
outbreak of war between the foreigners and the other men here in
the *cahob*. It was those captains of the *cahob* [who waged war] then; it
is we who pay for it today.

Today I have written that in the year 1541 the foreigners first arrived
from the east, [from the place] named Ecab. In that year occurred
their arrival at the port of Ecab, at the *cah* of [CBC:22] Nacom Balam,
on the very first day of the year of *katun* 11 Ahau. After the Itza were
dispersed, it was three hundred years until the foreigners arrived. The
cah of Saclahtun was destroyed; Kin Chil's *cah*, Coba, was destroyed;
the *cah* of Chichen Itza was destroyed; the *cahob* outside Uxmal, to

the south of Uxmal, named Cib and Kabah, were destroyed. The *cahob* of Seye, Pakam, Homtun, at the *cah* of Tixcalomkin, and Ake, Holtun Ake, were destroyed. The *cah* of Emal Chac was destroyed, Etzemal [Izamal], where the daughter of the true god, the lord of heaven, descended, the queen, the virgin,[25] the miraculous one. Then the ruler said: "The shield of the glorious Kakmo has come down; he was not declared ruler here. Declared here was she, the miraculous one, the giver of love. The rope has descended, the cord has descended from heaven. The word has descended from heaven." There was rejoicing over this lordship in all the *cahob*, who were told not to declare the lordship of Emal.

Then the great Itza left. Five thousand, two hundred was the number of their thousands, and six thousand the number of their hundreds, the principal men, the heretics, the Itza. But those who fed them [i.e. their servants] went also; many went with them to feed them. Thirteen measures of maize per head was their quota, and nine measures and three handfuls of maize. Many girls from the *cahob* went with them, before them, and behind them.

They did not wish to join with the foreigners; they desired neither Christianity nor the payment of tribute. The diviners of birds, the diviners of stones, the diviners of flat stones, the diviners of jaguars, they flayed the breadnut trees. Sixteen hundred years was the end of their lives, and three hundred years more, until the end of their lives, because they knew the count of their days. Complete was the month; complete, the year; complete, the day; complete, the night; complete, the breath of life as it also passed; complete, the blood, when they arrived at their beds, their mats, their thrones. They measured to find the good hours; they measured to find the good days; thus they measured to see the good stars enter [the period of] their rulership. They measured to observe the rulership of the good stars, all the good years [*tun*].

Then they were in agreement, of sound mind. There was no sin; they lived in their holy belief. There was no sickness then; they had no aching bones then; they had no high fever then; they had no pustule fever [smallpox] then; they had no burning chests then; they had no abdominal pains then; they had no consumption then; they had no headaches then; in sound health were the people then. The foreigners made it otherwise when they arrived here. They brought shameful things when they came. They lost their innocence in carnal sin; they lost their innocence in the carnal sin of Nacxit Xuchit, in the carnal sin of his companions. No good days were displayed to us then. This was the origin of the two-day throne, of the two-day rulership; this was also the cause of our sickness [or death]. There were no more good days for us; there was no sound judgement for us. At the end of our loss of vision, and of our shame, everything shall be revealed. There was no great teacher, no lord speaker, no learned lord, at this change of rulers when they arrived here. Sexually lascivious were their priests who came to be established here by the foreigners. Furthermore, they left their children, their sons, here at Tancah [Mayapan]. They then received their misery [or illness], having been bitten by these foreigners. These Itza came, the foreigners appeared, three times. This year, because it is the sixtieth year, they will relieve us from paying tribute, because of the biting by these men, these Itza. It was not we who did it; it is we who pay for it today. However there is an agreement at last, so that there might be peace between us and the foreigners. Otherwise, we will have a great war.

Excerpt from the Book of Chilam Balam of Mani

[CBM:70][26] The statement of the priest Xupan Nauat.

The prophecy of the priest Ah Xupan Nauat. My elder brothers, my younger brothers, prepare yourselves! Our elder and younger brothers the white men, the white-faced noblemen, will be coming now. In the time of the eighth year of *katun* 13 Ahau of the Maya rule the thirteenth idol [*ku u uich*] will come; on the day 13 Cauac of 13 Ahau will it be established; its seat will come.[27] The jaguar and the great eagle will be made into shoes by the white man, who will come wearing a visor, with a large mouth, thick lips, and bloody teeth and fingernails. There will come a great plague of ants. There will come too the burden of quarrelling. There also will come the substituting

of your white clothes; your white clothing will be permanently replaced. Baptism will come. The tribute solicitors shall come hopping
along, coming to bring an end to the wishes in people's hearts. Crazy
children, lazy children, will be disrespectful and bellicose; be warned
that they will come to disrespect you. Hairless dogs and vultures shall
come to assume the governorship [*batabil*]; they shall come and show
their faces [grow crops][28] in woodlands and on stony ground; they
shall come wearing visors, seated on carpets, slumped down, with
sleepy faces; they shall be motionless as though they were sick. The
priests and prophets, the great priests and great prophets, will be
replaced by nine wise men who shall appear on the nineteenth day of
the *katun* 11 Ahau. The foundation of the province, its center and
gateway, will from this day forth be the virgin mother—the holy virgin mother [*suhuy kulbil na*] is her name. Thus it is written in the book
of generations [*dzacab libro*], these [CBM:71] documents given to the
priests to revere, to look at, to deduce the *katun* count. It was given to
them because, according to the words of the book of Ah Uuc Satay, it
was at Chuncaan, and from Chuncaan it was taken, from inhabited
Ichcansiho.[29] The reason why this great aid, the seven-generation
book, was given to them to revere was because Hunab Ku had collected the plumerias there; he received each plumeria there.[30] Among
the houses that are seen there, the houses of thatch and the houses of
stone, the rule of the virgin will be established. The people do not
know these things, but at the thirteenth plumeria, they will behold
the holy mother [house];[31] it will be done to the flute and the trum-
pet. [The day] 10 Cauac is the start of the *katun* 11 Ahau; together with
the year-bearers [*u canhelob*] there is the serpent; this second force will
reach ears at the center of the province and, facing westward, invade
—it is war. There will come nine nights tied together, nine of them
before the coming too of much madness, much lust—the time for the
plumeria to open. Children will be conceived late; old women will
conceive them, old women of the plumeria; and old men shall conceive sons, old men of the plumeria. This will be possible because
there will be no youth. Children will now come to take notice of this,
to speak about it; our sons, you will be shipwrecked; you will be at
sea, your ship will list to the side, waterlogged, powerless with only

two or three oars, and it will turn over. One will be asked to go without sandals, to have sore feet, to get used to bruises that are not small;
one will be asked to immediately stop wearing Maya-style trousers
[*u maya exil*], to burn the trousers; we will be asked to have no more
of them. We will cease following the trail of the bird with the blue
arrow feathers.[32] We will become tight-lipped, so that our brothers be
strengthened for the time [CBM:72] when the *chibal* [lineage] will fight
the serpent, when the green lizard will be taken on with force, when
the jaguar [*balam*] will take on the weasel [*sabin*], when the jaguar
chibal will do likewise with the leopard [*chacbool*], with the puma [*coh*].
The trees will be snatched, the rule of the *cahob* will be snatched in 11
Ahau;[33] in the time of 11 Ahau, the jaguar and the leopard will bite
and claw each other; in the ninth year of the *katun* 6 Ahau the jaguar
and the puma—the puma that is a lion [*leon*], the chief rulers [*halach
uinicob*], shall claw each other.

[CBM:134][34] The *katun* arrangement since the departure from the land
and home of Nonoual. The Tutul Xiu were at West Zuyua for four
eras; the land they came from was Tulapan. Four *katunob* had passed
when they journeyed and arrived here with Holon Chan Tepeuh and
his subjects. When they set out for this province, 8 Ahau had already
passed; 6 Ahau, 4 Ahau, 2 Ahau, making eighty-one years [*haab*], as
one year [*tun*] of 13 Ahau had already passed when they arrived here
in this province; eighty-one years had passed when they journeyed out
of their land and came here to this province of Chacnouitan.[35] This
was eighty-one years [*años*].

8 Ahau; 6 Ahau; in the second Ahau Ah Mekat Tutul Xiu arrived in
Chacnouitan; they were in Chacnouitan a year short of a hundred
years. These years came to ninety-nine years.

Then the district of Ziyancaan, or Bacalar [*bakhalal*], was discovered. 4 Ahau; 2 Ahau; 13 Ahau; for sixty years they ruled in Ziyancaan,
then they came down here; during the years that [CBM:135] they ruled
Bacalar, Chichen Itza was discovered. Sixty years.

11 Ahau, 9 Ahau, 7 Ahau, 5 Ahau, 3 Ahau, 1 Ahau; they ruled Chichen Itza for 120 years. Then Chichen Itza was abandoned and they

went to the *cah* of Champoton [*chanputun*], where the holy men of the Itza people had their homes. These years came to 120.

In 6 Ahau the land of Champoton was conquered. 4 Ahau; 2 Ahau; 13 Ahau; 11 Ahau; 9 Ahau; 7 Ahau; 5 Ahau; 3 Ahau; 1 Ahau; 12 Ahau; 10 Ahau; in 8 Ahau Champoton was abandoned. Champoton was ruled for 260 years by the Itza people, who came back to their houses a second time. In this *katun* [i.e. 8 Ahau] the Itzas went to live beneath the trees, beneath the branches, beneath the foliage, where they suffered. These years that went by were 260.

6 Ahau; 4 Ahau; forty years, in which they came to establish their homes a second time and they lost Chakanputun. These years came to forty.

In *katun* 2 Ahau, Ah Cuytok Tutul Xiu founded Uxmal. 2 Ahau; 13 Ahau; 11 Ahau; 9 Ahau; 7 Ahau; 5 Ahau; 3 Ahau; 1 Ahau; 12 Ahau; 10 Ahau; for 200 years they governed along with the chief ruler [*halach uinic*] of Chichen Itza and [that of] Mayapan. These years that went by came to 200.

These *katunob* were 11 Ahau, 9 Ahau, 6 Ahau, and 8 Ahau, in which the *halach uinic* of Chichen Itza was overthrown due to the plotting of Hunac Ceel; this happened to Chac Xib Chac of Chichen Itza, due to the scheming of Hunac Ceel, the *halach uinic* within Mayapan. It comes to ninety years, for after ten years of 8 Ahau came the year of destruction caused by Ah Zuyteyut Chan, Tzuntecun, Taxcal, Pentemit, Xuch[CBM: 136]ueuet, Ytzcuat, and Kakaltecat—these were the names of the seven men of Mayapan. Ninety years.

In this eighth Ahau they went to bring down the ruler Ah Ulmil, because he had feasted with the Ulil ruler of Izamal [*Ytzmal*]. The *katun* cycle had turned thirteen times when they were overthrown by Hunac Ceel in order to teach them a lesson [*u dzabal u natob*]. It ended in 6 Ahau; thirty-four years; the years that went by were thirty-four.

6 Ahau; 4 Ahau; 2 Ahau; 13 Ahau; 11 Ahau; the territory of the fortress of Mayapan was conquered by those outside the wall, by factional rule[36] within Mayapan *cah*, by the Itza men with their ruler Ulmil. Eighty-three years. 11 Ahau had begun when Mayapan was destroyed by the foreigners from the hills outside Mayapan *cah*.[37]

Mayapan was destroyed in 8 Ahau; then came the *katun* 6 Ahau, 4 Ahau, and 2 Ahau, in which the year came when the Spaniards first passed through and were first seen in the land and province of Yucatan, sixty years after the fortress was destroyed. Sixty years.

In 13 Ahau and 11 Ahau there was great sickness and the dying of the Maya in the fortress.[38] In 13 Ahau Ah Pula was killed, when it was six years short of the end of 13 Ahau, the year-count was in the east, [the day] 4 Kan had passed, and [the month] Pop had come; the eighteenth of Zip, 9 Imix, was the day that Ah Pula was killed.[39] That year [*tun año*] that passed may be known in a count of numbers [*u xoc numeroil*], as 1536 years. This happened sixty years after the destruction of the fortress [i.e. Mayapan].

The count of 11 Ahau was not over when the officers of the Spaniards arrived; they came from the east when they arrived here in this land. Christianity began in 9 Ahau; baptisms took place. It was in this *katun* that the first bishop arrived, named Toral [*toroba*]. This year [CBM: 137] that went by was 1544.

It was in 7 Ahau that the first bishop, [Diego] de Landa, died;[40] in the *katun* 5 Ahau the first padre settled at Mani; this year was 1550.

It was in this year that went by that the padre settled on the river: 1552.

It was in this year that went by that the *oidor* [judge] came and the hospital [*ezpital*] was built: 1559.

It was in this year that went by that Doctor Quijada, the first governor here, arrived: 1560.

It was in this year that went by that hangings took place: 1562.

It was in this year that went by that the Governor Marshal came and the reservoirs were made: 1563.

It was in this year that went by that the great sickness [*noh kakbil*] took place: 1609.

It was in this year that went by that men of Tekax were hanged: 1610.

It was in this year that went by that the *cah* was written down [i.e. censused] by Judge Diego Pareja: 1610.

Excerpt from the
Book of Chilam Balam of Chan Kan

[CBCK:26] It was on six Muluc; it was on this day when foreigners conquered this land [*peten*] here. This is that date as they themselves measure it: it was in this year—fifteen hundred and thirteen years [*mil y
quinientas y trece anos*]—that this land was conquered by those foreigners. Eighteen hundred and twenty three [*canbaak catac lahukal catac
hunkal catac oxpel*] is the count of the year.[41]

A HYBRID PERSPECTIVE
The Accounts by Gaspar Antonio Chi

Gaspar Antonio Chi was born during the unsuccessful Montejo campaign of conquest in the early 1530s. His mother was of the Xiu *chibal*, his father a Chi nobleman and a senior political officeholder in Mani; when Gaspar Antonio was still a child, his father, acting as a Xiu ambassador, was mutilated and murdered in an ambush in Otzmal by the rival Cocom *chibal*. In the wars of the Conquest, the Cocom opposed the Spaniards and the Xiu allied themselves with the invaders, a decision that heavily influenced the fate of the young Chi; at fifteen he was baptized Gaspar Antonio de Herrera Chi, with the *adelantado* Montejo's wife, doña Beatriz de Herrera, as his godmother. Educated by the Franciscans in Spanish and Latin, by the age of twenty-five Chi was working as an interpreter; in this important capacity he appears as a Spanish judge's assistant during the great land survey and treaty in the Mani area in 1557.[1] It was also probably about this time that he drew a family tree for his Xiu relatives, a unique piece of iconography that featured Gaspar Antonio himself, along with other late sixteenth-century Xiu nobles, in a deep-rooted and sacred ancestral context (see Figure 8.1).[2]

It is not clear exactly when Gaspar Antonio came to the attention of the zealous Franciscan Diego de Landa, but he and Chi had begun working closely together by 1561, when the friar became *provincial*, or head of the Franciscans in Yucatan; the following year Landa took Chi with him to Mani to assist as interpreter (Landa himself spoke Maya) during the violent campaign against "idolatry" that constituted the final

Figure 8.1. The Xiu family tree, from the Xiu Chronicle. Courtesy of Tozzer Library, Harvard University.

phase of the Conquest in the north (see Chapter 1). When power within the Yucatec church shifted to the first provincial bishop, fray Francisco de Toral, who initiated an investigation into Landa's activities, Gaspar Antonio went to work for Toral as interpreter general. Landa meanwhile returned to Spain, where he wrote up his *Relación de las cosas de Yucatán*, an "account of the things of Yucatan." This unique manuscript must have relied heavily on Chi as a source of information on Maya culture and history—although Chi is never mentioned in the work and when Landa came back to Yucatan to serve as bishop from 1573 until his death five years later, Gaspar Antonio did not work for him again.

Gaspar Antonio Chi's career, in fact, had taken a turn away from the immediate orbit of the Franciscans, for he had soon left Toral's employ and taken up a post as choirmaster and schoolteacher in Tizimin, a Maya community (*cah*) with few Spanish inhabitants on the northeast edge of the colony (see Map II). He did not languish in the boondocks for long, however; by 1572 he had returned to his native Mani, now as governor of the *cah*, one of the most important political posts a Maya man could hold in colonial Yucatan. By the end of the decade, Chi was again resident in Merida, where he acted as a notary and senior interpreter until his death in 1610; in that year he served as interpreter at the trial of the Tekax rebels, and saw the baby son of his granddaughter, who had married a Spaniard, baptized Gaspar Antonio.[3]

In the final decades of his extraordinary career Chi's signature appeared on a wide variety of documents, including *probanzas* filed in 1580 and 1593, reports of service to the Crown intended to win a royal pension—which, sporadically, Chi was granted.[4] He also participated in the completion of the *Relaciones histórico-geográficas*, a compilation of responses to questionnaires sent out by the King of Spain in the 1570s to the provincial governors of the Spanish Empire, to be completed by *encomenderos* and other colonial officials; the questionnaires reached Yucatan in 1577 and were returned to Spain between 1579 and 1581. The purpose of the *relaciones* was an ambitious one—to collate detailed accounts of the histories, resources, and conditions of the subject peoples and territories of the empire, in order to facilitate their rule and exploitation. Two of the questions asked after the religious, political, and economic practices of the local inhabitants before the Spanish invasion; not surprisingly, some Yucatec *encomenderos* simply passed over these questions, but at least twelve of them turned to Gaspar Antonio Chi. In each of these cases Chi either co-signed the response or was acknowledged as its source by the Spanish respondent; judging from the dates of these twelve reports, and the orthographic variations in otherwise identical passages, Gaspar Antonio probably dictated responses to *encomenderos* on seven different occasions.[5] Of the three passages below, the first is from the *relación* of Tiab y Tec; the second and third are taken from the *relación* of Merida.[6]

The text translated below is the only Conquest account in the present volume originally written in Spanish rather than Yucatec Maya.[7] This fact is most significant, for it indicates that we are hereby given a brief glimpse of a hybrid perspective, an indeterminate mixture of native and colonialist understandings of the recent past—the view, in fact, of a Maya noble who lived most of his adult life in the Spanish world, working for Spaniards and speaking their language, but who remained connected in profound ways to the indigenous community into which he had been born.

Chi's cultural multivalency is visually apparent in the hybrid nature of the Xiu family tree iconography (Figure 8.1). The drawing is, like the *relaciones* authored by Chi, clearly European in form and structure (being based on the biblical Tree of Jesse and the Franciscan Tree of Life), but its substance is distinctly indigenous (featuring both central Mexican and Yucatec characteristics).[8] The names of the ancestors function as mnemonics, for example, prompting biographical and historical stories from the Xiu past. This use of a lineage list is similar to that of the opening section of the Title of Acalan-Tixchel (Chapter 3); the stories were probably told to an audience and the illustration was part of the oral recitation or performance. Another example is the importance given to women in the tree, reflecting the pre-Conquest Maya emphasis on the female line of descent; in particular the woman of Ticul, situated at the base of the tree like the Virgin in the European template, becomes sexualized as the fertile founding matriarch to fully complement the patriarch, Tutul Xiu.[9] The mixture of Mesoamerican and European iconographic elements reflects the fact that the tree was drawn both for Chi's Xiu relatives and for the colonial officials to whom it would be presented as part of the collection of Xiu papers proving noble status (the large Xiu *probanza* also excerpted in Chapter 10). But the mixture also reflects the complex cultural identity of Chi himself.

Chi's own voice in the brief accounts below of Conquest-era events can be seen in various ways. His identity as a Xiu comes through in his partisan summary of the history of his maternal *chibal*—his characterization of them as allies of the Spaniards to an extent that parallels the Pech accounts of the Conquest, and his condemnation of his father's Cocom murderer. Chi's indigenous perspective may also be reflected in his less than flattering account of what the Spaniards had inflicted upon the province, in particular his list of the Spanish practices and policies that decimated the indigenous population; in contrast, while pre-Conquest Yucatan may not have been very peaceful, it was, according to Chi, a well-governed, well-peopled land of great abundance. Still, such a view should not be overemphasized as evidence of a distinctly Maya outlook; Spaniards commonly lamented the decline of the native population, and the best-known critic of Spanish colonial practices was a Spaniard himself, fray Bartolomé de Las Casas. Likewise, Chi's explanation of the submission of the Xiu to the Spaniards as providential, with the Maya prophet Chilam Balam essentially acting as a pre-Conquest agent of the Christian deity, can be taken on the one hand as proof of Chi's Hispanization and the Christianization of the Mayas, and on the other hand as an example of the indigenous Mesoamericans' attempts to make sense of the Conquest by reinterpreting the pre-Conquest past (as discussed in Chapter 2). In the end, Chi's take on the Conquest is neither simply Maya nor obviously Spanish, but rather a personal perspective reflecting the complexity of his colonial Maya identity.

The Accounts by Gaspar Antonio Chi, from the Relaciones de Yucatán

When the Spaniards entered these provinces there were many lords in the region, and each community [*pueblo*] had its governors and bosses [*caçiques y mandones*]; and for just one province it had many divisions, according to the factions maintained by one lord against the other and

the wars which they had between them—up until the time the Spaniards, as I said above, invaded these provinces. The lords of this land
were well obeyed because, although they gave orders with little anger,
they executed justice and rigorously punished the vices and sins which
the priests held to be among them.[10] One province fought with another, and the aforementioned province of Mani was always at war
with that of Sotuta—[particularly] with a lord of the ancients of the
land named Nachi Cocom[11]—because of an ancient emnity which the
said Cocom had against the Tutul Xiu, saying that the Cocom were
native lords and the Tutul Xiu foreigners.[12] Thus after the initial invasion of the first conquerors, whom the lords of Mani received in
peace, without any resistance, giving obedience to his Majesty, the
aforementioned Nachi Cocom treacherously killed more than forty
lords of the said province of Mani, who were passing through his
province on a pilgrimage, unarmed and under safe passage—behead-
ing and putting out the eyes of Ah Kulel Chi,[13] who was the most
senior of them, because the said lords of Mani received the captains
of his Majesty in peace and without any resistance and had introduced them into this land, the said Spaniards being a foreign people
of another law.

There were some provinces which never made war on the Spaniards,
instead receiving them in peace—in particular the province of Tutul
Xiu, whose capital was and is the town of Mani, fourteen leagues
southeast of this city [Merida]. There in Mani, a few years before the
Spaniards came to conquer this land, there was an indigenous lord [*un
yndio principal*], who was a priest, named Chilam Balam. This man,
whom they [the Tutul Xiu] held to be a great prophet and soothsayer,
told them that there would shortly come from where the sun rises a
white and bearded people, who would bring raised up a sign like this
+, from which their gods would flee, being unable to approach it; and
he said that these people would become lords of the land, doing no
harm to anyone who received them in peace, but killing those who
waged war against them; and that the natives of the land would abandon their idols and worship only one God, who they [the invaders]
worshiped and about whom they would preach. And he said that they
[the Tutul Xiu] would become their tributaries; he had woven a cot-

ton blanket [*manta de algodón*], telling them that this would be the
kind of tribute that they would have to give. And he ordered the lord
of Mani, whom they called Mochan Xiu,[14] to offer this blanket to the
idols, so that it might be kept and guarded as a memorial. And he had
that sign of the cross and others made out of worked stone and
placed in the patios of the temples, where they could be seen by all,
saying that this was the green tree of the world;[15] and many people
came to see it, as something new, and apparently venerated it from
then on. And later, when the Spaniards came, and they [the Tutul Xiu]
realized that they [the Spaniards] brought the sign of the holy cross,
which was like the one their prophet Chilam Balam had depicted for
them, they took as certain that which he had said; and they determined to receive the Spaniards in peace and not to go to war, but
rather to be their friends, as they have always been ever since they [the
Spaniards] settled in these provinces, helping them with provisions,
warriors, and servants [*jente de guerra y de servicio*] for conquering and
pacifying other provinces.[16]

This land was populated with many Indians, a great many at the time
the Spaniards invaded. The causes of them having decreased are
understood to have been the war of the conquest with the Spaniards,
which finished off some of them. Also the change they made in their
customs after [the war] must also have partly wiped them out,
because in the time of their heathenism they used to get drunk on
a wine[17] which contributed greatly to their bodily health by being a
purgative, and they were stopped from drinking it as they had used
it with idolatrous ceremonies and rituals. Also their having been
brought together and congregated in towns and removed from their
ancient settlements in order to indoctrinate them has been a great
cause of many falling ill and dying. Also a further misfortune resulted
from this, which is that famines have occurred, because the people
who are now together in one town used to be divided into six and
eight, and as they were spread throughout the whole land and had all
of it occupied, no rain fell which did not fall on cultivated lands,
which was why in that era they had a great abundance of provisions.
Also the smallpox and other pestilences which have occurred have

THE POLITICS OF CONQUEST
The Letters of the Batabob to the King

Fray Diego de Landa's campaign against "idolatry" in the summer of 1562 caused considerable controversy. Not all the Spaniards in Yucatan agreed that the extensive use of torture by the Franciscans was justified or prudent. In fact, Landa succeeded in polarizing Yucatec politics in the 1560s. On his side, Landa had most of the Franciscans in Yucatan, and, reluctantly, Diego de Quijada, who held the important post of *alcalde mayor*, representing the Crown rather than the settlers. Even before Landa's campaign had reached its climax, opposition among Spaniards was coalescing around the provincial governor and the *cabildo* (municipal council) of Merida, representing the conquistador families. Yucatan's first bishop, Francisco de Toral, arrived during that fateful summer; although also a Franciscan, Toral was soon persuaded that the methods of Landa and his followers were counterproductive, that the "Indians" responded better to carrots than to sticks. Among Toral's allies were the few secular clergymen in the province.[1] (All of these protagonists—Landa, Quijada, Toral, the governor, the Franciscans, the secular clergy—feature in the documents presented in this chapter.)

While settlers and ecclesiastical opponents alike insisted that it was the cruelty of the persecution to which they objected, the dispute was also a political one over the control of the Mayas within the new colony. *Encomenderos* were concerned with the uninterrupted provision of labor and tribute from native communities, and with the continued maintenance of good relations with the *batabob* (governors of the Maya communities or *cahob*) upon whom the system depended. Toral's concern

151

was priest-parishioner relations; he wrote to the king in 1564 that, due to Landa's methods, when the Mayas "knew a friar was going to the village everyone absented themselves from it and ran off to the bush to hide, and others hanged themselves from fear of the friars."[2]

Meanwhile, the Mayas and their community leaders were themselves dealing with the aftermath of Landa's campaign and the battle among Spaniards for the sweat and souls of Yucatan's natives. The various responses among the Maya to the Spanish invasion, as demonstrated by the texts in the preceding chapters, should dissuade us from assuming that Maya opposition to Landa and his Franciscan allies was uniform. Not that any Mayas were likely to have condoned the maiming and the killing. But the role of Gaspar Antonio Chi (see Chapter 8), who in the early 1560s worked first for Landa and then for Toral, indicates something of the complexity of the situation for many native nobles. Furthermore, Maya manueverings during the previous Conquest decades would suggest that *batabob* sought a politically advantageous route through the 1560s and beyond.

Out of this complex context emerged a fascinating set of letters, written in Maya, signed by groups of *batabob*, and addressed to the King of Spain. The letters were accompanied by Spanish translations. Ten letters have survived (nine from 1567, one dated 1580), but more were probably written and may yet surface in the Spanish archives.[3] Added together, a total of one hundred and nineteen *cah* governors and other Maya *cabildo* officers had their names put to such letters. These signatures represented some seventy-five *cahob*, comprising a third of all Maya communities in the colony and almost all the communities in the districts that surrounded the colonial core of Merida (see Map II).[4]

Nine of the ten letters are written in favor of the Franciscans, requesting that more friars be sent to Yucatan to proselytize the Mayas (Letters i–vii, which are virtually identical, and Letters viii and x, which are longer variants). Letter ix, in stark contrast to the others, is an attack on the Franciscans. This anti-Franciscan petition is presented below with two of the other letters: one has been selected to represent the series of nearly identical pro-Franciscan missives (Letter ii); the other is the lengthier version which, in praising the Franciscans, also attacks the secular clergy (Letter viii).[5]

Scholars have traditionally viewed the pro-Franciscan letters as creations of the friars and thus as inauthentic expressions of the Maya viewpoint.[6] Such skepticism seemed justified by several factors. First, the existence of virtually identical letters from different regions of the colony suggested that the petitions had been copied from a master letter, which "considerably invalidated" the value of each letter "as a real expression of Maya sentiment."[7] Second, the Spanish translations accompanying the letters exhibit their own set of minor variations that do not correspond to the Maya textual variants. Third, it seemed to historians that, in the wake of Landa's campaign of torture, Mayas surely must have feared and loathed the Franciscans; that if any Franciscan were to be praised it would be Bishop Toral, who had effectively driven Landa back to Spain (Landa did not return until 1573, when he came as bishop himself). Fourth, this reading of Maya feeling was apparently borne out by the existence of the anti-Franciscan letter from Mani, a letter which alleged that the *batabob* were obliged to put their names to the lies written by friars in the other letters (Letter ix). Had scholars been aware of the 1580 version (Letter x), they no doubt would have taken it as evidence that the Franciscans were still using the same promotional technique thirteen years later; indeed in this version the authors comment, "we are writing this letter to you together with padre fray Gaspar de Najera, Maya speaker."[8]

But there are other factors to consider. First, as I have already implied, there was the considerable precedent of Maya nobles in earlier decades seeking to benefit from the Spaniards' presence. Outright confrontation was only practical where the foreigners could be expelled, as had sometimes been the case early in the Conquest period. But in the face of an increasingly permanent Spanish settlement, especially in the northwest, Maya leaders turned more and more to diplomacy in order to manipulate and mollify the invaders. Second, Landa's campaign had been centered on Mani, and it was this *cah*, along with three of its neighbors, who wrote the petition of protest (Letter ix). The seventy odd *cahob* who authored the pro-Franciscan letters were less affected by the persecution, some not at all. In fact, if we pull back from 1562 to look at the larger picture, we see that some of the pro-Franciscan letters came from communities whose accounts of the Conquest, going back to the early or mid-sixteenth century and running through the colonial period, stress a noble record of cooperation with the Spaniards and a ready acceptance of Christianity. One such letter, for example, was authored by don Pablo Paxbolon and his fellow principal men of Tixchel (Letter vi; see Figure 9.2 and Chapter 3); another came from Calkini, Nunkini, and other *cahob* in the region dominated by the Canul *chibal* (Letter i; see Chapter 5); and two of the letters came from twenty-three Pech *batabob* and three Pech *alcaldes* of twenty-five *cahob* in the Motul-Conkal region (Letters ii and iv; see Figure 9.1 and Chapter 6). For all these Maya leaders, the position taken in their letters represented a tenacity and consistency of political policy.

Third, the contrasts between the anti- and pro-Franciscan letters do not necessarily mean that the former were heavily Spanish-influenced and the latter not so. All of the letters were probably subject to various forms of Spanish participation. But there is a difference between a domineering Spanish influence and a meeting of common interests; a difference between a friar dictating a letter and Mayas taking advantage of Spanish expertise and interpretive abilities (as could have been fray Gaspar de Najera's role in Letter x of 1580). Furthermore, a concerted effort by friars to produce the letters might arguably have resulted in a single series of identical petitions instead of two series—let alone the longer letter of a month later featuring several new themes (Letter viii; see below) and yet another variation thirteen years later (Letter x).

If the pro-Franciscan letters seem to smack of Landa's efforts in the 1560s to win exoneration for his deeds of 1562, it should also be pointed out that the anti-Franciscan petition from Mani is equally reflective of the simultaneous efforts of some Spanish settlers and the secular clergy to bury Landa and undermine the Franciscan position in the province. This coincidence of political position is illustrated in similar letters from Spaniards to the king. In 1563, for example, the *defensor de los indios*, Diego Rodríguez Bibanco, asked the king to expel all the Franciscans from Yucatan, and in 1566 the friars were similarly denounced by Montejo, Pacheco, and the other conquistadors and prominent settlers on the Merida *cabildo*.[9] On the other hand, the Maya attack on the secular clergy in Letter viii was paralleled by a similar attack from Spanish officials in May of the same year, 1567.[10] Thus the Mayas, almost as much as the Spanish settlers, had become caught up in the jurisdictional struggle between the Franciscan order and the secular clergy.

Fourth, the identicality of letters within the series and the sincerity of the letters' message are not necessarily mutually exclusive—especially not from the Maya point of view. In a general sense, repetition was viewed as an effective stylistic device by Mayas and is found in various genres of uncontroversial colonial Maya texts.[11] In a specific sense, the notion of one community copying a text from another community, substituting only the names of the community and its leaders, also has clear parallels in other genres of Maya documents; see, for example, the intertextual parallels between versions of the Books of Chilam Balam (Chapter 7) and the long identical passages in the Titles of Chicxulub and Yaxkukul, documents so similar that I presented them above (Chapter 6) as one text.

Fifth, as one scholar has detailed,[12] the language of the Maya texts has far too many characteristics of colonial Maya discourse to be a mere translation of a Franciscan-authored document; there must have been some Maya input, at the very least. By this I mean that the way in which the letter's sentiments are expressed fixes the texts at a particular temporal and cultural point, a moment during the shift from Conquest to colonial times when the Mayas of Yucatan were adjusting their view of the world, and their expression of that view, to the influences of the Spanish presence and the requirements of Spanish rule. I would argue, for example, that the documents reflect the corporatist, *cah*-centric nature of Maya culture, as well as the role played by representation; that the letters, authored not by individuals but by *batabob* representing *cahob*, are community expressions. But the "we" of authorship also contains a further dimension, one relative to the "you" that is the king; this shift from the micro to the macro is underscored by the defining of "here" as "Yucatan" and the commentary on the distant location of the "there" that is Castile.[13] In other words, the Mayas have by no means abandoned their perception of the *cah* as the center of the world, but they are now aware that their *cahob* are part of another world centered far away.

The idea that the language of the letters to the king reflects both Maya culture and Spanish influences offers a solution to the riddle of

their sincerity. For the letters reflect not only the complexities of cultural interaction in sixteenth-century Yucatan, but also the complex
politics of the Conquest era. The contrasting letters for and against the
Franciscans reflect opposing political positions among Spaniards and
among Mayas, as well as between them; questions of authorship and
expression within the letters reflect the multiple dimensions of Maya-
Spanish relations. The letters may at first seem unlikely sources for
studying Maya views of the Conquest, but their highly conflictual sub-
text—and their close relationship to the perceptions of the protagonists rather than any objective realities—arguably make them extremely
relevant. It may be simpler to accept the anti-Franciscan letter from
Mani as the true Maya voice, and dismiss the rest as fakes, but it surely
is more interesting to view all the letters as both contrived and authentic. That they were both things, in a world where the Mayas could be
the conquistadors, is also more likely.

Letter from the Pech and Other Batabob and Alcaldes of the Motul Region to the King of Spain, February 12, 1567 (Letter ii)

Holy Catholic Royal Majesty.
Because all of your subjects—you, O ruler [ah tepale]—understand
that it is wished that all is done so that we be saved; for this reason,
you, O ruler, would be sure to have within your kingdoms [ahaulilob]
the guides who might illuminate and enlighten and teach those who
know nothing. Although we are distant and far from the kingdom of
Castile, we nevertheless understand that you are concerned, O ruler,
as though we were close by, and that you are also concerned that it be
spoken in your ear, that which is truly necessary to us—as befits our
low level of reason [ca cabalil ti cuxolal] and our material impoverish-
ment on this earth. For this reason, we are informing you—you, O
ruler—that from the beginning of our believing in Christianity, Franciscan friars have taught us the doctrines; and they, with their doc-

trines and their poverty, preached to us and preach to us the spoken word of Dios; and truly we love them like true fathers and they love us too like true sons. But through sickness and illnesses and the opposition of the devil [*ciçin*], they have really abandoned us and very seldom have come here to this land, and also others have not come out from the land of Castile because it is far and distant.[14] For this reason we are petitioning you—you, O ruler—to have mercy on our souls and decide to send us Franciscan friars to guide us and teach us the way of Dios. There are some in particular who were here in this land and went to the land of Castile; there were several of them; they really know our language now, having previously preached to us and taught us. Their names are fray Diego de Landa, fray Pedro Gumiel of the province of Toledo—especially that fray Diego de Landa, through whose really great benevolence [*tibilil*] and his goodness [*utzil*] in the eyes of our lord Dios we truly owe to him alone our Christianity— and fray Miguel de la Puebla, and the other padres that have served you—you, O ruler. And because we understand that it is not in vain that we have entered into your service, we now address you—you, O ruler—to bring all our wishes to your Christian heart. And we are confident that we shall be quickly assisted by you—you, O ruler. Our lord in Dios enlightens and continues to glorify you in his service. Here, Yucatan, on the twelfth day of February, the year 1567.

> Your humble subjects and servants kiss
> your blessed hands, you, O ruler.

Don Melchior Pech, governor of the province of Motul.

Juan Pech, *batab* and governor of Tichake.

Francisco Pech, *batab*, Tichac.

Juan Ek, *batab*, Suma.

Diego Pech, *alcalde*, Tichac.

Pedro Pech, *batab*, Kini.

Francisco Pech, *batab*, Uci [*ucuyi*].

Luis Pech, *batab*, Muxupip [*moxpip*].

Gaspar Oxte, *batab*, Bokoba.

Martín Pech, *batab*, Tixkumchel.

Luis Pech, *batab*, Dzemul.

Diego Pech, *batab*, Euan.

Luis Pech, *batab*, Cacalchen.

Agustín Canul, *alcalde*, Motul.

Martín Che, *alcalde*, Kini.

Francisco Pech, *alcalde*, Cacalchen.

Esteban Chi, *alcalde*, Tichac.

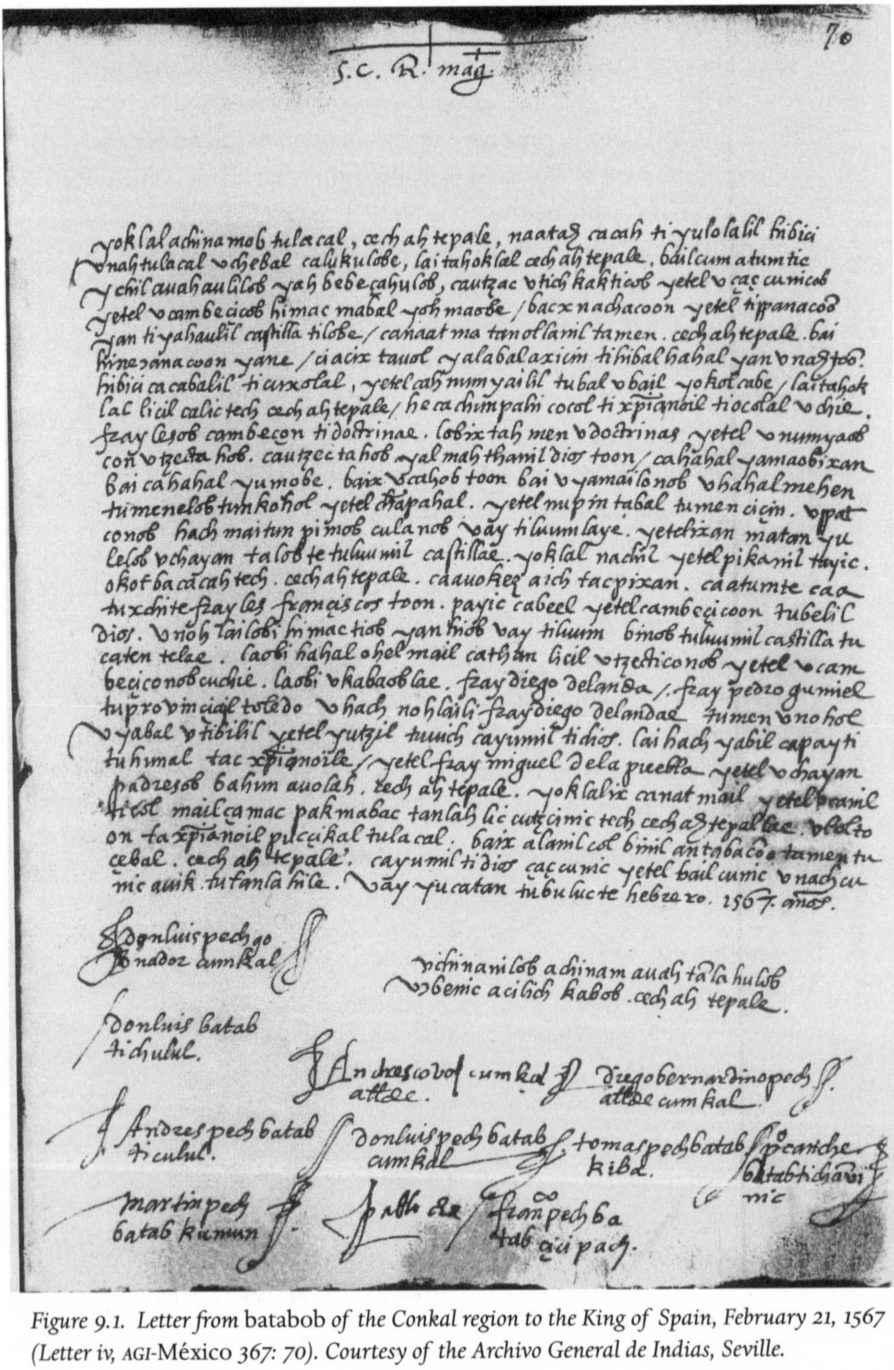

Figure 9.1. Letter from batabob of the Conkal region to the King of Spain, February 21, 1567 (Letter iv, AGI-México 367: 70). Courtesy of the Archivo General de Indias, Seville.

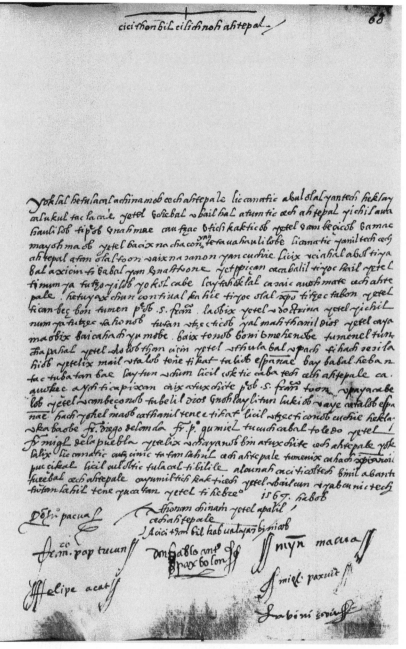

Figure 9.2. Letter from the principal men of Tixchel to the King of Spain, February, 1567 (Letter vi, AGI-México 367: 68). Courtesy of the Archivo General de Indias, Seville.

———   *Letter from the Pech and other* Batabob   ———
and Maya Officials of the Merida Region to the
King of Spain, March 9, 1567 (Letter viii)

Because we who are gathered together, we common men, understand
our lord Dios, and you who are the great lord ruler [*noh ahau ah
tepale*], we wish you to implement something that is necessary, for you
too. For truly we are humbled, all of us, beneath your foot, beneath
your hand, however many of us there are—we *batabob* and our principal men [*nucteylob*] who are here in this province of Yucatan. For
here in our land, we are also natives [*ah otochnalonixan*]. We wish to
recount something in your ear, you, O ruler, so that you may take the
necessary means. Here then we speak. There is truly a great need
here in the province of Yucatan for Franciscan padres [*sant franco
padresob*] for us, so that they might tell us the word of Dios, which is
the Christian doctrine, as it is called, and so that they might say mass
for us to watch, and so they might preach to us in the language of
here the word of our creator [*c ah çihçahul*], which is the gospel [*euan-
gelio*], as the Spaniards call it. Because it is truly necessary that they
come into our districts, for it happened that since the arrival of the
bishop whom you sent, named fray Francisco Toral, he brought and
distributed black padres [*ek padresob*]; they are falsely named clergymen [*clerigo*]. He then appointed them to take care of the *cahob* [com-
munities] within our district, that they might speak the word of Dios
to us, and also so that they might say mass for us to watch. Meanwhile, they preach to us through interpreters because they do not
know this language here. There are really no Franciscan padres for us,
because they have gone far away; they have scattered. Thus it is truly
necessary for us—it really is necessary—that they truly settle here
among us. For a very long time ago there came here those who knew
our Maya language [*ca maya thanil*] really well; at that time they
preached to us—they were wise men too. Therefore nowadays, many
times each day, we remember them. And although, because we are
just commoners [*chambel maçeualon*], we did not really understand the
nature of their thinking and were driven out of our minds in the past
by the Franciscan padres, they nevertheless verified their words to all

us common people; they appointed themselves to be judges of the *cah*, so as to put a lid on our wickedness. For previously we were truly suffocating under the pressures of the devil; for many times we traveled along the ancient path of our ancestors, which is our path too. We shall never learn our lesson while we speak with the devil, while we go along absorbed in the devils—which are common clay pots worshiped by us in our imaginations, while we make use of *balche* [native wine]. For there is no life in our heart when the forest people do not once see those padres. Truly did they soon give life to our hearts and also gave us the love of their preaching to us to prevent sin. Thus today we frequently remember them. For those clergymen never have anything to say; but the Franciscan padres speak well to us, truly and clearly preaching to us, and that is what we now wish for today. For many times they expressed a wish to learn our language here. Now they also baptize our children and baptize us too. Thus those ones that travel to us are really good, for they wish to join us to the son of Dios and also deliver us from guilt and from living in carnal sin. May your children be cherished, you, great ruler![15] Now too will they love us while truly giving us from their hearts a true understanding of the faith, you, chief ruler [*halach uinic*] that is here, for this is not yet known. Now too are these clergymen seen; their doctrine has the same meaning as that of the Franciscan padres, yet—and we are not insulting them—they do not love us nor are we in their hearts. Furthermore, we are not accustomed to being among them; we have spoken to them only a few times, to see this or say that. Neither do they know our language here, nor do we know their Castilian language. Nor do they really devote themselves to us, although we need them; thus do we engage them in vain. So now we are acquiring an understanding of the ways of the black padres. They often do not know how to trade, as they have their commerce with the Spaniards there; they will have no commerce with us. There are men with goods to sell, who have gone before a judge [*juezil*] so as to be given a license in order to trade with whomever they meet. [But the clergy] don't take them; they travel a lot, and so they are not able to; they really do not want different goods, because they would thus pile up every day too many things. Whereas the Franciscan padres are not used to doing that kind of thing; nor does anything arrest their hearts. But these oppressive clergymen get really angry at us while forcing us to work in their homes, [doing] whatever they tell us to. For those black men [*ek uinicob*] have their own homes and servants [*u palilobi*], and their own horses and rabbits. Furthermore, as they have settled in our *cahob*, we are providing them with food and household goods; they have neither paid a thing, nor do we ask them to. For they are ashamed of us and afraid of us too, although they are the *cah* guardians and are given the responsibility, and are asked, to go to each *cah*. And as they are not paid by the bishop's *cah*, the burden of it is given to us; but there is no salary. So now we give them much food, and they do not pay us. We now pay them, well and fully, to be guardians of many *cahob*. Meanwhile, may you reimburse us, you, great reigning ruler, with whatever the bishop that is here in the province of Yucatan orders! May you, the governor, don Luis Céspedes de Oviedo, see that we do not have many things, for we are always being robbed! This is the very reason why there is discord with the bishop that is here in this province and discord with all the black padres. Thus we are unhappy and tortured by them; and we are locked up in jail just for not going along with the authority created by your magistrates [*jusz^ao*], so we may be charged whatever money we have in our hands. This is the price we pay for our own homes. We do not know any reason for us to be tortured and damned by your magistrates [*justiçia*] and the other Spaniards, which we have lamented from the depths of our hearts. Thus what we have in our hands is not much, only our burial [clothes] and our tribute [goods]; we have now told of it all. We people that are here in this province, therefore, do not have the word; we truly need the doctrine, for we do not have it. For it to be born in our hearts, there must be Franciscan padres [here], for they all truly love us. They do not torture, but do good deeds; may they travel, then, to us today. For there are magistrates of good appearance; should they travel here, whatever tortures we may lament, there will be magistrates to help us. For whatever may be needed, these ministers of our lord Dios— and they are your ministers too, you, our great reigning ruler—would be truly good, if you sent them, you, our lord. May you allow the condemnation of that which we lament, the frequent sight of discord

among them, so they may help us. This is truly very necessary, therefore, that you, chief ruler that is here, bring them too; it would be
good for you to give them your license to really help us. And our *cah*
cries out to you to order Franciscan padres to be sent to us, so that
they may come and finish guiding the doctrine that they wished for
us. For they do it really well; truly and consistently do they do it well;
their walk is really good. Having said this, we are recounting their
ways because we really want to go there to heaven, from the depths of
our hearts. This then is the reason why we now wish for them to be
fathers to us, for they truly love us, and we love them too. This is the
reason why we wish there to be many of them. It would be good for
you to order their elders, the provincial [head of the Franciscans], to
send them a second time. These ones should be those who go, because they really know us, they who were here previously; and they
really had just taken to speaking Maya; and because they know what
we need in order to be worthy before Dios. And it would be good for
the rest of them to come too, to be distributed among us. So who will
now be given to us, who truly wishes to teach in our language here?
Because they should come every day, it would not be good for them
to desire money. It should not be the black-clothed padres; they really
take money; they really ask and ask for a great deal of money; they
drive us mad over money. Therefore these words that we say to you,
they are not lies; for this is really the truth. We will now prove it. For
there were many black padres, twenty-one, that came with the Spaniards, and not one of them knew our language here; only one of them
did, but that padre who entered did not teach. For at that time there
were no elders, really just boys; they traded in the other *cahob*. Moreover, they wished to say little, the black padres; those black ones, they
hated us. We are now recounting their ways to you, for every time
they piled up a lot of money, much cloth, and household goods which
Dios understands belong to us. For all these reasons, He truly understands that one Franciscan padre is better than many black padres. He
does not speak, but nevertheless He understands us. The way of fray
Francisco de la Torre, provincial here today, is very good; he knows
the language here; we truly love him, and he preaches to us often.
When he was taken ill with no small [attack of] consumption, our

hearts were saddened. And he has no substitute. It is now six years
since he traveled the road, since the *oidor* Loaysa came to count us
here [i.e. take a census]; very many of our people had died, and he really understood that you, don Luis, gave your license today so that he
count us. It is really a mercy given by Dios that he count us a second
time, for those from the *cahob* have brought themselves before the
chief ruler so that he be merciful and lighten their tribute. Now he
makes use of your license so that we shall truly be given mercy; it is
for this reason that we now jointly present ourselves to you, so that
you give us mercy regarding this our tribute to those lords and what
we give to you. The striped walls, really the sticks, is all we have.[16]
And now there are coming those who are not accustomed to us. Truly
we are afflicted. We have no property. Therefore you, the governor
that is here, truly do not make blind the way forward here in the *cah*
by placing the affairs of your *cah* subjects in the care of those who do
not wish to walk to the *cah*. So that the way not be closed, give your
license and authority for the coming of whatever good Christians that
will come quickly to respect us. We ask this so that we people here
will not be blinded. Truly the space between our *cahob* is great, but in
the end we quickly go the same way. For there are many *cahob* here in
Yucatan, truly so many hundreds of leagues of land here. This is the
reason we now truly present ourselves to kiss [you]; we are beneath
your feet, beneath your hands, you, O ruler; may you be quickly merciful to us. The power of the governor is great over your officers, chief
ruler. Thus we ask that quickly you give us a statement that is truly
good. We ask you, chief ruler, for [someone] who truly wishes us
good; who truly loves us; who truly will bring us happiness to the
bottom of our hearts; who is from Dios and from you, O ruler; who
understands that we are not accustomed to having what we have
turned upside down, that our hearts are truly good; who we may
truly love, because he loves us. Here then is our statement. We wish
for our protectors, those defenders, to give their signatures, so that
you may know that truly, coming from our hearts, do we petition you
and the governor; so that he may understand that which will truly
help us; so that you may know of the misery [or love; *ya*] of our *cah*,
you, great reigning ruler. This is the end. Here in the city of Merida,

Yucatan, on the ninth day of the month of March of the year 1567.
May Dios truly guard you for many years in your kingdom [*ahaulil*].
This is our statement, all of us *batabob*.

Your humble subjects and servants kiss
your blessed hands, you, O ruler.

Don Juan Pech; don Francisco Ucan; Francisco Chel; Francisco Chel;
Pedro Ek; don Pedro Canche; don Andrés Uitz; Diego Balam; Juan
Euan; Juan Tun; Andrés Chel; Pedro Che; Juan Pool; Pedro Tzul; Juan
Ake; Luis Pech; Pedro Cauich; Francisco Pech; Francisco Mutul; Juan
Chim; Francisco Ucan; Juan Maçun; Pedro Huchim; Juan Mutul;
Pedro Poot; Francisco Uicab.

Letter from the Xiu and Pacab Batabob *of the Mani Region to the King of Spain, April 12, 1567 (Letter ix)*

Sacred Catholic Majesty.

After the good came to us, that is, the knowledge of Dios our lord
as the only true god, leaving our blindness and idolatries, and your
majesty as temporal lord, before we could open well our eyes to the
knowledge of the one and the other, there came upon us a persecution of the worst that can be imagined; and it was in the year '62, on
the part of the religious of San Francisco, who had taken us to indoctrinate us, but instead of doing that, they began to torture us, hanging
us by the hands and flogging us cruelly, hanging weights of stone on
our feet, torturing many of us on the rack [*en burros*], pouring a great
quantity of water into our bodies, from which tortures many of us
died or were maimed.[17]

Being under these tribulations and burdens, trusting in your
majesty's justice [*justiçia*] to hear and defend justice, there came the
doctor Diego Quijada,[18] who at that time aided our torturers, saying
that we were idolaters and sacrificers of men, and other things far
from all truth, which even as infidels [*en nuestra ynfidelidad*] we did not
commit. And as we saw ourselves maimed by cruel tortures, and

many dead of them, and robbed of our property [*haziendas*], and yet
more, seeing disinterred the bones of our baptized dead, who had
died as Christians, we came to despair. And not content with this, the
religious and your majesty's justice held a solemn auto-da-fé [*auto*] of
inquisition at Mani, one of your majesty's *pueblos*, where they seized
many statues, and disinterred many dead and burned them there in
public, and condemned many to be slaves to serve the Spaniards for
eight and ten years, and they handed out sanbenitos.[19] And the one
and the other put us in great wonder and fear, because we did not
know what this thing was, having been recently baptized, and not
informed; and because we returned to our subjects [*vasallos*] and told
them to hear and guard justice themselves, they seized and imprisoned us and put us in chains, like slaves, in the monastery at Merida,
where many of us died; and there they told us that we were to be
burned, without our knowing why.

At this point came the bishop whom your majesty sent us, who,
although he took us from prison and freed us from death and took off
the sanbenitos, has not relieved us from the infamies and allegations
made against us, saying that we are idolaters, sacrificers of men, and
that we had killed many Indians; because, in the end, he is of the
habit of the religious of San Francisco and does for them. He has con-
soled us only by words, saying that your majesty will deliver justice.

A *receptor* came from Mexico to inquire into this, and we believe it
was the doing of the *audiencia*, and he has done nothing.[20]

Then came don Luis de Céspedes, governor, and instead of reliev-
ing us he has increased our tribulations, taking away our daughters
and wives to serve the Spaniards, against their will and ours; which we
feel so greatly that the common people have come to say that even as
infidels we were not so vexed and maltreated, because our ancestors
never took from anyone their children, not from husbands their wives
to make use of them, as your majesty's justice now does, even to
serve the blacks and mulattos.

And with all our afflictions and labors, we have loved the padres
and given them what was necessary, and we have made many monas-
teries for them, provided with ornaments and bells, all at our cost and
that of our subjects and natives [*naturales*]; although in payment of

our services they have treated us as so subordinated [*tan auasallados*] as to deprive us of the lordship which we inherited from our ancestors, a thing we never suffered as heathens [*en nuestra gentilidad*]. And we obey your majesty's justice, hoping that you will send us remedy for everything.

One thing that has greatly dismayed and upset us is the letters written by fray Diego de Landa, principal author of all these evils and burdens, saying that your majesty has approved the killings, robberies, tortures, slaveries and other cruelties done to us; to which we are amazed that such a thing should be said of so catholic and upright a king as is your majesty. If it is said there that we sacrificed men after being baptized, it is a very great and wicked testimony invented by them to gild their cruelties.

And if we have or had idols, we took them from the tombs of our ancestors to give to the religious, because they ordered us to bring them, saying that we had said under torture that we had them. But the whole land knows how we went to look twenty, thirty, and a hundred leagues, to where we understood that our ancestors had them and where we had left them when we were baptized, and with clean conscience. We should not be punished for this as they have punished us.

And if your majesty wishes to learn of this, send a person such as might ascertain it and perceive our innocence and the great cruelty of the padres; and had the bishop not come, we should all have been brought to an end. For though we truly love [*queremos bien*] fray Diego de Landa and the other padres who tortured us, only to hear them named causes our entrails to revolt. Therefore, your majesty, send us other ministers to indoctrinate us and preach the law of Dios, because we greatly desire our salvation.

The religious of San Francisco of this province have written certain letters to your majesty and to the general of their order, in praise of fray Diego de Landa and his other companions, who were those who tortured, killed, and put us to scandal; and they gave certain letters written in the Castilian language to certain Indians of their familiars, and thus they signed them and sent them to your majesty. May your majesty understand that they are not ours, we who are lords [*señores*] of this land, who did not have to write lies nor falsehoods nor contradictions. May fray Diego de Landa and his companions do penance there for the evil that they did to us, and may our descendents to the fourth generation be recompensed the great persecution that came to us from them.

May our lord Dios guard your majesty for a long time in his sacred service and for our good and protection.

From Yucatan, the twelfth of April, 1567.

Your majesty's humble subjects kiss your royal hands and feet.

Don Francisco de Montejo Xiu, governor of the province of Mani.

Juan Pacab, governor of Muna.

Jorge Xiu, governor of Panabchen.

Francisco Pacab, governor, Texul.

CONQUEST AS NEGOTIATION
The Perspective of Petitions

CHAPTER 10

The enthusiasm and skill with which Maya communities took to the colonial genre of petitions suggests that there was some form of petitionary precedent in Maya culture before the Conquest. This precedent probably involved a formal, oral presentation of grievances to the local or regional ruler. Indeed some of the language used appears to have survived into the colonial period. The term that Mayas usually used to refer to a petition, for example, was *okotba than*, which literally means "statement of request"; in her petition below, Catalina Cime states that she has presented herself in order to speak or recite her request.[1]

Elsewhere I have elaborated upon this language of request, its similarity to a parallel petitionary discourse in the central Mexican language of Nahuatl, and its persistence through the colonial period.[2] Suffice it to observe here that the overwhelming tone of such language was deferential. This deference involved an extended reverential greeting to the addressee, featuring all his titles of office and often some not properly due him, combined with self-abasement and self-effacement by the authors (the *cah* notary wrote such documents, but the elders, the *cabildo* officers, were the true authors). In the world of petitionary discourse, Maya nobles became humble, wretched children addressing Spanish officials as benevolent fathers; note that the oft-used Maya term *yum* meant both "lord" and "father."

Examples of such language can be found in the Tahnab petition and in the Xiu petitions below, and indeed in the previous chapter—for the letters of the *babatob* to the king are also examples of colonial Maya petitions. A question and an important point are raised by the fact that the earlier documents (the letters in Chapter 9 and the Xecpedz petition) feature less of this deferential language than later examples (such as the Tahnab and Xiu petitions below).[3] Does this mean that such language was Spanish in origin? Probably not, as the terminology used is Maya and the imagery seems more Mesoamerican than European (and native notaries did not hesitate to borrow Spanish terms when they deemed them efficacious). Furthermore, not all mid- and late colonial petitions use the formulas of deferential address. Yet mere inconsistency is an insufficient explanation. More to the point, while the language may be Maya in origin, the context of its usage was colonial. The presence of Spaniards, their colonial demands, and the colonial legal system with which Maya *cabildos* had to work, made such petitions necessary.

This point touches on a central theme of this book and allows the petitions below to act as a form of conclusion. For these documents, like those of the preceding chapters, not only tell us how Mayas viewed the Conquest and its colonial ramifications, but give us insight into the impact of conquest and colonialism upon Maya life and culture. Spanish influences on Maya ways of seeing and doing things are as myriad and multiple as the survivals and continuities from the fifteenth century, but the relationship between the two influences is so complex as to defy categorization or classification; terms like hybrid and composite, syncretic and bicultural, are (although I use them here and elsewhere) ultimately inadequate. It may be enough simply to recognize the complexity of the process and to explore its constituent elements without an agenda that seeks to classify cultural components or prove survivalism or acculturation. This is not to say that cultural interaction and intra-action are intangible and ineluctably complex. At the core of these processes there is some solidity. For example, whether Mayas were writing and rewriting history to accommodate the past to the present (as in the primordial titles), or depicting their current situation in a way that both reflected and reconfigured reality (as in the petitions), they were consistently attempting to make sense of the world as it appeared to them and to force that world to make better sense. In that sense, Maya motives and efforts are perfectly accessible.

The petitions below have been selected for two reasons. First, each represents subgenres of Maya petitions, which in turn reflect aspects of colonial rule. The Xecpedz petition[4] is an example of the subgenre of complaints against parish priests. This is the earliest such petition to survive; examples run into the nineteenth century. The most common gripe of Maya parishioners was negligence and malpractice—that priests performed their sacerdotal duties poorly, if at all. Also common were accusations of two specific abuses—violent behavior and sexual misconduct—which are not included in the Xecpedz petition but which were made by other communities against the priest in question, Andrés Mexía. For almost two decades this curate faced a sporadic Inquisition investigation into his conduct, finally receiving a modest punishment by an Inquisition tribunal in Mexico City in 1590.[5]

The petition by the *cah* of Tahnab[6] illustrates the subgenre of complaints against colonial exploitation, usually specific demands for labor and taxation. The Tahnab document reflects what was in many ways the essence of colonial life for the Maya. This was the daily burden of economic exploitation, and the relentless effort, largely using the Spaniards' own legal system, to curtail and limit that burden—in other words, to renegotiate the impact of the Conquest. Although this petition illuminates the fact that long before 1605 Spanish officials had institutionalized colonial obligations, note the similarity between Tahnab's complaints and the account in the Title of Calkini (Chapter 5) of Mayas being taken by Spanish conquistadors to be laborers and servants.

Thus the second rationale behind the selection of petitions below is that these early colonial examples help to illustrate the idea that colonial rule was an ongoing process of negotiated relations (and thus a more institutionalized and less overtly violent continuation of the Conquest). The first two petitions below show signs of the relationships between conqueror and conquered still in the early stages of being worked out. The language of deference and request is formulaic, but the specific complaints have a certain freshness to them. After all, at the time these petitions were being written, the violence of the Conquest era was barely a generation in the past, while the imposition of the colonial system was still very much in the present. The elders of Xecpedz, who drew up the first document below, surely had their view of priest-parishioner relations colored in some part by their memory of Landa's persecution campaign just eleven years before, by the arrival of Christian priests in their district probably less than a decade before that, and by personal memories of pagan priests and practices. Even at the time of the second document below, the complaint of 1605, some of the elders of Tahnab were old enough to have been boys when Spaniards first entered their *cah*—rather like the boys later christened as Alonso Canche (Chapter 5) and Gaspar Antonio Chi (Chapter 8).

However, more of a sense of temporal distance from the Conquest is present in the trio of Xiu petitions.[7] By the mid-seventeenth century, these negotiations are more delineated by precedent and more circumscribed by a legal system enjoying hegemony across the dividing line between conqueror and conquered. Indeed the blurring of that line in the form of Maya nobles asserting aspects of the status of Spaniards— seen most prominently in this book by the Pech claim to be noble conquistadors—is here institutionalized in the pro forma confirmation of *indio hidalgo* status for successive generations of Xiu nobles.

In a sense, Pech, Xiu, and other *indios hidalgos* in Yucatan were both conquerors and conquered. They were an elite category atop the Maya nobility (the *almehenob*) who enjoyed many of the privileges of Spaniards, and whose status was based not only on alliance with the sixteenth-century conquistadors but on an ongoing role in the military extension of colonial rule into the "unpacified" regions of Yucatan; note, for example, the early seventeenth-century activities of don Pablo Paxbolon (Chapter 3) and those mentioned in don Juan Xiu's petition below. Yet at the same time, these Maya noblemen were dependent upon the Spaniards for the maintenance of their status, were never seen as equals by the colonists, and as agents of colonial rule were also subject to it. Their collaboration was, in other words, a curse as much as a blessing. Such was the fate of the Maya conquistadors.

Petition by the cah of Xecpedz, 1573

I who am the *batab*, don Gaspar Cupul, with the *ah cuch cab* [councillor] Canche and the *ah cuch cab* Poot and the *ah cuch cab* Tzuc, and the principal men, make our declaration regarding our lord [*yum*] the padre Andrés Mexía: He is not in the habit of giving us what is owed; neither have we sold to him here in Xecpedz; nor does he send a man from Tiho.[8] Why? We ask nothing of him. As our lord the padre is good so he does well by us; yet because he gives mass here in a twisted fashion,[9] once again his children are left high and dry. What do you say to that? As to the question of eating: he also doesn't come because of that. In other words, there's nobody here in the *cah* because there's no food.[10] This is the reason why the priest does not come here; it is because we have no food, nor will we give him any. Our father the padre, he doesn't remember us, although we lead good lives. This is the reason that I, along with the principal men, have written, so that the goodness of our hearts regarding our father the padre be known. That's all. Here we write on the day of San Lorenzo, the tenth day of August.

This is my statement, I, don Gaspar Cupul.

Don Gaspar Cupul; Gonzalo Uayu; Francisco Poot; Francisco Hol, notary; Martín Tzuc; Alonso Cupul; Juan Canche; Francisco Nahuat, *maestro* [school/choirmaster].

Petition by the cah of Tahnab, 1605

For the Viceroy [*halach ahau*], who is in the great *cah* of Mexico. I who am don Alonso Puc, the governor, along with Simón Piste and Francisco Antonio Canul, the *alcaldes*, Juan Ucan, Gonzalo Poot, Gaspar Ku and Pedro Dzul, the *regidores*, we the *cabildo* have assembled ourselves in the name of God Almighty and also in the name of our redeemer, Jesus Christ. We now lower our heads before you, kneeling in great adoration in your presence, in honor of God, beneath your feet and your hands, you our great lord the king [i.e. the Viceroy], supreme ruler [*ah tepale*], in order that you hear our statement of petition, so that you will hear, our lord, what it is that we recount and explain in our said petition. O lord, we reside here in the heart of the road to the *cah* of San Francisco Campeche.[11] O lord, here is the poverty that is upon us, that we are going through. Here at the heart of the road, O lord, day and night, we carry burdens, take horses, carry letters, and also take turns in serving in the guest house and at the well. Here at the road's heart, O lord, it is really many leagues [*lubil*] to the *cah* of Campeche. Our porters, letter carriers, and horse takers go ten leagues as far as our *cah*, day and night. Nor are our people very great in number. The tribute that we give, O lord, is sixty cotton blankets [*mantas*]. The tally of our tribute adds up to sixty, O lord, because they add us, the *alcaldes*, and all the widows too. That is why we are relating our miseries for you to hear, O lord. Here is our misery. When the lord governor marshall came he gave us very many forced labor rotations,[12] seventeen of them, though our labor rotations had been abolished by our lord the *oidor* Doctor Palacio because of the excessive misery we experience here on the road. Our misery is also known by our lords the past governors [*halach uinicob*], and our lords the padres also know it, O lord. Every day there are not enough of us to do so much work, and being few, neither can we manage our fields nor sustain our children. In particular we are unable to manage the tribute burden that is upon us. Within each year we give a tribute of two *mantas*, two measures of maize, one turkey and one hen [*ix caxtilla*]. This is what we give, O lord, and we really cannot manage it, because of the great work load that we have. Thus our people run away into the forest. The number of our people who have fled, O lord, who have left their homes, is fifty, because we are burdened with so much work. O lord, this is why we humbly place ourselves before you, our great lord ruler, the King, in honor of our redeemer Jesus Christ, we kiss your feet and hands, we the worst of your children. We want there to be an end to the labor obligations under which we serve, with which we are burdened. Because our fathers, many of them principal men, along with our porters, letter-carriers and horse-takers, serve day and night. We want to look after you, our lord, and greatly wish that you will be compassionate and turn your attention to us. We have neither fathers nor mothers. We are really poor here in our *cah* in the heart of the road, O lord; nobody helps us. Three times we have carried our petition [*petiçion*] before you, our lord the *señor* governor, but you did not hear our words, O lord. Nor do we have any money in order that we may petition [*c okotba*] before you; our *cah* is poor. Here, O lord, is the reason why our people flee, because it is known that in the forest, through the use [sale] of beeswax, one is given money on credit by our lord Francisco de Magaña. It really is the governor's money [*u takin halach uinic*] that is given to people. This is our petition [*c okotba than*] in your presence, lord, our great ruler, the king, made here in the *cah* of Tahnab, today the ninth day of the month of July in the year 1605. Truly we give our names at the end.

Don Alonso Puc, governor; Pedro Ku, notary; Francisco Antonio Canul, *alcalde*; Simón Piste, *alcalde*; Juan Ucan, Gonzalo Poot, *regidoresob*; Gaspar Ku, *regidor*.

Three Seventeenth-Century Petitions by Xiu Nobles of the cah of Yaxakumche

[Doña Catalina Cime, the widow of don Alonso Xiu of the cah of Yaxakumche,[13] *petitions the Spanish authorities in 1632 to restore her privileges of nobility (XC:10)]*

Catalina Cime of Yaxa, wife of don Alonso Xiu, deceased; my respected lord *señor*, I declare that I present myself before you that I may recite the request [*okotba*] and also that you may grant my favor in your compassion to me, a widow. My respected lord, here are the edicts [*mandamientos*] granted to my husband.[14] I bring them for you to see. In them he was given a housekeeper while he lived. O lord, now that he is dead, my governor and the *alcaldes* have decided that I should pay tribute, and I have paid them seven *tomines*.[15] This is why you, my respected lord, you should grant me an edict so that I may pay them no longer. For I am poor and destitute, and I support my four little ones. You, O lord, this is why I present myself, so that you may help me, for the sake of God and of our great ruler, the reigning king. This is the petition [*okotba than*] for your compassion [*ta tzayatzil*], my respected lord. I who am the least of your daughters, Catalina Cime.

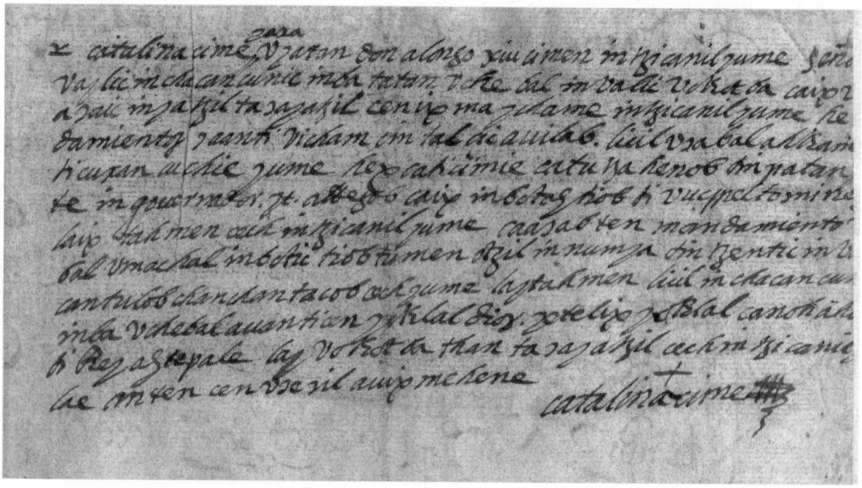

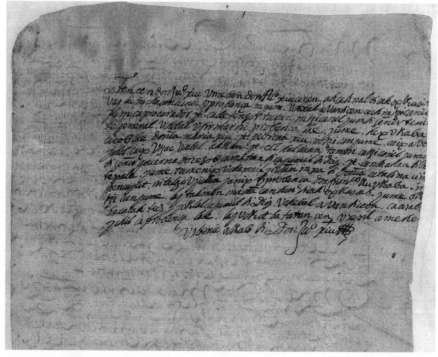

Figure 10.1. Petition by doña Catalina Cime of Yaxakumche, 1632 (xc:10). Courtesy of Tozzer Library, Harvard University

Figure 10.2. Petition by don Juan Xiu of Yaxakumche, 1640 (xc:13). Courtesy of Tozzer Library, Harvard University

[Don Juan Xiu of the cah *of Yaxakumche petitions the Spanish authorities in 1640 for confirmation of the privileges of nobility for himself and his mother, doña Catalina Cime (xc:13)]*

I who am don Juan Xiu,[16] son of don Alonso Xiu, deceased, resident
[*ah cahnal*] of the *cah* of Oxkutzcab, hereby present the *probanza*
[proof of status] of my father, so that you, my respected lords, our
attorney and our defender,[17] may help me before my respected lord,
the *señor* Lieutenant General, so that he sign the *probanza*. These, O
lord, are the names of my older sisters—doña Maria Xiu and Petrona
Xiu. My respected lord, may you inform him that a field hand should
be given with a cultivated cornfield; may you tell our respected lord
the *señor* Governor that this is by the grace of our lord God and our
great ruler, the reigning king, O lord. It is also because my mother,
doña Catalina Cime, has taken a husband in Pencuyut. Her husband
is an *hidalgo*[18] and has a *probanza*; don Francisco Ku is his name. My
respected lord, this is why you are petitioned, so that for the sake of
our lord God you help us to get our *probanza* signed. This is the petition before you. I am the least of your sons, who kisses your hand,
don Juan Xiu.

[Don Juan Xiu of the cah *of Yaxakumche petitions the Spanish authorities in 1662 for permission to carry a musket (xc: 35)]*

I, don Juan Xiu, am resident [*ah cahal nalen*] at the *cah* of our patron,
the blessed San Juan Yaxakumche, adjacent to the great *cah* of Oxkutzcab. My greatly respected lord, I now come here to bow down to
your feet, my greatly respected lord, *señor* Nicolás de Cárdenas, interpreter [*ah tzol than*] for us Maya men,[19] that you may translate my language into Castilian, in order that my petition may be heard.[20] This
is because I am asking to be given a license [*liçençia*] for my musket
[*escopeta*], because, lord, it is very necessary to us for the service of
God and our great ruler, so that we may capture the forest people[21]
and bring them to be baptized here among Christians. And because
it was we, the people of my *chibal* [lineage], who brought back the
bones of Mirones and the chalice which they had previously taken
along with the Church property. Just as they brought them all in, so

do we bring them in, and we shall go, God willing, that they may be baptized.[22] Furthermore, the *chibal* is a noble one [*u chibal almehen*]; our *probanza* provides for my cornfield to be cultivated by the community and I have a housekeeper—a young man and a woman—come each week. For these reasons I wish for a license to be given me by the *señor* Governor for the musket, not that I may do harm damaging things, because I do not know how.[23] This is my petition to you, along with the copy that is in my *cah*; this is my petition to you, my beloved, respected lord. I, the least of your boys, kiss your hand. Don Juan Xiu.

Notes

PREFACE

1 See León-Portilla's *The Broken Spears: The Aztec Account of the Conquest of Mexico* (1992: xxiii) for Klor de Alva's suggestion of a bones / spears pun in this phrase made famous by the English edition; see Lockhart (1993: 313) for an assertion that "bones" —not "spears"—is the correct translation.

2 Recent publications aimed primarily at nonspecialist audiences include López Portillo (1992), Wright (1992), Le Clézio (1993), Thomas (1993), and Marks (1994). Examples of recent scholarship by specialists offering various perspectives, some of them revisionist, are Cline (1988), Borah (1991), Wood (1991), Hassig (1992), Kicza (1992), Klor de Alva (1992), Gruzinski (1993), Lockhart (1993), and Schroeder (1995).

3 Pagden (1986); Elliott (1989).

4 León-Portilla (1992) is the most obvious example. The Nahuas, whose language was Nahuatl, inhabited central Mexico at the time of the Spanish invasion; the Aztecs (or Mexica, as scholars prefer to term them) were the Nahuas of Tlatelolco-Tenochtitlan, the city-state that dominated central Mexico.

5 Mesoamerica and New Spain only approximated each other in area, roughly comprising today's Mexico and most of Central America. (Mesoamerica is a modern term that describes an indigenous culture area whose boundaries are subject to debate; New Spain was a viceregal administrative area whose boundaries shifted during the colonial period. Yucatan lay clearly within both areas.) The number of recent studies of the Spanish Conquest in the subregions of Mesoamerica—see, for example, Warren (1985), Clendinnen (1987), Chance (1989), Kramer (1994), Romero Frizzi (1994), and Knaut (1995)—is tiny relative to the historical literature on the Conquest of central Mexico. Similarly, works with a continent-wide approach to the European conquests in the Americas, such as Todorov (1984), Koning (1993), and Trexler (1995), tend to devote more attention to central Mexico than to other regions of Mesoamerica. Nobles (1997) is quite even-handed with respect to Mesoamerica, but the book's focus is primarily North America.

6 Some readers may lament my failure to include my transcriptions of the Maya texts as well as my translations; this decision was made in order to maximize the accessibility of the material. I suggest that a logical additional volume would not be one containing the Maya texts of all the manuscripts featured here, but a book on Maya primordial titles featuring the Maya texts presented here in Chapters 3, 5, and 6, with fully annotated English translations.

7 Stern (1987: 12), citing Jesús Sotelo Inclán, *Raíz y razón de Zapata* (Mexico City: Editorial Etnos, 1943), 201–203.

8 Bricker (1981: 3–28).

CHAPTER 1. *Conquests*

1 TC:12–13, 16–17. Citations of the translated Maya texts presented in Part II, such as the Title of Calkini (TC), give the original page or folio numbers so that readers will be able to find cited passages not only in this volume but in other editions, or in the original Maya-language manuscripts.

2 Mesoamerica was a civilizational area comprising most of what is today's Mexico and Central America; it was more or less consistent with the colonial viceroyalty of New Spain.

3 See Lockhart (1972), Chance (1989), Kramer (1994), and Knaut (1995) on other Spanish American regions. For details of an example from the Conquest of Yucatan—the first Montejo campaign of 1527–29, financed largely by doña Beatriz de Herrera (a wealthy widow of Seville whom Montejo soon married), and consisting of unsalaried priests, merchants, physicians, cannon engineers from Flanders, and other "investors," a few of whom brought their wives—see AGI-*México* 3048: 18–24, 76–81; Landa (XI–XIII); Cogolludo (2, I and V); Chamberlain (1948: 32–33); Kicza (n.d.: Chapter 7); and note 44 below.

4 Bernal Díaz del Castillo is one example of some of these patterns; dissatisfied with his reward for being one of the first conquistadors of Mexico, he wrote from Spain an extended report, or *probanza*, which includes accounts of the early Spanish expeditions along the Yucatec coast (Díaz 1963: 16–68). The Montejo family are another example; members of this Castilian family participated in conquest expeditions in Central America and Hispaniola (Cuba), in an early expedition to Yucatan (that of Grijalva), in the Cortés-led conquest of central Mexico, and in the series of campaigns that led to the establishment of a colony in Yucatan (Chamberlain 1948).

5 The story appears not in Columbus's own writings, but in the biography by his son (Colón 1947: Chapter 89). I agree with Clendinnen (1987: 4) that the description and location of the traders strongly suggest that they were Mayas, possibly Yucatecans. Her suggestion of a link between the Columbus encounter and the prophesies in the Books of Chilam Balam is less convincing.

6 Bricker (1981: 15).

7 Under Juan de Valdivia, the ship had been en route from Panama to Santo Domingo when it ran aground on a reef; a number of Spaniards made it in a small boat to Yucatan, at that time entirely unknown to Europeans. According to Díaz (1963: 64–65) the men were mostly killed or died of disease, and the women worked to death; in the versions by Landa (III) and Cogolludo (1, VII), Valdivia was sacrificed.

8 Díaz comments on the Spaniards' pleasure at having acquired an interpreter (1963: 66); they must have presumed, or hoped, that the language Aguilar had learned in Yucatan would be understood by all the "Indians" they encountered, a hope en-

couraged by Aguilar's ability to communicate with local rulers in Tabasco (1963: 69). When Cortés's expedition then entered Nahuatl-speaking central Mexico, Aguilar remained useful due to the acquisition in Tabasco of a woman who spoke Nahuatl and Maya (this was doña Marina, or La Malinche; see Karttunen 1994: 1–23; 1997). This chain of communication did not last long, as doña Marina soon learned Spanish, but Aguilar has nonetheless gone down in history as crucial to the Cortés campaign. Aguilar went on to be one of the early settlers of colonial Mexico and had two children by a Nahua noblewoman, doña Elvira Toznenitzin of Topoyanco (Carrasco 1997: 95); this fact, and the statement in the Pech Titles that during his years in Yucatan he was made the son-in-law of a Cozumel lord (TY:4v; TCH:8; in Chapter 6), belie Aguilar's claims of being piously chaste with indigenous women (Pérez Martínez 1936: 51).

9 The quote is from Oviedo (XXXII, III), whose source is Alonso Luján, who came to Yucatan with Montejo but not before (Jones 1989: 26–27). Aguilar, as reported by Díaz (1963: 65), is the source on Guerrero as a Maya war captain. Landa (III) also tells the story, naming Guerrero's Maya patron as a Nachan Can. Oviedo also claimed that in 1528 Montejo heard in Chetumal that a Spaniard was living among the Mayas nearby, and so sent him a letter reminding him he was a Christian, to which the Spaniard, allegedly Guerrero, replied, "I am a slave, I am not free, although I am married and have a wife and children. And I am at peace with God. And you, sir, and the Spaniards will have a good friend in me." Montejo's men insisted nevertheless that Guerrero was behind the organized local resistance shown to them (Oviedo XXXII, III; Clendinnen 1987: 22; Jones 1989: 27–28). A 1536 report by a Spanish official serving in Honduras claimed that a Mayanized Spaniard named Gonzalo Aroça had been killed in a local skirmish, and that this was the Gonzalo Guerrero "whom they say brought to ruin the *adelantado* Montejo," that is, caused the conquest campaigns of 1527–34 to fail (Tozzer 1941: 8). In the Spanish mind, there were two sides, Spanish Christians and their enemies, and nothing in between; perhaps too it was easier for a Spaniard to believe that only another Spaniard could so prolong the Conquest.

10 Landa (III); Díaz (1963: 16–43); Chamberlain (1948: 11–14); Clendinnen (1987: 4–16).

11 Landa (IV); Díaz (1963: 39–87); Chamberlain (1948: 14–16).

12 Chamberlain (1948: 18–34).

13 The town, named Salamanca after Montejo's hometown in Spain, was never built other than a few temporary structures; Montejo had the habit of naming almost every town he founded Salamanca, although none that survived retained the name. Montejo destroyed his ships to prevent any of his lieutenants slipping back to Cuba, Mexico, or Spain to seek direct royal patronage, just as Cortés, Montejo, and many other conquistadors had done. Despite the frequent repetition of the image of burning ships (e.g. Bricker 1981: 16), the sources only state that the ships were maimed, scuttled, grounded, or broken up, both by Cortés (Díaz 1963: 128–30; Pagden 1986: 52 [Cortés's Second Letter]) and by Montejo (Chamberlain 1948: 35–40). Pagden (1986: 461) suggests the myth of the burning ships originated with the Spanish historian Cervantes de Salazar in 1546.

14 Chamberlain (1948: 40).

15 Chamberlain (1948: 41–66); Clendinnen (1987: 20–22).

16 CD,13:86–91. Indeed it is possible that Montejo and his followers may have so down-played this initial failure in later years that they effectively eliminated it from the Spanish memory of the era; Landa (XII), for example, writing in the 1560s, elides the first *entrada* with the second, with Montejo's forces going more or less directly from the east coast (where the first expedition under the elder Montejo was in 1527) to Chichen Itza (where part of the second expedition under the younger Montejo was in 1532–33). As Bricker comments (1981: 26) and Chamberlain details (1948: 347–48), this edited version of early events took hold in the late sixteenth century and remained standard until Chamberlain's study centuries later.

17 See Chapter 3 for the Chontal Mayas' own account of Cortés's visit. Landa (XIII) states that the younger Montejo accompanied Cortés to "California," which Tozzer (1941: 53) suggests may be a euphemism for the Pacific coast regions; the younger Montejo's own *probanza* of 1563 states that he served as a page boy on the Honduras expedition (Chamberlain 1948: 69).

18 Chamberlain (1948: 69–175); Bricker (1981: 16–17); Jones (1989: 29–41).

19 There are some parallels here between the protracted conquests in Yucatan and the northern sierra of Oaxaca (and even parallels of personnel in the Pacheco family); on the sierra, see Chance (1989: 16–34), and on other aspects of the conquest in Oaxaca see Terraciano and Sousa (1992) and Romero Frizzi (1993).

20 Chamberlain (1948: 175).

21 CDI:XII.

22 García Bernal (1978: 247–423; 1979); Patch (1993); Bracamonte (1994:69–84).

23 On the 1536–40 Champoton settlement, see Chamberlain (1948: 188–96). The flight of Montejo's followers to Peru in 1534 illustrates the fact that for the Spaniards the Conquest of Yucatan was more about conquest than it was about Yucatan. This is also reflected in the ambitions and fate of the elder Montejo. Not only did he seek more than his *encomiendas* in central Mexico, but he also hoped to carve out for himself a province far larger than the colony of Yucatan was destined to become. At various points in his career Montejo was granted the governorships of Tabasco, Yucatan, Honduras, and Chiapas; his ambition was to unite all these areas into one territory, using the broad base of the peninsula (the area that today runs from Honduras across Belize and northern Guatemala to Chiapas and Tabasco) as the heartland of a province that included the whole Yucatan peninsula. Such a plan could not easily be reconciled with the geopolitical realities of either Maya settlement or Spanish administrative policies. As a result, he never completed his campaign of conquest in Yucatan, instead taking up the governorship of Honduras in 1537, and then, forced out by Alvarado's ambitions in Guatemala, the governorship of Chiapas in 1539–40. Following Alvarado's death, Montejo resumed the Honduran post in 1542–44, and in 1546 returned to Yucatan, where he still was technically the *adelantado*, to take up the governorship of a fledgling colony created by his son and

nephew. Removed from office by royal officials in 1551, he went to argue his case in Spain, where he died two years later (Chamberlain 1948: 155, 179–85, 292–310).

24 Landa (XIV). Wars are usually economically devastating to the regions in which they are fought, but the Spaniards could be especially destructive during their initial conquest campaigns; Hassig's point with respect to central Mexico, that the Spaniards wrought economic havoc by fighting, unlike their indigenous opponents, without regard for "seasonality and agricultural manpower demands" (1992: 96) is also applicable to Yucatan.

25 AGI-*México* 299; Chamberlain (1948: 197–99).

26 Chamberlain (1948: 203).

27 For an excellent discussion of these factors, see Clendinnen (1987: 32–36). For two different discussions of the role these factors played in the Spanish Conquest of central Mexico, see Clendinnen (1991) and Hassig (1992). Kicza (n.d.) emphasizes military factors in his discussion of Spanish conquests in the Americas. Romero Frizzi (1994) devotes some attention to the "mentalities" factor in the Conquest of Oaxaca.

28 Landa (III, XIII, XIV); Cogolludo (3, VII–XIV).

29 Carrillo y Ancona (1880: 49). This short work is structured around a series of "lessons" containing questions and model answers; it was designed by the bishop as a tool for teaching Spanish-speaking students in Yucatan about their land and history (as seen by the bishop, of course).

30 Tozzer (1941: 53); Chamberlain (1948: 168). Also see Ancona (1878–80) and Blom (1936). Mitchell's work entitled *The Conquest of the Maya* begins with the dawn of civilization in Yucatan and ends with "the fall of Zotuta" (Sotuta) in 1542, with which "the Conquest of the Maya may be viewed as complete" (1935: 268). Bricker was the first to suggest that the Conquest did not end before 1547, or even before 1697; she characterizes the 1546–47 war as "The Maya's Last Stand," and only as a parenthetical "rebellion" (1981: 18–19), and includes the 1695–97 incorporation of the Peten Itza in her discussion of "The Conquest of Yucatan" (1981: 21–24). Clendinnen is also appropriately ambiguous in her treatment of the Conquest's end, suggesting by the title of her study (1987) and her focus on the early 1560s, an approximate date of 1570. Jones, in his study of southern Yucatan (1989), pushed the Conquest into the turn of the eighteenth century. Hanks (1996: 278) finesses the issue by stating that "the *official* conquest of Yucatán by Spanish forces was in 1547" (emphasis mine). Kicza (n.d.: Chapter 7) refrains from giving the Conquest an end-date, citing the Caste War of the mid-nineteenth century as evidence of a certain degree of Maya independence even after the colonial period.

31 Cogolludo (5, II); Landa (a passing reference; XVII); Chamberlain (1948: 237–52).

32 Chamberlain (1948: 239), quoting Montejo in 1549.

33 In the words of Chamberlain (1948: 241). Kicza (n.d.: Chapter 7) also notes that "The Great Maya Revolt" is a serious misnomer.

34 Chamberlain (1948: 250). Chamberlain offers a blatant apologia for Spanish practices in the east, characterizing Spanish violence as restrained and according to due legal process, justifying the atrocities committed by the younger Montejo, and giving the father credit for magnanimously freeing slaves and declaring women and children innocent of the crime of rebellion (1948: 237–52).

35 See comments by contemporary Spaniards in CDI (XII) and RY (II: 36–41).

36 Cogolludo (5, I).

37 Scholes and Roys (1938); Clendinnen (1987: 45–207); Tedlock (1993).

38 Scholes and Roys (1938), Tozzer (1941: 80–81), Thompson (1977: 29), Bricker (1981: 20), and Farriss (1984: 291) accepted that the confessions more or less described actual Maya practices; Clendinnen (1987: 121–26, 161–89) questioned this to some extent, but it was Tedlock (1993) who persuasively cast serious doubts on the veracity of the Maya statements extracted by torture.

39 Chamberlain (1948: 232–52); Landa (XV); Jones (1989: 26–276).

40 The topic has been studied sporadically in the second half of this century. Little of note was published in the decades immediately following Chamberlain (1948). Recent publications have tended to cover the Conquest in a few introductory pages (García Bernal 1978; Farriss 1984: 20–25; Restall 1997a: 1–5) or less (Patch 1993); they have limited their discussion to one chapter of a broader work (Bricker 1981, Karttunen 1994; Kicza n.d.) or focused on one part of the story (Clendinnen 1987 and Tedlock 1993 on Landa's anti-idolatry campaign of 1562; Jones 1989 on the southern frontier; Quezada 1993 on early colonial Maya political organization; the present volume on the Maya perspective).

41 CD,13:86–91.

42 CDI:XII. This Catalina is the daughter that Landa (XIII) mentions as being married off to Lic. Alonso Maldonado, president of the *audiencia* or royal high court in Guatemala.

43 Chamberlain (1948: 153).

44 According to Herrera's own *probanza* of 1554; her request for royal support was based not only on her pedigree as widow of the *adelantado* and as matriarch of the first conquistador family, but as a major investor who "gave to the *adelantado* a great quantity of money for the costs of the people and fleet that came to these provinces for their conquest and pacification, which assistance the said *adelantado* took and thus carried out the said conquest, as is common knowledge (*como es puco y notorio*)" (AGI-*México* 3048: 18–24, quote from 21–22).

45 See, for example, *probanzas* in AGI-*México* 104, 105, and 3048. In one such case, Juana de Contreras asked in 1588 for an annual pension of 300 *pesos* and 100 *fanegas* of maize on the grounds that her uncle and aunt had provided at their own expense weapons, horses, and servants for the Conquest and had been "the first Spaniards and conquistadors to be married in the province" (AGI-*México* 3048: 76–81).

46 Chamberlain (1948: 345).

47 Chamberlain (1948: 1).

48 Carrillo y Ancona (1880: 49).

49 Landa (XVIII).

50 See Landa and various entries in RY.

51 British Library, London, MS 17, 569: 181.

52 Pendergast 1967: 154, 184. Also see Stephens (II-IV). The other side to this coin is the tendency of a century of published studies of the Mayas to end with the Spanish invasion, reflected in the traditional and somewhat neocolonialist disciplinary divisions between archaeology and history. Scholars of the precolumbian Mayas have for a long time studied early colonial ethnohistorical sources, but overwhelmingly with a view to discovering what they reveal about precolumbian Maya civilization (of numerous examples, two recent ones are Marcus 1993 and McAnany 1996).

53 Thompson (1956: 99).

54 As most vividly illustrated in a 1936 *National Geographic* article; Morley (1946: 211–12); Tozzer (1957: 128–29); Gillespie (1989: 201–207); Jones (1997: 281–83).

55 Thompson (1956: 105; 1970); Tozzer (1957); Coggins (1987); Coe (1993: 155).

56 As Gillespie (1989: 207) notes, this is not really a new idea; see Kubler (1961), for example.

57 Sabloff and Andrews (1986); Ringle (1990); Sabloff and Henderson (1993); Sharer (1994: 348–408); Jones (1995).

58 The Itza Mayas are associated in the Chilam Balam texts with various places within Yucatan but with none outside of it (CBC:20; CBM:135–36).

59 In a passage in the Title of Calkini the authors assert that, as Maya noblemen of the Canul dynasty, they came from the east, "from those people of West Zuyua" (TC:36); the Book of Chilam Balam of Mani comments that the Xiu came "from West Zuyua" (CBM:134). This is presumably the same Zuyua mentioned in the Chilam Balam of Chumayel passage which, headed "'The speech and understanding of Zuyua [*zuyua than y naat*],'" consists of a series of riddles interpreted variously as a test for rulership (Roys 1933: 88–98; Edmonson 1986: 168; Marcus 1992: 78–79) or as a parody or mockery of ruling-class pretensions (Burns 1991: 35; Sigal 1995). Going back a century, scholars have asserted that Zuyua is Nahuatl-derived and in central Mexico, the birthplace indeed of Kukulcan-Quetzalcoatl (Brinton 1882: 110; Roys 1933: 88; 1943: 59, 151; Edmonson 1982: 38; Thompson 1970: 23; Coe 1993: 171; Sharer 1994: 406); a variation on the theme has Zuyua in the Tabasco region (Carmack 1981: 46 and Okoshi Harada 1993: 5). Yet, as one linguist has pointed out, there is "no convincing evidence that *Zuyua* has anything to do with Nahuatl place names, the Nahuatl language, or central Mexico" (Karttunen 1985: 6). Indeed, the Canul nobles asserted that "West Zuyua" was east of Calkini—the opposite direction to central Mexico. The Mani reference (CBM:134) gives two other toponyms as Xiu provenances; although one of them, Tulapan, seems central Mexican and could be Tula, the other, Nonoual, symbolizes (like Zuyua) some place distant, for-

eign, and important but otherwise unidentifiable. Other colonial references to the Mexican origin of Maya nobles are also, I would suggest, reflections not of an historical migration or invasion, but of the Maya elite's complex culture of legitimacy-assertion. For example, a statement made in 1618 by a Maya man in Valladolid, written down in Spanish as part of a lawsuit, repeats the folk-historical belief of the time that the Cocom and other local nobles were descended from lords "who came from Mexico," one of whom was related to Moctezuma. Local Kauil and Camal noblemen are cited as sources by the Maya witness (document reproduced in Brinton 1882: 114–18; quoted at length in Roys 1962: 66, where it is erroneously dated 1718). Although knowledge of one or both the Moctezumas may have circulated in precolonial Yucatan, it seems more likely that tales of him arrived with the Spaniards and/or their Nahua auxiliaries. Besides, the Cocom name has been identified in Chichen Itza heiroglyphs dating from long before the Moctezumas ruled in Mexico (Stuart 1993: 346–47). As Brinton observes (1882: 120–21), the names in the Valladolid document of these putative ancestral migrants (such as Suhuykak Camal) are entirely Maya, not Nahuatl. In addition, some misinterpretations in the historical literature have served to distort the evidence on the origins of the families ruling Yucatan at the time of the Conquest. For example, Roys (1957: 41) misread into the Pech titles (see Chapter 6 below) evidence that the Pech nobles arrived in the region north of Merida not only after Mayapan's fall but "in conquest times" (the claim by the Pech author to be "the first noble conquistador [*yax hidalgo concixtador*] here in this land" refers to his acquisition of the prestigious Spanish title, not the initial arrival of the Pech in the region); Farriss (1984: 245) then took Roys's comments as the basis of her characterization of the Pech as "parvenu 'adventurers'." For other Maya origin myths with similar elements, see the Chontal example of Auxaual of Cozumel in Chapter 3 (TAT:69v) and various Cakchiquel parallels, from the assertion that lineage ancestors came from "Tulan, Zuyua" to the claim to be descended from Abraham and the ancient Israelites (in the Xpantzay primordial titles from Tecpan; Cakchiquel texts and Spanish translations in Recinos 1984: 120–21, 168–69). On Nahua migration myths see Gillespie (1989), Christensen (1996), and various other studies cited by these authors. For a discussion of the role of foreign origins and connections in the ideology of rulership elsewhere in the world, see Helms (1993).

60 See Lockhart (1992) and Restall (1997a; 1998b) as well as many other studies cited in these works and in Restall (1997b).

61 Karttunen (1985: 14).

62 Sharer (1994: 348).

63 Culbert (1973); Lowe (1985); Sabloff (1990); Stuart (1993).

64 Sabloff and Henderson (1993); Sharer (1994: 338–408, 462–63).

65 Quote by Jones (1997: 285) characterizing the views of others.

66 Morley (1946: 88; the quote); Pollock et al. (1962); Sabloff and Andrews (1986); Sharer (1994: 408–21).

67 Gaspar Antonio Chi (see Chapter 8), a Xiu on his mother's side, asserted in his 1582 *relación* (in the AGI; English translation in Tozzer 1941: 230–32) that the Xiu were lords of Mayapan. Landa (XIII), perhaps attempting to reconcile what he had been told both by Chi and his other informant, Nachi Cocom, states that the Cocom were the dominant lords but that they introduced slavery and tyranny (thus justifying the Xiu-led revolt).

68 Although scholars tend to give the impression that the "voluntaristic confederation" of the Mayapan arrangement is well-evidenced (e.g. Marcus 1993: 117; Quezada 1993: 28), the ethnohistorical evidence actually centers on a single phrase in the Books of Chilam Balam, *mul tepal*, "group rule," i.e. rule by a council or oligarchy rather than an individual. The phrase is usually glossed as "joint government" or "joint rule" (Brinton 1882: 103; Roys 1962: 72; Craine and Reindorp 1979: 139, all on the Mani book), but Edmonson (1982: 10) gives it a different spin in the Tizimin text, linking it not to Mayapan's system of government but to its breakdown — "crowd rule" — and I have similarly translated the phrase in the Mani text as "factional rule" (see CBM:136 in Chapter 7 below). Note that Cogolludo (2, I) states that Mayapan was under the "monarchical rule" of a "supreme king." I suspect that the reality was, as implied below, not dissimilar to the colonial-era Maya system — that is, rule by an oligarchical council of elders who were divided into factions and more or less dominated by the municipal governor (termed *batab* both before and during the colonial period).

69 The *cabildo* was the Spanish municipal council that was imposed upon, and variously used and reinterpreted by, indigenous communities throughout colonial Mesoamerica; Restall (1997a: 61–97). For an interpretation that stresses greater contrasts in Maya government between the Chichen Itza, Mayapan, post-Mayapan, and colonial periods, see Quezada (1993: 21–126).

70 See Chapter 2 below for a discussion of the nature of these post-Mayapan polities.

71 TC:13 is the specific reference to Mayapan, but see the various settlement passages in the Calkini and Pech texts (Chapters 5 and 6). The assertion by Maya landowners that their ancestors settled empty lands following the fall of Mayapan can also be found in mundane land records (documents which are titles of a sort but which, although written in Maya, are too brief and stick too closely to Spanish land-record formats to be called primordial titles). Take, for example, this excerpt translated from a Maya land title of 1569 (TT:32):

> They placed stone markers along the edge of that forest. Then they cut the borders of the forest at Chiche, which belongs to Blas [*balas*] Pox, whose uncle is [Juan Pox, mentioned earlier in the document]. Blas Pox's father was called Napuc Pox. He was the eldest son of Nadzul Pox, who died with Ahpulha. He was the oldest man of the first settlers at the foot of the mound of Tixdzitkuk. They settled there before the time of the coming of the Spaniards; the men of the forests were alone. Nadzul Pox was the first to settle at Ahtocoyna [Place of the Abandoned House] at one of the four abandoned houses that there were in these forests. Nadzul Pox was the first of the men. Nadzul Pox was the fourth son of one woman. This was

Nadzul Pox. They came from within the *cah* of Mayapan when they settled the territory [*lum*] of Chichican. When they left they went to Tinum, where the mound of Puluzuoo is, and thus they settled Tocoyna at the foot of the mound of Ahpuluzuoo. It is called Ahcalomkin. These are the landmarks of the forests of Nadzul Pox, which are at Tinum. When Nadzul Pox was settled there, they gave the borders landmarks.

72 Rubio Mañé (1941) is the only study of the Montejo house; other relevant works offer only an illustration and brief comment on the façade [see, for example, Perry and Perry (1988: 94–95); Early (1994: 121–22); Fernández-Armesto (1995: 266–67); and Mullen (1997: 11–12)]. There is no hard evidence for the Maya role in the designing and building of the façade beyond the rationale that in 1549 there were in Yucatan a few hundred Spanish conquistadors, none of whom appear to have been masons, and hundreds of thousands of Mayas, some of whom obviously were—an observation made by commentators from Stephens (IV) to Molina Solís (1896, I: XI) to Rubio Mañé (1941:18–19, also quoting the previous two authors). The façade, as Figure 1.1 shows, boasts many other features that appear to reflect both Spanish and Maya cultural influences; Rubio Mañé (1941) points out parallels, for example, to buildings in Chichen Itza and Valladolid, Spain.

73 In Classic Maya culture, "the boundary between the living and the ancestors was a permeable one" (McAnany 1998: 292). There are various examples of the Maya concept of some form of life surviving in the disembodied human head; see, for example, the fate of the severed head of one of the hero twins in the Popol Vuh (Tedlock 1985), or the role played by disembodied ancestor heads in ancient Maya iconography—of particular relevance here is the existence of such heads carved into stone façades (such as Stela 31 at Tikal) (McAnany: 1996: 27–47; 1998; personal communication). For pre-Conquest Maya images of captives at or under the feet of captor lords, including some with open mouths (but not with severed heads), see Schele and Freidel (1990: 142, 145, 148, 166, 190).

74 It is worth noting that this interpretation of the open mouths of the stone heads could be seen as still relevant almost exactly three centuries after Merida was founded and the Montejo palace built; in the so-called Caste War, which began in 1847 and dragged on to the turn of the twentieth century, the Mayas momentarily reclaimed almost the entire peninsula from the descendents of the Spaniards but suffered through a bloody civil/race war and a brutal suppression of Maya resistance to Hispanic domination through most of the nineteenth century (Patch 1991; Rugeley 1996; Dumond 1997).

CHAPTER 2. *Recontextualizing Calamity*

1 Chamberlain (1948: 1).

2 Le Clézio (1993: 176).

3 Restall (1997a: 67–69) on the notary. On Maya alphabetic writing see Restall (1995a; 1997: 229–303; 1997b; 1998b).

4 The eyewitness authenticity of Maya accounts is even more compromised than that of Nahua accounts (Lockhart 1993: 27–46), written down twenty-five to fifty years after the fall of Tenochtitlan but subject to less subsequent interference.

5 Las Casas (1992: 80); Landa (XV).

6 We are reminded of the young Alonso Canche witnessing the seizing of Mayas in Calkini. In another episode recorded by Las Casas, the dogs of a Spaniard savaged a baby that had been tied to the feet of a Maya woman who had hanged herself (in vain "thinking to soften the hearts of the Spaniards"); Las Casas (1992: 79–87).

7 Landa (XV; XXXII); Restall (1995b). Landa occasionally gives the name of one of the Spanish perpetrators, although he claims that Montejo (the chief villain in the Las Casas piece) "was not guilty of any of those cruelties."

8 Leon-Portilla (1992: 137).

9 Lockhart (1993: 313).

10 See Chapter 9 for the letter in full; AHN *caja* III.

11 CBC:20, 22.

12 TAT:74v (in Chapter 3); AGI-*México* 367, etc. (in Chapter 9); CBT:60 (in Chapter 7).

13 CBM:70–72 (in Chapter 7). The *Songs of Dzitbalche* consist of fifteen brief texts, apparently the lyrics of songs which accompanied dances; the manuscript, discovered in the 1940s in the *cah* of Dzitbalche, dates from the end of the colonial period (Barrera Vásquez 1965).

14 Indeed, in one passage Maya priests seek to reassure the people that the Conquest had been anticipated by their religious officials and that, although they "would suffer greatly in the future, their souls would benefit from all these misfortunes" (CBM:74 in Chapter 7).

15 Chapters 3, 5, and 6 below present examples of Yucatec Maya primordial titles; the genre is discussed more fully in the introductions to Chapters 3 and 5.

16 TY:3v; TCH:6; TY:5r; TCH:10. Of course, from the perspective of those who resisted, the collaborators are to blame for the continuing, demanding presence of the Spaniards, no doubt one of the meanings of the Chilam Balam of Chumayel phrases: "It was not we who did it, [but] we pay for it today" and "we are paying for the war with the foreigners . . . it was those captains of the *cahob* then; it is we who pay for it today" (CBC:22, 21).

17 TC:17–19.

18 Particularly the Tlatelolco account mentioned above and the account in Book Twelve of the Florentine Codex (Sahagún 1978; León-Portilla 1992; Lockhart 1993: 48–273).

19 Lockhart (1993: 15) has commented on a similar lack of moral judgment of violence in Nahua accounts of the Conquest. The same point can be made with respect to some of the highland Guatemalan Maya accounts. In the Title of Coyoy, the Quiché Maya authors are as concerned with the details of battle preparation

and dress as they are with the battle itself and its outcome; the emphasis is not on judging the Spaniards for bringing war, but on evaluating the dignity of the Quiché reaction to the invasion (Carmack and Zapeta 1993). In the Annals of the Cakchiquels (which is also a primordial title that could be called the Title of Solola), both the Spanish and Cakchiquel Maya forces engage in military activities that are presented as neither gory nor gratuitous, but simply as the expected glories and horrors of war; the devil in the piece is the *adelantado* Pedro de Alvarado, not the Spaniards as a whole (Recinos 1950; Recinos et al. 1953).

20 TY:5r; TCH:10.

21 See TAT:72 in Chapter 3 for the full Chontal account. Different versions of the story are offered by Cortés (Pagden 1986: 365–67; the Bernal Díaz version is similar), in which a Mexica lord reveals Cuauhtemoc's conspiracy and the Chontal Mayas play no role at all, and by the Nahua chronicler Ixtlilxochitl, who asserts that before he even met Paxbolonacha, Cortés invented the conspiracy as a pretext for executing the Mexica lords (Scholes and Roys 1968: 113–15).

22 CBC:20, 22. Roys describes this list of woes as "stereotyped phrases usually employed to describe a riot or the plundering of a town" (1933: 79).

23 Just as, according to the Chumayel, conquest and colonization have added church fees (*limosna*) to the traditional burden of tribute (*patan*), so have Spaniards (*Españolesob*) and colonial public prosecutors (*fiscalob*) been added to a list of pre-Conquest officers who continue to require service (*meyahtabal*)—priests (*ah kinob*), community governors (*batabob*), and teachers (*camzahob*); CBC:20.

24 See, for example, the Chilam Balam of Tizimin (Chapter 7), in which non-elite Mayas are the implied victims both of the violence accompanying the Spanish invasion and the inadequacy of the Maya rulers of the time; the native "wise men" are denounced as "lords of idiocy" (CBT:63), and the Maya warrior elite are condemned for being two-faced (presumably for attempting to maintain status in the Maya community as well as to appease the Spaniards) (CBT:67).

25 In a land survey of 1569 from Dzan, for example, the author, Juan Pox, not only gives an all-Maya name for his father, Nadzul Pox, but also a pre-Christian name for his older brother, Napuc Pox. Aside from the change in naming patterns, the Conquest seems to have had no effect on the family land tenure that is the subject of the document (save for the need to draw up the document); the Conquest is simply a temporal reference—"they settled there before the time of the arrival of the Spaniards (*tijili cahanob ti manan u tal u kin yulel españores*)" (TT:32r).

26 TCH:4. Don Alonso Pech, the "author" of the Yaxkukul title, puts it even more succinctly: "My father, whose Maya name was Nacan Pech, was ruling his governorship when he was given a name" (TY:3r).

27 Stendhal Collection, Benson Library, University of Texas, Austin: MS. 1964.19; Whitecotton (1990); Zeitlin and Thomas (1992); Alvaro Hermann (1996); Zeitlin (1997).

28 The Chontal account adds only one Conquest-related detail, a one-line reference

to Cortés's visit (TAT:70r-v in Chapter 3). Later on in the Acalan-Tixchel title, when a little more detail is provided regarding Christianization, it is still the change in names that serves as the symbol and prominent feature of the conversion (TAT:74v). The Quiché title briefly and dispassionately mentions the arrival of *"donadi"* (Tonatiuh, as the Nahuas and Guatemalan Mayas called Pedro de Alvarado), that a couple of rulers were hanged by the *"castilan winak"* (Castilian men), and that tribute payments and baptisms then took place (Carmack and Mondloch 1989: 71, 87). Note that the Chontal and Yucatec Mayas, unlike the Quiché Mayas, Nahuas, and many other Mesoamericans, are utterly consistent in retaining their patronyms after conversion (on the importance of Maya patronyms, see Restall 1997a: Chapters 2, 4, 6, 7; 1998).

29 Straightforward, undramatic references to the transition to Spanish rule can also be found in Nahua primordial titles, where the Conquest period is simply the time of "the coming of Cortés" or "the coming of the faith" (Lockhart 1991: 59; Wood 1991). In the brief Conquest account in Nahuatl from Cuauhtitlan, the Spaniards merely pass through en route to Tenochtitlan, with the only sign of any aftereffects being the fact that one local ruler now has "don Pedro" prefixed to his indigenous name; a comparable account from Cuauhtinchan reports that in the wake of Cortés's passage through nearby Tlaxcala and Cholula, the local "ruler Tequanitzin died, and don Alonso de Castañeda [a baptized Nahua successor] assumed the rulership." In both accounts further details are reserved for information on tribute arrangements and payments, an aspect of intercommunity relations that also represented continuity from prehispanic times (Lockhart 1993: 280–81; 282–87; Leibsohn 1993: 40).

30 Lockhart (1993: 282–87); Leibsohn (1993); Wood (1991); Chapters 3, 5, and 6 below.

31 Scholes et al. (1936–38, 1: 13–25).

32 TY:5v; TCH:11. The Chontal title likewise praises this same judge for eliminating a long list of items from the tribute record as well as requiring that Spaniards pay Mayas specified sums for transporting tribute items and other goods (TAT:75r).

33 Alonso de Maldonado and Alonso López de Cerrato; Recinos et al. (1953: 131, 136–39).

34 *ah makopilobe ah dzudzopob*; "never before had custard-apples been eaten, so when the Spaniards ate them they were called custard-apple eaters" (TY:4v; TCH:9); "they were the first to eat the custard-apple for breakfast, and thus were called the custard-apple-sucking foreigners" (CBC:21).

35 The Alonso Canche narrative discussed in Chapter 1; TC:12–13, 16–17 in Chapter 5.

36 Lockhart (1993: 15) has remarked that the Nahua perception of the Spaniards as "formidable adversaries who wanted much the same thing as . . . themselves" was the Mexica rationale for opposing the Spaniards, as well as, conversely, the rationale for other Nahua communities "to play power politics with them against the Mexica." The similarity of Maya perceptions is illustrated by the fact that the Cocom killing of the Xiu was possibly revenge not only for a Xiu massacre of Cocom

lords a century earlier, but also the Xiu use of an alliance with Spaniards against the Cocom a few years earlier.

37 Lockhart (1993: 16). Hence the initial Maya acceptance of the *encomienda* in many areas, followed by its rejection as soon as Spanish heavy-handedness became apparent; see Chapter 1.

38 The incorporation of the Chontal Mayas into the colony came about through a protracted series of tribute negotiations and population relocations; the eventual decline of the Chontal was caused not directly by Spanish conquest but indirectly, as a result of epidemics, pirate attacks, and the southward migration of Yucatec Mayas into Acalan (TAT in Chapter 3; Scholes and Roys 1948: 88–315). The Pech titles (Chapter 6) describe how the Pech rulers of the region left Chicxulub and Yaxkukul on a number of occasions in order to participate in the Conquest-era wars and diplomatic meetings, but, according to their account, they never fought against Spaniards nor did Spaniards ever engage in hostilities in or near those two *cahob*. See Chapter 1 for a discussion of the protracted nature of the Conquest of Yucatan.

39 Tedlock (1992); Florescano (1994).

40 Klor de Alva (1992); Lockhart (1993: 50–56; 1994: 245–46).

41 Burkhart (1996: 96).

42 Wood (1991); Lockhart (1991: 57–63).

43 Farriss (1984: 25); the quote does not do justice to the sophistication of Farriss's understanding of Maya concepts of time, most fully argued in Farriss (1987).

44 Bricker (1981: 7–8, 24–28); Clendinnen (1987: 169). A related issue is that of the decision by the Peten Itza at Tayasal (at the southern central foot of the peninsula) to voluntarily submit to Spanish rule and conversion in 1695, allegedly determined by the Chilam Balam prophesies and the onset of a new calendrical cycle (Bricker 1981: 21–24; Jones 1989: 241–76).

45 Chapter 4; Edmonson (1982: xvii–xviii; 1986: 12–14); Farriss 1987.

46 With respect to the Peten Itza issue, one might argue that as the only extant sources on the Itza surrender of 1695 are Spanish, they are compromised by the Franciscans' desire to see the hand of God at work. Furthermore, calendrical determinist theory bears traces of the Spanish perception of Mesoamericans as superstitious Indians who in central Mexico saw Cortés as the god Quetzalcoatl and in the Peten even deified the horse he left behind. Even if the ambassadors sent by the Itza to Merida were motivated by a belief in a preordained surrender, they must have represented a mere faction within their community, for the Itza obliged the Spaniards to take Tayasal by force in 1697. It would be more in line with the broader context of evidence to see the 1695 embassy as an active political initiative rather than an attempt at passive surrender. Also persuasive is the notion that Franciscans, armed with their knowledge of the Maya calendar, attempted (with partial success) to convince the Peten Itza ruler to surrender on the calendrically auspicious day in 1697. The historiographical legacy of 1697 thus becomes the Spanish perception of

the Maya perception of time. (No doubt Grant Jones's forthcoming book on the Conquest of Peten Itza will clarify this and related issues.)

47 In fact, archaeologists have dated the Maya use of a cross symbol back many centuries to the Late Formative period; McAnany (1996: 85–86). The Chi account is in Chapter 8 below. For other Maya interpretations of the Conquest as anticipated and preordained, see the prophecy sections of the Pech titles (Chapter 6) and the Books of Chilam Balam (Chapter 7).

48 TY:2v; TCH:1.

49 TCH:15. On Maya patronym-based lineages or *chibalob* see Restall (1997a: 17, 87–102; 1998c).

50 TAT:76r-v in Chapter 3; the third Xiu petition in Chapter 10.

51 Note the psychological parallel here with colonial Andean *kurakakuna* self-representation, in which indigenous nobles asserted their association with colonial as well as pre-Conquest authority (Cummins 1991).

52 Terraciano and Sousa (1992). The document is one of a pair of *títulos* written in the 1690s by neighboring Oaxacan communities, one Mixtec and one Nahua, with competing local territorial claims. The Nahuas' title claims that with Cortés's sanction it was they who conquered the cannibalistic Mixtecs, and that when this Spanish-Nahua alliance collapsed, the Nahuas still emerged as conquerors. Conflict broke out between the Spaniards and the Nahuas, according to the Nahua account, over a particular hill and the Spaniards' anger over the Nahuas' ability to "raise the water from beneath the ground" (note the water/hill symbolism that evokes the Nahua term for municipal community, *altepetl);* "Cortés saw how nobody dared to kill us. Then he told us, 'Let there be no more war; let us live as brothers; we shall willingly settle next to the Mexicans as brothers.' [But] when they saw water [still] ascending, the Spaniards were angry that we raised the water over the hill. They began to battle with great strength and fought us until we, the Mexican people, defeated the Children of the Sun [the Spaniards]. Then they said: 'That is enough, let it be.' 'You are truly the famous Mexican people,' he [Cortés] thus declared. Just like the Spaniards we died in battle and we sought war. We captured two blacks. Also like the Spaniards, with war and gunpowder we won it" (Terraciano and Sousa 1992: 49; I have slightly edited their English translation but not altered its substance).

53 This follows Hill's persuasive interpretation (1992: 1–8). The *fiesta* was held from early to mid-colonial times in the city that is today's Antigua. Cakchiquels constructed a large wood-framed replica of a volcano and covered it with live foliage, captive animals, a small "temple" on the summit, and a defensive force of about a thousand young men in precolonial warrior attire. Descendents of Tlaxcalans, dressed as Spanish soldiers, then stormed the hill, drove off the Cakchiquel defenders, and captured their "king." Finally, all participants paraded out of the plaza. The volcano/mountain was to Guatemalan Mayas both the home of their animal-spirit companions, or *tonas* (a term of Nahuatl origin), and the symbol of indigenous municipal integrity (here Mesoamerican imagery of pyramid and mountain

combine); in this mock conquest, however, neither the plants and animals nor the small temple-like structure built atop the volcano were captured or destroyed by the invaders. Even the "king" (playing Sinacam, the last Cakchiquel ruler and leader of the 1526 "rebellion") is merely captured (an honorable fate for Mesoamericans anyway) and never ritually killed or sacrificed. Just as Cakchiquels were allowed to build and dismantle a structure laden with indigenous political symbolism year after year, so was Sinacam able to return to his "subjects" time and again.

54 Despite their use of terminology for "the Mixtecs" (*tay ñudzahui*) and "the Mexicans" (*mexicatlaca*), the authors of the Oaxacan titles are defending the territorial claims not of their ethnicities but of their individual communities, the *ñuu* of Chapultepec and the *altepetl* of Mexicapan—indeed, the principal men of Chapultepec wrote (or, as they claimed, produced from their archive) their title as part of a lawsuit against a fellow Mixtec noble from neighboring Cuilapan (Terraciano and Sousa 1992). For more on colonial-era Mixtec writing, culture, and society see Terraciano (1994).

55 This corporate-community perspective is visible in the wider body of primordial titles in Nahuatl (Wood 1991; Lockhart 1991: 39–64; 1992: 410–18) and also in Nahua Conquest accounts in other genres. The concerns of passages recounting the Conquest in annals from Cuauhtitlan (Lockhart 1993: 280–81) and Cuauhtinchan (Lockhart 1993: 282–87; Leibsohn 1993) are distinctly and overwhelmingly those of the *altepetl*, while the account in the Florentine Codex presents events so as to place Tlatelolco in a favorable light and to slight the sister-*altepetl* of Tenochtitlan, implying that the latter, not the former, was to blame for the defeat (Sahagún 1978; León-Portilla 1992; Lockhart 1993: 48–255).

56 Roys (1943; 1957: 3); Farriss (1984: 147–48); Marcus (1993); Quezada (1993: 32–58).

57 In the words of Marcus (1993: 120). While ultimately asserting the integrity of these "provinces," both Roys and Marcus offer evidence of their instability and loose definition Roys (1957: 3, 109, 113–14, citing sources in RY, and Marcus 1993: 116–21, which includes a schematic representation of the three province types suggested by Roys). Quezada (1993: 50–58) argues that a Maya term, *cuchcabal*, is preferable to "province," but he also asserts that these regional units had considerable integrity; both he (1993: 59–155) and Farriss (1984: 148–52) view the colonial-era localization of Maya geopolitics as a destructive ramification of the Conquest rather than a consolidation of pre-Conquest tendencies. Also see Okoshi Harada (1994) and McAnany (1996: 148–54). The lack of bipolarized centralized states comparable to the Tlaxcalan-Mexica rivalry, the Quiché-Cakchiquel hostility, and the Inka civil war, prevented a rapid Conquest in Yucatan; however, once the Spaniards were able to negotiate their way into the labyrinth of local rivalries, the decentralized nature of Yucatec politics actually worked to the advantage of the Spaniards.

58 The names signed to the 1567 letters of the *batabob* to the king (Chapter 9) are one illustration of these relationships; also see Roys (1943; 1957). On the taboo on *chibal* endogamy, and the fact that class considerations on rare occasions inspired individuals to break the taboo, see Restall (1997a: 131, 397) and Chapter 6, note 44, below.

59 Farriss (1984: 22–23); Roys (1957: 9–81).

60 The Acalan-Tixchel primordial title represents the Paxbolon *chibal*; the Chicxulub, Yaxkukul, Motul titles promote the Pech position; and the Calkini title reflects the viewpoint of the Canul, Canche, and other ruling *chibalob* in that region. Further evidence is offered by the letters to the king authored in 1567 by members of these *chibalob* (Chapter 9). The Xiu support for the Spaniards is reflected, albeit less directly, in accounts presented in Chapters 4, 7, and 8. A less conciliatory position adopted by Xiu and Pacab rulers in the Mani province in 1567 is contained in one of the petitions included in Chapter 9.

61 Farriss argues both ideas; see Farriss 1984: 23 and 412 respectively. As discussed in Chapter 1, there is insufficient evidence to support the notion that there were separate Mexican and Itza invasions and that the Yucatec elite came from migrant stock and thus differed in some ethnic sense from the Maya masses. The east-west contrast persisted throughout the colonial period (during which the east was never fully colonized) and into the nineteenth century, when Mayas from the east rose up against the descendents of the Spaniards and established an independent indigenous region that lasted half a century (Rugeley 1996; Dumond 1997).

62 That is, the *repartimiento de bienes*, by which Maya communities were forced by Spanish officials and their partners to sell goods at below-market rates (García Bernal 1979; Farriss 1984: 43–47, 83–85; Patch 1993). On the *encomienda* in Yucatan, see García Bernal (1978: 169–474) and Patch (1993).

63 TT:32r; CBC:22 in Chapter 7.

CHAPTER 3. *The Insinuated Conquest*

1 The marriage only lasted six years, as Catalina died in 1597, but their son Martín became the Paxbolon heir and appears to have grown up mostly in Tixchel. The boy helped to cement the Paxbolon-Maldonado alliance, one which offers a fascinating example of how the Conquest and colonial rule often took the form of collaboration between Spanish settlers and native elites; Paxbolon used Maldonado to represent his interests before the colonial authorities, while Maldonado's acquisition of lands near Tixchel, no doubt in part through marriage to Catalina, helped launch his career as a successful colonist—*estanciero*, captain, and *alcalde* in Campeche. The continuation of this relationship long after Catalina's death is demonstrated by the collaboration of Paxbolon and Maldonado in planning and carrying out their 1604 conquest campaign in the area east of Acalan (Scholes and Roys 1948: 249–98).

2 The Paxbolon papers consisted of a document written in Nahuatl probably in 1567 and translated by Paxbolon into Chontal in 1612 (this is the first part of the text through the list of *cah* names), followed by a lengthier chronicle of events (the rest of the text) written in Chontal in 1610–12. The papers were copied in Tixchel in 1612 and sent to Campeche, where they were translated into Spanish a few months later. A second-generation copy was then made in Merida in 1614 and presented to the

Council of the Indies in Madrid in 1618; it is this copy that survives in Seville (AGI-*México* 138). Maldonado was not granted the right to claim a specific *encomienda* until 1629, when he requested that the Mayas conquered in 1604 (and later resettled in the Sahcabchen area nearer to Campeche) be divided among his two sons, Martín and Nicolás. This request was still in the courts when the *encomienda* of Calkini (see Chapter 5) became vacant and, in 1630, went to Nicolás alone. In view of the importance given to the Paxbolon connection, it is ironic that in the end it was Nicolás, Maldonado's fully Spanish son by a second marriage, who received the reward, and one not directly related to Paxbolon or Acalan (AGI-*México* 97; 138; 2999; Scholes and Roys 1948: 291–98).

3   I have made my translation of the title from the facsimile of the Chontal Maya text reproduced by Scholes and Roys (1948: between 366 and 367). Also of use was the contemporaneous (1612) Spanish translation transcribed by Scholes and Roys, who also translated the Spanish text into English, inserting glosses where the Maya and Spanish versions differ (1948: 367–405). In fact, these differences are more extensive than Scholes and Roys recognize but as Smailus (1975) makes clear; the two originals tell essentially the same story but are very seldom phrase-by-phrase parallel texts. Also of use to me was the Smailus study, in which the Chontal text is transcribed and translated into Spanish. My version below represents the first attempt to translate the Chontal text directly into English. This endeavor was made possible by the fact that early colonial Chontal, despite being in the Cholan rather than Yucatecan language group, was very similar lexically and syntactically to early colonial Yucatec Maya (for an introduction to Mesoamerican languages, see Justeson and Broadwell 1996; on Chontal, see Smailus 1975; for an argument that puts Chontal and Yucatec in the same language group, see Schumann 1985). This similarity no doubt facilitated the virtual disappearance of Chontal by late colonial times as Yucatec speakers migrated in increasing numbers into Acalan-Tixchel, in which region Chontal is no longer spoken (Scholes and Roys 1948: 299–315).

4   Tedlock (1985).

5   Recent studies of central Mexican titles include Wood (1989; 1991; 1998); Borah (1991); Haskett (1992; 1996); Lockhart (1992: 376–92); and Gruzinski (1993: Chapter 3). Robert Haskett is currently writing what will be the first book-length treatment of *títulos* in Nahuatl. Terraciano and Sousa's "The 'Original Conquest' of Oaxaca" (1992) is a study of Mixtec and Nahuatl titles from Oaxaca. Restall (1997a: Chapter 21) discusses Yucatec Maya titles. Quiché and Cakchiquel Maya primordial titles, although they are not necessarily discussed as such, can be found in Brinton (1885); Recinos and Goetz (1953); Carmack (1973; 1995); and Carmack and Mondloch (1983; 1989). Restall (1997b) discusses primordial titles in the Mesoamerican context.

6   Marcus (1992).

7   For example, the significant intersection of literary-oral and political traditions is nicely illustrated below by the image of the aged notary-governor don Pablo Paxbolon reading out loud to the assembled community elders an account of the lineage and past conquests of the Paxbolon dynasty (TAT:70v). On orality in colonial Mesoamerican texts and its pre-Conquest antecedents see the articles in *Ancient*

Mesoamerica 1 (1990); Lockhart (1992: Chapter 8); Boone and Mignolo (1994); Restall (1997a: Chapter 18; 1997b).

8 I here follow the folio numbers written on the 1614 text which are clearly visible in the Scholes and Roys facsimile; my paragraph breaks also follow those of the Chontal text, which are mostly indicated by item marks in the margin. The Chontal text begins on the last line of folio 69r, following Martín Maldonado's formal request in Spanish to have the papers copied.

9 The Maya text uses the Spanish loan-phrase *escriuano publico* (*escribano público*); Paxbolon was of course the governor of Tixchel, not *the* notary, but his prominence, his literacy, and his role as translator of this document made him *a* notary and allowed him to lay claim to what was in Mesoamerica before and after the Conquest a prestigious status.

10 The text reads *mexico than*, meaning Nahuatl, which was spoken in the Chontal Maya area—as evidenced by the fact that the original text was written in that language, and by the assertion of a Spaniard that "the Mexican language . . . is the most common language in this province [Tabasco]" (RY, II: 415); indeed the word Chontal is presumably derived from a Nahuatl term for "foreigner," *chontalli*. Although Yucatec Maya contains words of Nahuatl origin (Karttunen 1985: 4–14; also see Chapter 1 above), the central Mexican language was not spoken in the peninsula east of the Chontal area.

11 As Scholes and Roys observe (1948: 383), Auxaual is not a very Maya-sounding name; in fact, it is more likely Nahuatl in origin, and indeed a community called Taxagual (which might be "translated" as Axaual's Place) appears on a 1579 map of Tabasco located west from Tixchel along the Gulf Coast (Scholes and Roys 1948: 16 facing; Izquierdo 1997: 185). Frances Karttunen (personal communication) suggests that Auxaual could derive from the Nahuatl *a-xahual-li* and be read as "waterfall." The appeal of Cozumel was probably that it symbolized remoteness, being at the very opposite end of the Yucatan peninsula from Tixchel; its role as an ancient pilgrimage site and Chontal-Itza trading port in the Postclassic period may also have been relevant. In other words, Cozumel's remoteness and sacred associations, together with the non-Chontal derivation of Auxaual, make these terms typical elements of a Maya origin myth (see Chapter 1 for the same point made using the example of Zuyua). The myth, of course, has historical roots; note, for example, that Auxaual's principal men all have common Chontal Maya names and were thus the ancestors of those alive when the document was written and copied.

12 The Maya term used here, *chuc*, means "take" or "take over," strongly suggesting but not necessarily meaning "conquer," which is how I have glossed it throughout the text.

13 As Frances Karttunen (personal communication) suggests, this is probably composed of *pax*, the lineage name element, and *chimal-li*, Nahuatl for "shield" (the *xch* would elide to *ch*); the same elements are in the sixth ruler's name below (also see Scholes and Roys 1948: Appendix C).

14 These places lie along the route from what the Spaniards called Laguna de Térmi-

nos out to the Gulf of Mexico, an important section of the trade route between Yucatan and central Mexico (Scholes and Roys 1948: 384; Izquierdo 1997).

15　Smailus glosses the Maya *chan kal* as "four" here and later as "twenty" (1975: 29, 32); in fact it means "four twenties," i.e. "eighty," probably an approximate number or a metaphor for a certain quantity.

16　The 1614 Spanish translation glosses this toponym as Xicalan (i.e. Xicalango), the Nahuatl name rather than the Chontal Maya one.

17　In other words, the Chontal Mayas under Paxua migrated south and inland to a series of sites centered on the Candelaria river; see Maps I and II. There are exhaustive discussions of the location of the Acalan region and its main settlements in Scholes and Roys (1948: 406–69) and Izquierdo (1997).

18　The Maya term, *dzulob*, "foreigners," is usually used in colonial-era Maya documents (including the titles in Yucatec Maya in the chapters to follow) to refer to Spaniards; however, here it seems to indicate people from the southwest, the area that is today Tabasco and northern Chiapas. If these were the same foreigners as those mentioned in the next paragraph of the text, they were, judging by the name of their leader, Nahuatl-speakers. It is also possible that this is a reference to the colonial-era region of Dzuluinicob in what is today northern Belize (Jones 1989), south of the Chetumal region also mentioned in the next paragraph.

19　Written in the Spanish translation as Balancan, which is a site on the Usumacinta river just south of the modern Campeche-Tabasco border. This is obviously a separate episode from that of Chetumal.

20　This of course was Hernán Cortés, whose visit is recounted later in the text.

21　The Chontal term, *a ototnalob*, like its Yucatec equivalent, *ah otochnalob*, contains within it the word for "home," thus conveying more of a sense of community identity and membership than the nearest English terms, "resident" or "citizen," suggest; a synonymous term was *ah cahnalob*, "cah member" (Restall 1997a: 15–18).

22　This is the Martín Maldonado, mentioned in the introduction to this chapter, who had his grandfather's papers copied, through which circumstance the Title of Acalan-Tixchel survived the colonial period.

23　The precise meaning is not very clear here; Smailus (1975: 42) translates the phrase *ya chunuani cappan kin ya* as *allí se estableció capitan sol allí* ("there settled Captain Sun"), while the Spanish translation of 1614 reads *que tuvo veinte días Cortés* ("where Cortés remained for twenty days") (Scholes and Roys 1948: 370, 388).

24　The text uses Western numerals ("67"), an error for "76," the actual number of *cahob* listed.

25　In fact, as Scholes and Roys point out (1948: 390), it was don Martín's father who passed through Acalan, and in 1525.

26　The Maya authors have blended earlier and later titles held by Cortés; Cortés later became the Marqués del Valle.

27 Literally, "I cannot then have two words, two hearts (*namach yuual cachelbel chappel than chappel puççikal*)."

28 The Maya phrase, used here and above (TAT:71r), *tzepci u lukub*, literally means "his neck was cut"; the passage makes it clear, however, that the blow resulted in full decapitation, singularly ironic in view of the baptism ritual that preceded it.

29 To again repeat Scholes and Roys's observations (1948: 392), Cortés did in fact cross to the Itza *cah* of Tayasal (the name is a Hispanization of *ta itza, ta* being a locative), located on an island in the middle of Lake Peten, and from there continued east. The Maya account seems to have elided details of Cortés's visit with those of Alonso de Ávila's 1530 expedition, which did not go as far as Tayasal but did go on from Acalan to Champoton. The Itza communities of the Peten region were not conquered by Spaniards until the 1690s.

30 The Yucatan referred to would be the area in the peninsula's northwest that became the early colony; the Spanish translation skips over this sentence. Scholes and Roys (1948: 393) argue that the previous sentences most likely refer to events that took place in 1531–32, but with Champoton as an error for Campeche. The point, I would suggest, is not how the Chontal account correlates with what we, like the Spaniards, would consider the historical sequence of events (the Maya version probably elides details of the 1530 Ávila expedition, which is more clearly evoked in the paragraph before, the 1531–32 visit by the *adelantado* Montejo, and the use of Champoton as a base by Montejo the son around 1540); rather more to the point is the Maya presentation of the repeated roles and relationships of people and places during this portion of the Conquest era.

31 The Chontal Maya phrase, here and earlier in the text, is *u yochel haa tu pam uinic*, "men's heads enter the water" (Scholes and Roys's literal gloss is "the water enters to the heads of men" [1948: 394]); the equivalent Yucatec phrase can be seen in the Pech text below (TY:2v; TCH:1 in Chapter 6).

32 As with other lists of names in the text (see TAT:69v above, for example), this appears to be a mixture of Nahuatl and Maya names, with the obvious Nahuatl ones here being Caltzin and Buluchatzi (this could be Boluchatzin, with *boluch* being Chontal ["eleven"] and *-atzin* being Nahuatl). (Frances Karttunen, personal communication, comments on the text's names; also see Scholes and Roys 1948: Appendix C.)

33 The Maya phrase, *u xin chan yithoc namach checel*, literally means "the middle of the sky which is not visible." Smailus suggests that the reference is to the world, rather than heaven (1975: 82).

34 Here and elsewhere in the text I have variously translated the Maya term *ciçin* (pl. *ciçinob*) as either "devil" (the literal translation) or "idol" (as it is clearly to pre-Christian religious images that the reference is made).

35 The deified quasi-legendary ruler(s) sometimes referred to in the literature by the translation of his name, Feathered Serpent—Kukulcan in Yucatec, Quetzalcoatl in Nahuatl (see Chapter 1).

36 These were presumably patron deities of the four subdivisions either of Itzam-kanac or of the Acalan region, as three of the names appear above [TAT:71v] as those of "subject communities."

37 The first of these, Ek Chuah, or Ek Chauah, written *ykchaua* in the Chontal text, is often referred to by scholars as God M, the patron deity of merchants and cacao; the third, Ix Chel, was Goddess I, linked to healing, childbirth, and divination, and her principal shrine was on Cozumel; the fourth may be God F, Chabtan (or Buluc Chabtan), a deity of war and violence (Sharer 1994: 526–39).

38 In other words, Palma, Aranda, and García were Acalan's early *encomenderos*, granted the right (in trust, or in *encomienda*) to tax the communities in goods and in labor. On the history of the first *encomiendas* in the Acalan area see Scholes and Roys (1948: 142–55) and García Bernal (1978: 525).

39 See glossary.

40 A *tostón* was half a *peso*; two *tomines* (two "coins," i.e. two *reales*) was equal to a quarter of a *peso*.

41 That is, to return to the Tixchel site up the Candelaria and near the Gulf Coast, where the title tells us the Acalan Mayas had lived several generations earlier, having been pushed inland up the river basin by coastal warfare [TAT:70r].

42 Meaning that the long process of relocation was formally completed on that day. The assertion that the *encomendero* also ordered the move (the Spanish version states merely that *lo quería*, "he wanted it") is not borne out either by common sense or by other evidence. Clearly the relocation—or *congregación*, as Spaniards called such moves—benefited Pesquera and the other friars based in Campeche, but it meant a considerable loss of revenue to the *encomendero*, not only during the move but also in its wake, when many Acalan Mayas quite understandably continued to resist such an atrocious policy (as detailed in the title). In fact, Antón García later claimed in court that Pesquera ordered and organized the whole thing without his knowledge or consent while he was away in Guatemala (Scholes and Roys 1948: 169).

43 Don Luis Paxua was of course the Acalan ruler; his flight to Chiuoha, a Chontal Maya community southeast of Tixchel, was presumably an expression of his opposition to the forced relocation. Scholes and Roys (1948: 171) point out that the assertion that Paxua's death was a natural one looks like an effort to quash any suspicions of foul play on the part of his successor, don Pablo Paxbolon, the alleged discoverer of his death. Scholes and Roys also argue (1948: 171, 397) that the title confuses this 1558 trip by Paxbolon to Chiuoha with his conquest of the *cah* (in his role as colonial agent) in 1574. I would characterize this as an elision of events. Besides, Scholes and Roys base their comment on the Spanish version of the text, which has don Pablo "discovering the people of Chiuoha"; the Maya text, as my translation above tries to show, makes more sense.

44 Although the old site of the Acalan Mayas lay between Tixchel and the Lacandon people to the south, the passage through was not as easy as fray Pesquera allegedly

suggested. The *oidores* (colonial administrators holding the office of judge on the *audiencia* or imperial high court) of Guatemala had sent the Ramírez expedition into Chiapas in 1559 against unconquered Lacandon Mayas, where Topiltepec and Pochutla (presumably the "Poo" area cited in the title) were subdued; Ramírez had ordered assistance from Yucatan, which was the force under Francisco Tamayo Pacheco that entered Tixchel the same year. Tamayo's force then proceeded to round up the Chontal Mayas still in Acalan, possibly under Pesquera's suggestion (as the title states) and/or because Tamayo and his men found Acalan both a dead end (there was thick rainforest and river rapids between there and the Lacandon area) and full of Mayas living outside colonial controls (as Juan Vela later testified) (Scholes and Roys 1948: 173–74).

45 The notary copying the Chontal Maya text in 1612 apparently omitted several pages which were nevertheless included in the Spanish translation; the following ten paragraphs are therefore based on the Spanish version, with terminology and spellings of people and places surmised from the rest of the text or adjusted to be consistent with it.

46 In fact the Chontals appear to have settled on a Maya name (Zapotitlan is Nahuatl), Ticintupa, and the *cah* is named thus later in the title.

47 For a description and illustration of the practice of using Mayas to transport Spaniards, see Bracamonte (1994: 80–83).

48 The Spanish term here, *los cimarrones*, " the runaways," is used later in the title as a translation for the Chontal term *a ppecheob*; I suggest that context makes "refugees" a better gloss than Scholes and Roys's "fugitives."

49 In 1569 don Pablo Paxbolon presented to the governor of Yucatan a longer account of his conquest campaign against the Mayas of Zapotitlan (Ticintupa), including testimony of Maya witnesses from Tixchel and Zapotitlan (Scholes and Roys 1948: 187; Paxbolon's *probanza* is in AGI-*México* 97).

50 The Spanish text actually says "his Chontal people," but elsewhere in the title the Spanish translation uses "Chontal" where the Maya text uses "Mactun" (the people) or "Tamactun Acalan" (the place).

51 The Spanish text says "Spaniards" but the Chontal version almost always uses the phrase "Castilian men or people."

52 Haircutting, like the ritual of baptism also mentioned in the text, was a symbol of Christian conversion.

53 Located on the Gulf Coast north of Tixchel and just south of Champoton (Scholes and Roys 1948: 402).

54 The Spanish text has *se llaman Aquebob*, "they were called Aquebob"; the Maya phrase would be *Ah Kebob*, meaning people of the Yucatec Maya patronym-group or *chibal* named Keb. The patronyms of many of the protagonists of these events of the 1570s and '80s—Ceh, Chab, Chan, Keb, Tuyu, Balam, Tzuc, Cauich—as well as place-names such as Hecelchakan, underscore the fact that Paxbolon was dealing increasingly with Yucatec speakers; his people were gradually being pulled

into the colonial Yucatec orbit just as the protracted process of Spanish and Spanish-sponsored conquest and colonization was pushing Yucatec Mayas south into the expanding Chontal area (Scholes and Roys 1948: 221–48).

55 *Ah cuch cab* was a Yucatec Maya title of political office that survived unevenly into the colonial period (Restall 1997a: 68–70; Quezada 1993: 108–109) and which might loosely be translated as "officer," or "councillor"; *açitiache* appears to be a Chontal equivalent.

56 This account omits the fact that don Pablo Paxbolon went to Merida to obtain a license (signed by both the governor, don Francisco de Solís, and the visiting *oidor*, Dr. Palacio) to round up not only the Hecelchakan refugees, but any other Mayas living near the Chontal region but outside colonial controls; as Scholes and Roys detail (1948: 229–31). As the title goes on to demonstrate, Paxbolon was able to take advantage of this and similar situations to consolidate and extend his regional authority.

57 Like Tomás López mentioned earlier in the title, Dr. Diego García de Palacio was an *oidor* appointed by the Crown to review the state of the colony; he was empowered to issue decrees as well as make recommendations for administrative improvements. Despite the title's assertion, Palacio's visit was in 1583–84 (García Bernal 1985; Quezada 1993: 141–42, 153–55).

58 Here the translation of the Chontal Maya text [TAT:76r] continues.

59 These acts of banditry were presumably being carried out not by May's gang but by Maya refugees who had resorted to such a way of life because any settlements they had tried to maintain were threatened by other Mayas—be they outlaws under May or Chontals from Tixchel operating as colonial agents. That these Maya refugees (*a ppecheob*) had once been under colonial authority is indicated below by the fact that most the adults were already baptized.

60 The Defender (or Protector) of the Indians, a Spanish attorney assigned by provincial authorities to represent the interests of indigenous communities in the colonial courts; for most of the colonial period the services of the *defensor* were free of charge.

61 During the three centuries of colonial rule the Franciscans very gradually lost control of most of the parishes on the Yucatan peninsula, primarily the less desirable ones (that is, those less densely inhabited and further from Spanish towns) (Farriss 1984: 92–96); among the earliest to be transferred was Tixchel, which along with three parishes in northern Yucatan was secularized by royal decrees of March 9 and May 1, 1602 (Scholes and Roys 1948: 405).

62 The Chontal Maya phrase, *tu pat hun ca kalay*, more literally translates as "on the back of the document of our history." The names in question appear not to have been transferred onto the surviving copy of the document.

63 The Chontal text actually has "1614," but the Spanish version's "1604" is a more likely date considering that the Chontal text is followed by a statement in Spanish

dated 1612 referring to the papers in the Chontal language that Francisco Maldonado has just had copied into the legal record.

CHAPTER 4. *Conquest as Chronology*

1 Lockhart (1992: 376–92).

2 On the "apparent flatness of Nahuatl annals entries," see Lockhart (1992: 383–84).

3 The nature of this impact is not always clear; for example, the *cah* of Dzidzantun, mentioned in these annals, is some distance to the north of the Mani area (see Map II). Oxkutzcab can also be found to the right of Mani on the Mani map (in Figure 7.1 it is to the far center-right; its name has been destroyed by the separation of the map into two).

4 Restall (1997a; 1998c); Lockhart (1992). This is arguably true of pre-Conquest Mesoamerican cultures too (for Maya examples see Culbert and Rice 1990; Marcus 1993; McAnany 1995: 131–56).

5 For an example, see Lockhart (1992: 379).

6 There are a few other orthographic rarities in the text (for example, this is the only instance I have seen of a *y* in *españoles*, written as *espayoresob*), while the use of the term *maya* to refer to people, rather than the language, was also highly restricted in colonial-era indigenous texts (Restall 1997a: 14–15). Neither of these examples necessarily help date the text. On how the Mayas wrote their language in the colonial period, including their writing of Spanish loanwords, see Restall (1997a: 293–303, 368–73).

7 The Xiu papers (xc) remain at Harvard, now in TLH, where I was able to consult them (for a scathing note on how Harvard came to possess xc, see Gates 1937: 125; for the context of Gates's comments, see Cortez 1995: 262–65). The annals page was in fact once published—in an early archaeological report on the site of Copan in Honduras (Morley 1920)—but Roys's 1941 translation of the whole collection was never published (it too is held by TLH). Sergio Quezada and Tsubasa Okoshi Harada are currently working on a Spanish-language edition of the xc to be published in Mexico. Chapters 8 and 10 below feature additional documents from xc. Archived in TULAL are a completely different set of Xiu documents usually called the Crónica de Mani.

8 They seem like chances because we cannot be sure of why don Juan Xiu copied these annals, or whether the "original" and / or his copy was longer than the surviving fragment, or if it is significant that the annals end the year the Franciscans arrived—bringing the alphabet with them.

9 The annals are on a single page (xc:154). These first four dates, 1534 through 1537, are written in the margin. In the first, the final digit is illegible; Morley (1920: 507) and Roys (1941: 677) estimated it to be a 3, but a 4 seems more logical. In the second, the text actually reads *153* with no final digit. It can be seen in Figure 4.1 that

the Maya dates are written out—*hunte pop* etc.—while the Spanish dates are written in numbers with the loanword for "years"—*1538 años* etc.

10 The *tun* was the 360-day year of the Maya calendar (the 365-day solar year, or vague year, called the *haab*, included the *tun*); equally significant was the 260-day year, called variously the ritual calendar or sacred almanac by scholars. Each day was given a name in both calendars, one of twenty "month" names and a number between 1 and 13 in the ritual calendar, and one of eighteen "month" names and a number between 1 and 20 in the *tun* (a nineteenth 5-day month created the *haab*). Thus the purpose of the Maya dates given here is not only to identify the year, but the day, identified in both Maya calendars, upon which the year began; in each of the years listed here the Maya year began in July (Morley 1920: 509; for a clear and detailed explanation of Maya calendrics see Sharer 1994: 559–75).

11 The original text is missing here due to document deterioration; I have followed Morley (1920: 507, using a translation made by Gates) and Roys (1941: 677) in filling the gap. For both Morley and Roys, the primary value of this document was its utility in correlating Maya and Western calendars, although they pointed out errors made by the Maya copyists and offered corrections accordingly. As my interest here is somewhat different, I have left all dates exactly as they appear in the original document.

12 Literally meaning "true men," this was a title of office reserved for the most senior rulers, usually the highest regional authorities; after the sixteenth century, Mayas tended to reserve the title for the Spanish governor of the province of Yucatan.

13 In other words, these officials had made the pilgrimage to Chichen Itza on a previous occasion. This time they never arrived, being ambushed and killed under the orders of Nachi Cocom, the ruler of Sotuta, a district to the north of the Xiu-dominated region of Mani. This massacre of some forty pilgrims or ambassadors actually took place in 1536, according to most of the various colonial-era versions of the Otzmal incident. These include accounts by Spanish chroniclers (such as Cogolludo 3, VI, Herrera, and Landa XIV) and the three Maya-language accounts presented in this volume. These are the one above, the Chilam Balam reference from Mani (CBM:136) in Chapter 7 (there is a similar reference in the Chumayel [Roys 1933: 138] and a longer Mani version [Craine and Reindorp 1979: 187–88]), and the account in Chapter 8 by Gaspar Antonio Chi, whose father, Ah Ziyah Napuc Chi, is one of the ambassadors listed above in the Annals. (It is possible that "Ah Ziyah Napuc Chi" is a reference to two individuals: Ah Ziyah [Chi or Xiu], a relative of Gaspar Antonio's; and Gaspar Antonio's father, Napuc Chi.) *Ah pulhaob*, which I have translated as "rain-bringers," actually means "water throwers," or "those who offer water," no doubt reflecting a detail of the ceremony at Chichen Itza; as Gates observed (Morley 1920: 509), the pilgrims' purpose was obviously to end the drought. According to Landa (XIV), the massacre brought years of warfare and famine. See Cogolludo (3, VI) for a drawing that commemorates the Otzmal massacre (the drawing is also reproduced as the cover illustration to Quezsada 1993).

14 The word *Xul* is not written in the original but follows Morley's (1920: 507) and Roys's (1941: 677) calendrical calculations. In the 1539–44 entries I have added "the

year-bearer" and "the *tun*" where it can be inferred from the context that this is the intended meaning.

15 Roys suggests (1941: 678) that this was probably the Maya name of the ancient man-made mound (popularly termed pyramids) in Tiho upon which the Franciscans built their monastery. As other Maya sources assert that this main mound was called Chuncaan (TY:4v; TCH:9 in Chapter 6 and CBM:71 in Chapter 7), it may be more accurate to take Pocobtok as the name of one of Tiho's mounds.

CHAPTER 5. *The Community View*

1 An historical footnote also links the Conquest story of the two areas: as mentioned in Chapter 3, Francisco Maldonado, the Spanish son-in-law and ally-in-conquest of the Chontal ruler don Pablo Paxbolon, had a son by a second marriage who became *encomendero* of Calkini in 1628–31 (AGI-México 242; Scholes and Roys 1948: 296–97).

2 Okoshi Harada's emphasis is slightly different, giving greater primacy to the *cah* of Calkini and to the Canul lineage (1993: Chapters 2–3).

3 Gates (1935: 6).

4 Craine and Reindorp (1979: xv); Barrera Vásquez (1957: 11); Okoshi Harada (1993: 5–6). This is the same Bishop Carrillo y Ancona mentioned in Chapter 1.

5 Barrera Vásquez (1957: 14).

6 Teobert Maler took the late nineteenth-century photos, and in 1910 the manu-scripts traveled to Philadelphia to be photographed by G. B. Gordon. Gates made the 1915 photostats, either from original Gordon photographs or prints made by Gordon from Maler's plates; a set is in Harvard's Tozzer Library, where I was able to make my translation from them. (According to Cline [1975: 379], there are also copies at Brigham Young University, in the Library of Congress, and in the New-berry Library.) Gates later published his photostats in a facsimile edition (1935; no transcription or translation) and Barrera Vásquez also used them in his edition (1957; facsimile and Spanish translation). Roys made a transcription and translated the first three pages (1929) but these were never published. I closely consulted the Barrera Vásquez edition while making my translation, and, subsequently acquir-ing the Spanish translation and extensive commentary by Okoshi Harada (1993), found it also to be of considerable use; Okoshi Harada's dissertation is the sole in-depth study of the Calkini manuscript to date.

7 Barrera Vásquez (1957) and Okoshi Harada (1993) respectively.

8 The surviving manuscript begins midsentence at the top of the eleventh page (TC:11).

9 There is some ambiguity in the text's use of "Calkini," which sometimes refers specifically to the *cah* and sometimes to the region it dominated (as seems to be the case here); I have not inserted any qualifying terms, as in most instances the con-

text is clear, and because the ambiguity reflects the way in which Calkini is promoted and projected in the manuscript.

10 The Maya words are lost here due to document damage, so this phrase is a guess based on the sentences that follow. The pre-Conquest political hierarchy being outlined here consists of the *batab* as the senior officer, beneath whom is a deputy or officer (*kul* or *ah kul*), followed by a second and third speaker (*ah can*). *Kul* and *can* are effectively interchangeable terms here, as the listed deputies are by implication the first speakers, while many of the second and third speakers are referred to with the title *Ah Kul*. In this and the other texts presented in this book I have translated *kul uinicob* as "principal men." Okoshi Harada (1993: Chapter 2) and Quezada (1993: 38–58) discuss these titles of office at some length. Also see their usage in the Pech titles (Chapter 6 below).

11 Called Chican throughout the text. Colonial Maya documents do not spell place names consistently, often attaching or dropping locative prefixes such as *te*-, *tix*-, *tu*- or *x*-; I have thus used modern spellings of place names wherever possible, though I have not hispanized them by adding accents.

12 Roys (1929), Barrera Vásquez (1957: 21), and Okoshi Harada (1993: 2) read this as *batab nauat u batabob*, which they respectively glossed as "Batab Nauat was their chief," "*tenían por Batab a Batab Nauat*," and "*tenían a Batab Náuat como su batab*." This is a very plausible reading, as Nauat is indeed a Maya patronym and a Batab Nauat is mentioned later in the text, but it leaves unclear Batab Nauat's role in the paragraph's story and the reason for the different styling of his name. Furthermore, there is a worm hole obscuring the first part of the *n* of *nauat*. I have therefore taken the phrase as *ma uat*, "there was no break, or a very small break," assuming that the author is thereby emphasizing continuity in Becal's *batab*-ship despite the change in personnel.

13 Named Tipakam or Pakam in the text; see note 11 above.

14 Sisal or henequen, the *Agave sisalana*, or *ci* in Maya, is a native Yucatec plant whose fibre is used to make cord or rope. Spanish demand somewhat stimulated sisal production in the colonial period (Patch 1993); international demand created a boom in the nineteenth century (Wells 1985); in the early twentieth century the industry was taken over by the Mexican government and subsequently collapsed as demand fell; *ci* cultivation survives largely as a local domestic industry.

15 Several encounters with invading forces have probably been elided into one, although the most notable unopposed entrance of Spaniards into Calkini was that of 1541, in which case "the Captain" here is Francisco de Montejo the nephew (for the Spanish side of the campaign, see Chamberlain 1948: 207); because of the ten missing pages, it does not become clear until this moment that the gathering of officials and goods is for the benefit of a newly arrived Spanish-Nahua army.

16 As discussed in Chapter 1, these were the Nahua forces brought by Montejo from central Mexico, whose conquest had taken place the previous decade. As well as being a specific referent to the people of Culhuacan, a Nahua town in the Valley of Mexico, "Culhua" (in the Nahuatl plural, "Culhuaque") was also used to refer to

the Mexica (whose twin-city of Tenochtitlan-Tlatelolco dominated central Mexico at the time of the Conquest) and more generally to all those subject to the Mexica. This multiple usage was due in part to the Spaniards' vague grasp of regional identities and nomenclatures, and in part to the fact that Culhuacan had briefly dominated the Valley in the fifteenth century, before being conquered by the Mexica, who continued to claim the legacy of earlier Culhua authority—the ruler of Tenochtitlan, for example, was titled Culhuateuctli (Gibson 1964: 10–11; Lockhart 1992: 109). The Maya use of "Culhua" to refer to central Mexicans in general, as evidenced above, is supported by Bernal Díaz's claim (1963: 33) that at one point the 1518 Grijalva expedition was met with Yucatec Mayas urging the Spaniards to go west, saying "Colua, Colua" and "Mexico, Mexico."

17 On the ritual role and cultural significance of this tree, *Ceiba pentandra*, see Hernández Pons (1997); Okoshi Harada (1993: Chapter 2) cites additional sources.

18 Presumably of cotton cloth or *manta*, a common item of barter and tribute before and after the Conquest, although *sap*, "arm span," was a unit of measurement also applied to land.

19 The text uses the Spanish term *carpintero*, and then explains it with the Maya equivalent, *ah men che*; thus the sentence might also be translated: "Then came Carpintero, as a carpenter is called."

20 The Maya phrase used is *ma señorai*; although some Spanish titles, such as *don*, were incorporated into the internal Maya system of social deference, colonial-era Mayas used the titles *señor* and *señora* exclusively to refer to Spaniards (Restall 1997a: 41–46, 88–92).

21 The Maya phrase, *u nucil uinicob* ("the principal men, or elders"; synonyms in Maya documents are *u noh uinicob* and *u kul uinicob*), refers to the traditional ruling body of the *cah*, formalized in the colonial period in the form of the *cabildo*, or municipal council; see, for example, the officers whose names and titles end this first section of the Calkini text.

22 A reference to the collapse of the federation at Mayapan; see Chapter 1.

23 Okoshi Harada reads this as "they settled among the Itza" (1993: 9; my citations of this work are of the page numbers to Okoshi Harada's Spanish translation of TC). I suggest that this invocation of the Itza name is neither evidence of, nor intended as a claim to, the foreign origins of these ancestors; the term is simply a status marker, partially removed from its historical context and employed as a bestower of prestige—similar to the use of *zuyua* and *hidalgo conquistador* elsewhere in the Maya sources.

24 I follow Okoshi Harada's suggestion that this is a toponym (1993: 10).

25 This is probably a reference to the small *cah* of Siho, just northwest of Nunkini, not to Ichcansiho, also called Tiho.

26 Barrera Vásquez (1957: 35) and Okoshi Harada (1993: 12) both translate this toponym into "the savannahs."

27 Okoshi Harada (1993: 13) reads this term, *katun*, as a patronym, making "Batab Katún."

28 "Where he had been hanged" is a guess based on context; a worm hole has destroyed the Maya phrase. "A Canche doorway" could also be simply "a wooden doorway," as *canche* is not only a patronym but also means "wooden bench or plank." For a different reading see Okoshi Harada (1993: 14).

29 The Napot Canche in this paragraph I take to be the grandfather or great-uncle of the author, not the Napot Canche who was his father and who is mentioned in the next paragraph and elsewhere in the text.

30 This is the only instance I have seen in the colonial-era Maya literature of this unlikely looking name, but it is clearly what the Maya text says; this was, after all, a boyhood name.

31 *Kul uinicob* (see note 21 above), a reference to the Spanish and Nahua officers mentioned earlier; the narrative now returns to Calkini's reception of Montejo, with the digressive account of the Canche *chibal* reduced to a secondary role.

32 Molina Solís (1896: 614; quoted by Okoshi Harada 1993: 18) states that a Gonzalo Méndez, as captain of a squad of native Mexican auxiliaries, militarily occupied at least one *cah* in the Calkini area, transporting "as provisions a great quantity of pigs."

33 This ritual of firing warning shots was a standard Spanish practice; Mayas would witness it again when, for example, armed Spaniards arrived at the edge of Tekax in 1610 during a large riot and fired off a round before entering the *cah* (AGI-*Escribanía* 305a; also see brief mention in CBM:137 in Chapter 7).

34 The Maya term is *tupil*, used for low-ranking community officers. The reference here is presumably to constables of the central Mexican auxiliaries; indeed there is a cognate Nahuatl term, *topile*.

35 Okoshi Harada (1993: 22–23) puts here, rather than a few lines below, the transition in topic from the list of those seized to the list of Calkini elders.

36 The Maya term for "nickname" is *u coco kaba*, "joking or jesting name"; the last two listed here mean "he with a potter's-wheel belly button" and "owl face" (on Maya naming patterns see Restall 1997a: 41–50; Roys 1940).

37 *u kul uinic*, "principal man, official" (see note 21 above); possibly a catch-all reference both to Montejo and to the various Spanish officials who made labor demands upon generations of Calkini residents. (Okoshi Harada 1993: 24 simply glosses the phrase as "the Spaniards.")

38 Although the text initially accuses Mayas of resorting to theft, this sentence could well pass for a description of a Spanish practice termed *repartimiento* in Yucatan, where colonial officials and private agents together forced Maya communities to sell local products on credit or at below-market prices (Patch 1993; also see Chapter 2). Indeed the passage goes on to detail a variety of abuses committed by "the foreigners."

39 The Maya term used is *chuc* (not *chuc*). Both can mean seize or take: Barrera Vásquez (1957: 53) translates the phrase as *miedo de ser cogidos* ("afraid of being seized")
and Okoshi Harada's translation is similar, only he avoids all sexual suggestion in
his translation of the succeeding passage (1993: 26–27). However, *chuc* has strong
sexual overtones, often with implications of involuntariness. The text goes on to
clarify this context of sexualized violence, while avoiding any explicit sexual terminology, presumably so as not to suggest that the experiences described were in
any way humorous or pleasurable for the Mayas (on Maya sexuality in the colonial
context see Restall 1997a: Chapter 11; also see Sigal 1995).

40 This was the city upon which the Spaniards founded Merida in 1542, although Tiho
was the name most commonly used by Mayas throughout the colonial period to
refer to the city and its communities. For further discussion of Tiho's name and
colonial history, see Restall (1997a: 29–37).

41 Champoton is mentioned in the Chontal account (Chapter 3) as a stopping point
between the Chontal Maya area and Yucatan and a springboard for the Spanish
Conquest of the latter.

42 I had read this simply as "many drinks," but Okoshi Harada (1993: 29) makes a good
argument for *haa* as "chocolate."

43 The fact that Tzemes has *akal*, "lake, lagoon," after it, whereas Dzalal does not,
suggests that Tzemes was a permanent lake and Dzalal was a rainy-season one;
Okoshi Harada (1993: 30) makes a similar point. If this is so, it should be applicable
throughout the text. Lake Tzemes is located just south of Matu (see Map II).

44 *Ah yidzin sucunilon*, literally "we are of younger sibling and older brotherhood,"
refers to metaphorical, not consanguineal, fraternity. This speech has the feel of a
ritual declaration made at all such occasions; another such admonition follows below (TC:22). (Similar phrases were used in Maya testaments to admonish heirs not
to quarrel over their inheritance; Restall 1997a: 241–42.)

45 At first I translated this term ("hillock of palm trees"), but Okoshi Harada (1993: 33)
actually located a savannah still called Tzucxan in the Lake Tzemes area.

46 In other words, Nachan Canul, *batab* of Calkini at the time of the border conference, had earlier been *batab* of Becal and, before that, Tepakan (both smaller *cahob*
in the Calkini area).

47 This is one of the few examples in the Maya text of a borrowed Spanish noun: the
phrase is *u sicinil* (later *u sicinail*), "the corner(s) of," the loan-word being *esquina*.
The same term appears in TY (Chapter 6). (On Maya use of Spanish loans see Restall 1997a: 293–302, 368–373.).

48 Okoshi Harada (1993: 36) suggests that this is a reference to the *congregación*, or
forced resettlement, of smaller *cahob* into Calkini in 1550.

49 Another Spanish loanword, *título*, rendered here in the Maya text as *titoloil*. In this
same paragraph the word for "signature," *firma*, is also a loan, as is of course the
date phrase.

50 The Motul dictionary (Okoshi Harada 1993: 38) identifies a nobleman of this name as a late sixteenth-century governor of Tepakam. As only Chim is given the "don" title due every *batab*, and placed at the top of the list, and as each of the participant *cahob* in the treaty (or each group of participants) would have had their own copies of the agreement, this may have been copied from the Tepakam version.

51 Identified below (TC:25) as *batab* of Nunkini.

52 The Maya term, *mul* or *muul*, can mean a natural hill but more often refers to a manmade mound such as a platform or pyramidal structure. I have written "Kochyol" to be consistent with earlier references to the place, but the Maya text actually reads Xcochyol; this could therefore be a reference to the archaeological site of Xcochol in modern Campeche state.

53 These two trees are *uas* (*Crescentia cujete*) and *bec* (*Ehretia tinifolia*) respectively; on trees mentioned in other colonial Maya texts see Restall (1997a: 203–05).

54 The Maya term, *auat*, is actually more specific than this; it means "to shout" and thus, in this context, indicates the distance from which a cry can be heard. Four *auatob* equalled one *lub*, which was the distance between resting points, coming in the colonial period to mean a league (about three miles).

55 *Alcalde* and *regidor* were Spanish offices, loosely translatable as "judge" and "councilman," which came with the institution of the municipal council, or *cabildo*, imposed by colonial authorities; however, Maya communities adapted these offices to local practices and needs while continuing to maintain compounded or parallel indigenous offices—such as *ah cuch cab*, an office that may have been seen as an equivalent to *regidor* by some communities, such as Nunkini in the above example, and thus might also be loosely translated as "councilman." (Restall 1997a: 61–72 details Maya *cabildo* composition.) Quezada (1993: 117) argues that the late sixteenth-century *ah cuch cab* retained from before the Conquest specific fiscal responsibilities.

56 *Ah lukul benal*, "departed officer"; Barrera Vásquez (1957: 77) has "*caminero*"; Okoshi Harada (1993: 42) has "*oficial jubilado.*"

57 The Maya phrase used here and later in this paragraph is *kul uinic(ob)*, usually a reference to indigenous community elders or officers; however, on the following page the term *dzul*, "foreigner," is used in a similar phrase, strongly suggesting that *kul uinicob* is here being used as it was previously used in the text—as a reference to the Spaniards and the Conquest.

58 Okoshi Harada (1993: 44–45) translates *toc* (which appears three times in the above sentence) as *quitar*, "leave, quit," rather than "defend," making the sentence a comment on forced resettlement (*congregación*).

59 In other words, to confirm land access or ownership through a ritualized border survey recorded on paper, resulting in this title.

60 One is struck by the similarity between this Maya phrase of self-identity—*coon uayil uinic lae*, "we the here-people"—to the Nahuatl phrase *nican titlaca*, translated by Lockhart as "we people here" and used as the title of his 1993 volume on Nahua accounts of the Conquest.

61 The use of the Spanish loanword *testigo*—"*destigosob*"—reflects the fact that, although this is an indigenous ritual of pre-Conquest origins dealing in part with pre-Conquest matters, it is still a post-Conquest document whose partial purpose is to stand up in the colonial courts.

62 A worm hole has obliterated the final digit of the year. Context would seem to suggest that this is a continuation of the previous document, and I have presented it as such; however, as discussed in the introduction to this chapter, the intertextual relationship between the documents that make up the Calkini title appears to have been complicated by the role of copyists up to and including that of 1821.

63 Barrera Vásquez (1957: 105) reads *chac* as "destroyed," Okoshi Harada (1993: 57) as "crossed over," which is more likely; I suggest that the intended meaning is "surrounded," as this makes geographical sense (a triangulation of the Cupul, Ceh Pech, and Calkini regions would converge, or "cross over," in the Xiu region).

64 *Coon ah maya uinice*; this is the only instance in this text of the term "Maya" being used (the term is very seldom used as an identity reference in Maya sources; see Chapters 4, 6, and 7 and Restall 1997a: 14–15 for discussion of how this relates to questions of Maya identity); *uinic* usually refers to men but is not necessarily gender-specific, so the phrase could also be glossed as "we Maya people."

65 *Ah chikin suyuaob lae*; as discussed in Chapter 1, Zuyua also appears in the *Chilam Balam* texts associated with noble lineage. Although there is no evidence for its location in central Mexico, as so often claimed by scholars, it was presumably a distant place (or supposed to be taken as such), so that the Canul are here trying to establish both their prestige as a *chibal* of external origins and their legitimacy as deep-rooted local natives; note that in the text they also lay claim to other places of origin, including Peten Itza (see my comment above on "Itza").

66 The Maya for noble is *almehen*, a term whose constituent parts are more easily seen as written in the text here—*yal u mehen*, literally "child of a woman, son of a man." This is of course another way of saying "descendents," with implications of social status.

67 The Maya phrase *peten itza* does not necessarily mean the region of that name in what is now northern Guatemala; in fact, as Okoshi Harada argues (1993: 14–18), it most likely refers to an area closer to Calkini, such as the Chichen Itza region.

68 The area around Tiho (the Spaniards' Merida) was called Chakan; Barrera Vásquez (1957: 109) translates *chakan* to make "*las sabanas de Tihó* (the savannahs of Tiho)" and Okoshi Harada (1993: 60) likewise has "*la sabana de Tihó.*"

69 The Cordemex/Porrúa dictionary has this as a toponym (Barrera Vásquez 1980: 617), but Barrera Vásquez (1957: 111) may be correct in translating it "*en los términos de cielo,*" in which case I would read the phrase as, "The Canul seas end at the horizon." Okoshi Harada (1993: 61) leaves the phrase as a toponym. These coastal sites are not found on modern maps.

70 In other words, the governors of the *cahob* in the area were present at the ritual completion of the new colonial roads linking Calkini to its neighbors; presumably

those roads ran into the central plazas of the *cahob* as part of the Spanish imposition of a municipal grid onto the clusters of houses that had surrounded pre-Conquest plazas (Restall 1997a: 20–24). This is probably a copy of a fragment of the record of that occasion; at the very least a list of *batab* names would have followed, and indeed the final phrase could read, "Here are all the *batabob*. . . ." Okoshi Harada (1993: 62), by reading *cati* as *kati*, has the *batabob* "wishing it."

71 This entry is written in Spanish by Crespo, who signs his name with a rubric (he wrote no other parts of the text).

72 The Maya phrase, *yantiob tumenel*, which I have translated as "made for them by," literally means, "that is to them because of." Don Francisco de Montejo Xiu (also mentioned elsewhere in this book) was governor of Mani in the sixteenth century, when the Mani maps (see Figure 7.1) were probably drawn. There are other extant versions of the Mani map (see Stephens 1841; Gates 1935: 133; Roys 1941; 1943; Riese 1981) and it is interesting therefore that Mani was viewed as a map center of sorts, such that the elders of Calkini traveled there to verify the boundaries between the Mani and Calkini districts even as late as the final year of the colonial period. Calkini is mentioned in a Spanish notation on one version of the Mani map to the left of the page, more or less in the direction of the Calkini area. No map accompanying the Title of Calkini has survived.

73 The Maya phrase—*yum alcalde dzul constitucional y ayuntamientos*—could be read "lord constitutional and municipal *alcalde* Dzul." I have translated *dzul*, rather than treating it as a Maya patronym, because Maya officials were usually cited with their Christian names and because it seems likely that a senior postindependence official in an important community like Mani would be a Spaniard.

CHAPTER 6. *Maya Conquistadors*

1 Various sets of Gates's photostats of the nineteenth-century Regil copy have survived; I used copies in TLH and TULAL, also consulting Ávila's 1864 Spanish translation (the photostat of the unpublished handwritten manuscript is also in TLH), Brinton's 1882 transcription and English translation of part of the manuscript, and Pérez Martínez's 1936 Spanish translation of the same part (reprinted in Yáñez 1939: 191–215). There are also nineteenth-century translations in French (by Brasseur de Bourbourg, first five pages only) and Latin (by Charency), neither of which I consulted.

2 No English translation of the Yaxkukul manuscript (TY) has been published. Martínez Hernández's Spanish translation (1926), published first in the *Diario de Yucatán* and then shortly afterwards printed as a limited edition, now has rare book status. Prior to the present volume, the whole Yaxkukul manuscript had appeared only in these editions of Hernández's translation; details on prior publication of the land survey section are given below.

3 In the interests of textual integrity I have translated the Title of Yaxkukul intact and unaltered, even to the point of only using those paragraph breaks indicated in the

original document (that is, a 1769 copy). The variations contained in the Chicxulub text (TCH) are presented in full in footnotes, with the exception of a fairly long passage near the end of TCH which is not found in TY and which is thus included in the body of the translation. Page or folio references from both TY and TCH are inserted into the body of the translation.

4 Likewise, the final section of the Title of Chicxulub (TCH:22–26) is another nearly identical version of the account in the opening section of the same manuscript (TCH:1–7) (thus I have not included that final section).

5 Martínez Hernández (1926: 37); Barrera Vásquez (1984: 98).

6 The Franciscans, who introduced alphabetic literacy to young Maya nobles, did not arrive until 1545; as the friars were so few, just four at first, it is probable that trained native notaries were not working in *cahob* until the early 1550s. The earliest extant alphabetic Maya document is a land record dated 1557 (Restall 1997a: 230–31, 409). For a detailed discussion of the dating of primordial titles, focusing on textual evidence of late-colonial composition in the land-survey portion of the Yaxkukul title, see Restall (1997a: 281–92).

7 *Concistadores dzulob* (TCH: *Concixtadores dzulob*); I have glossed the Maya term *dzul* according to its original meaning of "foreigner," as the text also uses *españolesob*, but note that during the colonial period (when this account was written) *dzul* came to mean "Spaniard" specifically, and, ultimately, to refer to white people in general. Note that *dz* was actually written in the colonial period with the invented letter ɔ (a backwards *c*).

8 Martínez Hernández (1926: 30) comments that, following the Spanish chronicler Cogolludo, the above list is complete but for Juan de la Torre and Blas González. These officers comprised the first *cabildo* of Merida (called in the text below by its Maya name, Tiho). Note that with Spanish personal and place names in this title I have modernized spellings [or corrected the surnames, after Martínez Hernández (1926: 30), following Cogolludo] where the original manuscript uses variants commonly used by Spaniards at the time (such as *s* for *z*), adding in parentheses the original spellings where they reflect how the Maya notary may have spoken the name. TCH variants are Pallego (for Gallegos), Samar (for Azamar), and Ficon (for Picón); TCH likewise lists the Spaniards in parallel columns.

9 As stated earlier, the Spaniards founded Merida on the Maya site of Tiho, which name the Mayas continued to use throughout the colonial period to refer to the city and its indigenous suburbs; here, however, the Maya text uses the variant name *ychcansiho* [translated by Edmonson (1986) as "Heaven Born Merida"], a more poetic or literary toponym reserved for nonmundane texts such as this title.

10 TCH begins the paragraph at this point.

11 TCH: "therefore their names are written down so that they be well and widely known."

12 TCH omits this final name.

13 TCH begins here with the heading "Conquest and Map" (*Concixta y[etel] mapa*); no map has survived.

14 TCH: "I who am Nakuk Pech, I, the first of the noble conquistadors [*yax hidalgos con-cixtadoren*] here in this land, of the district of Maxtunil, I was appointed to the principal *cah* of the district, Chicxulub [*Chac Xulub Chen*], which my lord Ah Naum Pech gave me to guard." Note that I have throughout rendered Chacxulubchen as Chicxulub, its post-Conquest name. Unless otherwise stated, everywhere that TY names Yaxkukul, TCH names Chicxulub.

15 TCH: Nakuk Pech states that Chicxulub was his first governorship, adding, "this *cah* has two districts: Chichinica; and Chicxulub here."

16 TCH: "My name was Nakuk Pech before I was baptized [*ococ haa tin pol*, my head enters the water]; I am the son of Ah Kom Pech, don Martín Pech, of the *cah* of Xulkumchel." Unless otherwise stated, everywhere that TY names Ah Macan Pech, TCH names Nakuk Pech. The pronominal perspective is inconsistent in both texts, shifting between the first and third person. The fact that pre-Christian names are frequently used in the text suggests that the narrative was aimed as much at Mayas as at Spaniards.

17 TCH: "When we were given the districts to guard by my lord Ah Naum Pech, from the *cah* of Motul, who promoted me to guard the district of Chicxulub . . ."

18 TCH: "They only stayed here in this land, in the district of Maxtunil, for three months."

19 TCH inserts: "passing through to arrive at the *cah* named Tixcuumcuuc; and they left there . . ."

20 TCH: "Namox". Dzidzantun was the principal *cah* in a small region dominated by the Chel *chibal* in the sixteenth and seventeenth centuries (and probably before and possibly after this). Letter iii of 1567 to the king of Spain, discussed in Chapter 9, was from three Chel and five other *batabob* of the Dzidzantun region.

21 TCH: "Foreign warrior, rest in those stepped houses!"

22 TCH: "six years."

23 TCH: "I went there with my companions, Ah Macan Pech and his younger brother Ixkil Itzam Pech, ruler of the *cah* of Conkal [*cumkal*], and my father, who was in the *cah* of Xulcumcheel." The contrasting and potentially confusing details of who traveled on this occasion (TCH implies that the authors of both texts went together, in which case why are different companions named? Likewise why does TCH not state "*our* younger brother"?) are an example of how titles such as this should not be evaluated for their strict historicity as we would understand the concept, but rather appraised for their intended meaning (in this case, the fact that a number of Pech *batabob* brought tribute to Montejo).

24 TCH: "because he knew that he [the *adelantado*] did not know their language, for they first stayed in his house when they came here, and because they told him to accompany them when they went for the tribute."

25 TCH: "coats and cloaks and shoes and rosaries [or necklaces; *u*] and hats."

26 TCH: "[We], Ixkil Itzam Pech of Conkal, and our companions Ah Macan Pech of Yaxkukul, and my father Ah Kom Pech, the most senior among us."

27 TCH adds: "on the road from Campeche."

28 TCH emphasizes "and I went a second time."

29 TCH: "I, Nakuk Pech, of the district here of Chicxulub, and Ah Macan Pech, of the district of Yaxkukul, and Ixkil Itzam Pech, the senior *batab* of Conkal, with me, Nakuk Pech, *batab* here in the *cah* of Chicxulub, went to give them gifts a second time at Dzibilkal; and this second time we delivered them an embarrassing quantity of gifts . . ."

30 TCH prefixes Captain General with "first" and Francisco de Bracamonte with "don." I have taken a parenthetical mark here (TY) and at the end of the next paragraph to indicate section breaks; there are no equivalent marks in TCH.

31 TCH: "I delivered tribute to the conquistadors [*concixtadoresob*] in Tiho, as I was *batab* here in the district of Chicxulub."

32 TCH: ". . . came to Tiho and all of us were taken over."

33 Literally, "he served in the governorship, the *cah* burden . . ." (*lay tanlic u batabil cuch cah ca*); *cuch* was a term associated with office and thus *cuch cah* could be taken as a title similar to *ah cuch cab*, "councillor, officer." However, the TCH variation suggests a notarial slip altered the phrase in one of the versions: *ten tanlic in batabil cuchi ca*, "I served in the governorship at the time that . . ."

34 In addition to the obvious TCH substitutions in this passage of Ah Macan and Yaxkukul with Nakuk and Chicxulub, the *encomendero* named for Chicxulub is don Julián Doncel, and TCH names Alvarez [Albares] instead of Suárez as *alcalde mayor*. Whereas TY's references to the Pech *batab* and text author are third person in these sentences, TCH uses the first person.

35 TCH: "I who was previously called Nakuk Pech was baptized [*ca oci ha tin pole*] and I received baptism [*bautismo*]; my name became don Pablo Pech and I ceased to be called Nakuk Pech. We [were made] *hidalgos*, principal *batabob*, by the captains."

36 TCH: ". . . king; the members of our *chibal* will be *hidalgos*, all of our descendents, until the time comes when the world shall end."

37 "Dios" is omitted in TCH.

38 TCH: "all the subject people of the *cah*."

39 This phrase is omitted from TY.

40 TCH erroneously grants López the title "don" here, later in the same paragraph, and again at TY:5v; TCH:11 below.

41 The use in both texts of *xicin*, which meant "ear" but was also used as a term of measurement, especially of the width of a piece of cloth, suggests that the reference here is to tribute *mantas* or sheets of cotton cloth, the primary unit of tribute in colonial Yucatan.

42   TCH: "Then I delivered my baton to my son, don Pedro Pech . . ."

43   Neither text indicates a paragraph break here, but, as Martínez Hernández observes (1926: 11), there is a partial shift here to narration by the next generation of *batabob*.

44   This passage is quite different, and much clearer, in TCH: "This was the number of the year when I received the rod from my father, Nakuk Pech, don Pablo Pech, Ursula Pech his daughter-in-law, here in this district of Chicxulub, in order to serve Dios and our great ruler, the reigning king, in order that I may govern this *cah* here in this district of Chicxulub." A note on "daughter-in-law": this is my translation of the Maya *ixan*, which I have taken to be *ixhan* or *ixhaan*, meaning a person's mother-in-law or daughter-in-law, thus making Ursula don Pedro's wife. Note, however, that this remains problematic, both grammatically and because the *chibal* was endogamous (although the Pech feature strongly in the few examples of intra-*chibal* marriage; see Restall 1997a: 397–98).

45   TCH adds "to the *cah* of Yaxkukul, to the *cah* of Xulkum Chel, and to the *cah* of Maxtunil" and specifies that these officers were "of the principal *chibal*, that of Macan Pech, of Ah Kom Pech, and of Xulkum Chel."

46   TCH: ". . . when they came to the district of Yaxkukul we also came to this district of Chicxulub."

47   TCH reverses the generations of Nakuk and Ah Macan's immediate ancestors: "I Nakuk Pech was appointed by my father, Ah Kom Pech, son of Ah Tunal Pech . . ."

48   TCH also names the deputy Chuc; the word order in these officer-naming sentences is a little different in TCH but conveys the same information as TY.

49   Brinton (1882: 200) transcribes this name as Kan, which is thus a potential TCH variant, but in the original TCH manuscript (the Regil copy) the word could just as easily be Kuu.

50   TCH substitutes "they" for "I," specifying at the start of one sentence "Ah Nakuk Pech"; the time period is also specified as "the coming of the Spaniards here to the land."

51   TCH states that the gathering together (of Chicxulub) was done by "I, don Pablo Pech, and my father don Martín Pech, conquistador, [and] Xulkum Cheel."

52   The Maya phrase *u yumil kuluinicil* most commonly refers to native officers, but here, and for the rest of this paragraph, it seems to refer to the Spaniards (for a parallel use of the term to refer to Spaniards in the Calkini text, see TC:27 in Chapter 5). The "Cochuah tribute" would thus be the payments made by the Pech in support of the war against the Cochuah Mayas, whose region was far southeast of Ceh Pech and on the southeast edge of what was becoming the colony of Yucatan.

53   These Spanish terms are discussed in the glossary and elsewhere. Colonial Mesoamerican notarial documents tended to be peppered somewhat indiscriminately with Spanish legal-document genre terms in an effort to further validate a document in Spanish eyes; thus the authors of TY/TCH are not only referring to the text

itself with their use of *información, título,* and *probanza,* but are invoking the system of authority that granted them and their fellow Pech the status of *hidalgo* and the concomitant privileges of both Spanish and Maya nobility.

54 Compare this sentence to the prophesies in Chapters 7 and 8; written after the invasion, these prophesies were part of the Maya appropriation of the Conquest (see Chapter 2).

55 Here begins the section which I have dubbed the Title of Saci-Sisal. Although TCH shows no break here, TY indicates a paragraph or section break (I have treated double or triple dashes as approximate paragraph markers; see Figure 6.1), and Martínez Hernández (1926: 15) titles the section that follows "Cronica de Yaxkukul: Segundo Documento." Indeed, the section's emphasis upon events in the east (centered on the Cupul *cahob* of Saci and Sisal, upon which the Spaniards founded Valladolid), and its chronological return to the moment of first contact with the Spaniards, suggests that it must have originally been an account from a Cupul community; as discussed above, some Pech-related passages may have been inserted when the account was copied into the Yaxkukul and Chicxulub manuscripts.

56 Unlike the previous section of the titles, the names are identical here, along with the rest of the text, in both TY and TCH.

57 TCH omits the Montejo reference.

58 In translating *hantabi* in this way I follow Pérez Martínez (1936: 28, on TCH), whose version is more persuasive than that of Brinton (1882: 226, on TCH) or Martínez Hernández (1926: 16, on TY), who both have Aguilar being eaten by Ah Naum Ah Poot, an historical impossibility considering Aguilar's subsequent rescue by Cortés and role in the Conquest of central Mexico (see Chapter 1).

59 TCH omits this date.

60 *ah makopilobe ah dzudzopob;* the second term is here in TCH only.

61 Chuncaan was the name of the manmade pyramidal mound near the center of Ichcansiho (or, as it became at this time, Tiho-Merida). The second sentence of this paragraph is omitted in TCH. There is also a reference to Chuncaan in CBM:71 in Chapter 7.

62 TCH includes the year here but otherwise omits this sentence.

63 TCH has "Guerrero."

64 TCH omits this second reference to Juan López de Mena, a local *encomendero* included in the list above of the "foreign conquistadors."

65 According to Martínez Hernández (1926: 21), this was a friar named Villagómez; the texts borrow the Spanish word for "hermit," *ermitaño,* but write it as *ertanyo* (TY) and *emitanyo* (TCH).

66 *ca noh ahau ti Rey de castilla;* TCH inserts *ah tepal,* "reigning, he who rules," after *Rey.*

67 TCH omits the phrase relating to commissions; TY uses a Spanish loan, creating *u comisionil.*

68 Presumably Ah Macan Pech was here requesting permission from the Spaniards to capture a leader of the Maya resistance against the Spanish-Pech alliance; note that in the subsequent section of TY Ah Ceh Pech is credited with capturing Kul Chuc, who Montejo then "gives" to Ah Macan Pech.

69 There are some small differences between the two texts in this sentence: TCH omits the phrases "to the *cah*" and "the first conquistador [*yax concixtador*]"; TCH inserts "to the district of [*cab*]" before "Yaxkukul" (note that Yaxkukul is named in both texts). Although TY indicates no break here, the TY and TCH texts diverge at this point, and the content that follows makes it clear that this is the end of the section that I have called the Title of Saci-Sisal; it seems significant that the only mention of Yaxkukul in the Saci-Sisal section is its final word, and symbolic that with Ah Macan Pech's return to Yaxkukul the manuscript also returns to focus on events in the west.

70 The following section is found only in TY (with the exception of a few sentences that appear down in TCH:14); the corresponding passage in TCH is slightly shorter and reads as follows: "From the year 1519, when the Spaniards came here to the communities [*cahal*] of we the Itza, here in this land of Yucatan, I have indicated the days, the months and the years as above—I, don Pablo Pech, the son of don Martín Pech of Xul Kum Chel, I, conquistador [*concixtadoren*], here in Maxtunil and Chicxulub [*chac xulub chen*]—in which we received the Spaniards with good will and heart. Nor did we wage war against them, against don Juan de Montejo, *adelantado*, and the rest of the captains whose names are in the book [*ti libro*]. We also first received Christianity, we conquistadors don Martín Pech, son of don Fernando Pech, and don Pablo Pech, son of don Martín Pech, on the thirteenth day of the month of October, 1518 [sic]. My subjects [*in mektan cahilob*] received baptism all together [TCH:12] in Maxtunil; they were baptized by the first bishop to the Maya people [*maya uinicob*], don Francisco Toral; and when he baptized us, our lord bishop showed the images of the saints to all the *cahob*, images of San Pedro and San Pablo and San Juan and San Luis and San Antonio and San Miguel and San Francisco and San Alonso and San Agustín and San Sebastián and San Diego; and they desired unction [*oleos*], and he who became named Pablo [or Pedro; *Pº*] took unction. Such is the history [*u kahlail*] of everything I have collected together here in this book [*uay ti librose*], in order that it might be understood by the people, by whomever wished to know it, according to the will of our great lord Dios almighty." Note that there was no *adelantado* named don Juan de Montejo; the son of don Francisco de Montejo the younger was don Juan de Montejo y del Castillo (d.1603) and his son was don Juan de Montejo Maldonado (d.1642) (Rubio Mañé 1941: 29–75, 117).

71 This may be the same Ah Kul Chel who appears as a prophet in the Books of Chilam Balam; see Roys (1933: 165) for an example and various citations.

72 This is a play on *chuc*, which means "seize, take, assault, conquer"; Kul Chuc could thus be translated as Officer Conquest.

73 The Maya term used here, *kaxob*, literally means "forests" but can refer either to forested or cultivated land; its sense is land that *can* be cultivated, whether it is at

that moment or not (on colonial-era Maya land terminology, see Restall 1997a: 189–211).

74 Martínez Hernández (1926: 24) may be right to read this phrase, *y[etel] cutzuc*, as a name: "and Cutzuc."

75 Here begins the section that I have called the Title of Motul. (Martínez Hernández [1926:25] titles it "Chronicle of Ah Naum Pech, named don Francisco de Montejo Pech, Cacique [i.e. governor] of Motul.") Although TCH shows no break in the text here (a continuation of TCH:12), TY has a half-page space and begins a new page with the underlined heading *1541 años*; the two texts are once again parallel and virtually identical.

76 The Maya texts borrow the Spanish term *mesón*; *messone* (TY) and *mensone* (TCH). Maya *cabildos* (municipal councils) appointed or contained an officer responsible for maintaining the *mesón*, in accordance with Spanish requirements, as it was intended primarily to house visiting Spanish officials (Restall 1997a: 55, 72, 80); the "*cah* home" mentioned just above is either a reference to the church or to the room or building where the *cabildo* conducted their business—the town hall.

77 TY has *yucal*, TCH *yocol*; it seems to me that if we take this name to have originally been Yukal Peten, which means "the whole land," or Yokol Peten, which means "this land" or "on this province" or even "the world," it is a very likely pre-Conquest name for the peninsula. (The term *cab*, meaning "district, region, world" is virtually synonymous with *peten*, and *yokol cab* is a common colonial-era phrase for "on this earth" or "the world.") It is quite credible that the Spaniards found "Yukal Peten" or "Yokol Peten" to be a mouthful and very quickly reduced it to "Yucatan." However, there is a better-known (but not better?) explanation that circulated in the colonial period and is included by the Pech titles; see below and accompanying note 81.

78 The Maya phrase used here, *hunab ku*, is an interesting choice, as Hunab Ku was the name of a pre-Conquest Maya deity, arguably the deity that best corresponded to the Spanish Dios, for he was some sort of supreme being who incorporated at least one other deity (Itzamna) (Sharer 1994: 530; Landa XXXIV–XX; also see the reference in CBM:71 in Chapter 7 below). Compare this paragraph to the prophecy passages in the Books of Chilam Balam (see Chapter 7 for an example) and in the *relaciones* accounts by Gaspar Antonio Chi (Chapter 8).

79 Note that chickens were Old World fauna introduced by the Spaniards; the Mayas called them *caxtilla u luum* ("Castilian turkey"), soon shortened to *cax* (the term used in the text here). Clearly the Mayas would not have had chickens to offer Spaniards at the time of the Conquest; this fact and the use of the abbreviated term *cax*, added to other evidence in the text, indicate it is a mid- or late colonial composition, albeit probably drawing upon earlier copies (see discussion in this chapter's introduction).

80 TCH omits the previous two sentences.

81 This has become the conventional explanation for the name "Yucatan," going all

the way back to Landa (II), writing in the 1560s; however, it is problematic, for although *ca than* (in colonial orthography, pronounced similar to "-catan") can mean "our language," "yucatan" as such has no meaning in Yucatec Maya. By the seventeenth century the matter had become even less clear, as Cogolludo's (2, I) multiple explanations demonstrate.

82 TCH adds, "in Mani."

83 TCH omits the Tixkumcheil episode, substituting instead the following (note that the final sentences are nevertheless identical): ". . . in their jurisdiction of Yaxkukul. Don Pablo Pech, Ah Macan Pech, was chief ruler [*halach uinic*] of the whole district here to the west; moreover, all the captains did not give up heart, for they had been appointed by me to guard the district of Chicxulub, because the commoners had been given monthly duties; their end was shown by the will of Dios in the *cahob*." This paragraph marks the end in both texts of the section that I have called the Title of Motul.

84 TCH simply has, "This is now the history [*ytoria*] of all . . ."

85 TY ends this section with, "in those years, when they had just established the holy church [*santa yglesia*] here." TY then goes straight on to its land-survey section (to which I subsequently return below). Thus the remainder of this lengthy paragraph is material found only in TCH.

86 This passage, from "Two or three years. . . ," appears in near-identical form above in TY:6r.

87 TY:8r continued; here begins the land-survey section of TY, a portion of the title which is referred to in the scholarly literature as the Deslinde ("demarcation"). There are two extant versions of the Deslinde from Yaxkukul, one (Deslinde #1) is dated April 30 and survives as a separate document, the other (Deslinde #2) is dated May 8 and survives as the final part of TY; there is also a parallel and very similar land-survey section from Chicxulub (TCH:16–18). Reconciling these three texts proved impractical, so I have simply presented here my translation of Deslinde #2, as it is an immediate continuation of the TY text that I have primarily been following (and because none of it has been published in English before). Martínez Hernández's Spanish translation (1926: 33–37) is reproduced in Barrera Vásquez (1984: 91–98), and there are also two complementary discussions of the Deslinde documents by Hanks (1987), who analyzes the language of both documents but quotes from Deslinde #1, and Restall (1997a: 276–292), in which I make a case for categorizing the Deslinde as a primordial title, analyzing and quoting from Deslinde #1 only.

88 This sentence appears to have been added to the text after the rest of the 1769 manuscript was copied. Martínez Hernández (1926: 33) erroneously transcribes the date as *8 de mayoile 1544*; it is *8 de mo de 1522 ã*, with the ambiguity of *mo* resolved only by the repetition of the date near the end of the text. His argument that the 1522 should be read as 1544 because "in ancient documents the letters 2 and 4 are easily confused" (1926: 37) is entirely unpersuasive; Barrera Vásquez (1984: 10–11, 106) compounds the error by suggesting that the Maya notary actually meant to

write 1554, not 1544, thus placing the document the right side of the 1542 founding of Merida. Any attempt to "correct" the date here or elsewhere in the TY (or in any primordial title) is based on a misconception of the nature of the document; the date of 1522 was written down deliberately not in that year or even in the sixteenth century, but in 1769, because it was the Maya understanding that such a date helped to give the document a veneer of validity, both in Maya and Spanish eyes. It is very possible that an earlier version of the land survey featured the date of the actual border agreement, which very likely took place in the 1550s or 1560s, when much of the colony was surveyed; it is also possible that between then and 1769 a copyist of the survey decided that an earlier date—perhaps 1542, the symbolic date of Merida's founding, and later, 1522—made the document more impressive; but this must remain mere speculation based on our understanding of primordial titles as the product of centuries of compilation and copying. For further discussion of the dating issue, see Restall (1997a: 290–91).

89 This account of a border walk is what I have termed an ambulatory land description; note how the rhythms of the description reflect the rhythms of the actual procession along the community's territorial boundary. To place this land survey in the context of Maya practices of land description and concepts of land ownership in the colonial period, see Restall (1997a: 189–220).

90 I.e., given each *cah* official status as a self-governing indigenous *pueblo* of the colony.

91 There is a space here of about half a dozen lines before a final list of prominent Pech noblemen, their descendents, and the Spaniards whose authority they cite.

CHAPTER 7. *The Cruel Cycle*

1 Because some manuscripts are fragments, some may be excerpts from others, and some are unpublished, one can only make an estimate of the number of surviving Books of Chilam Balam. In addition to the texts that are published—see Roys (1933, 1946); Barrera Vásquez and Rendón (1948); Solís Alcalá (1949); Makemson (1951); Craine and Reindorp (1979); Hires (1981); Edmonson (1982, 1986); and Gubler (1997)—there are several more texts that are unpublished, and a further half a dozen for which there are references but as yet no extant manuscripts.

2 I have consulted the photostat copy of the original Tizimin manuscript in TULAL (the original document is in Mexico City's Museo Nacional de Antropología), but I made my translation of the excerpt below mostly from the transcription in Edmonson (1982); his translation was also of use. The cited numbers are pages in Edmonson (1982) followed by folios in the original manuscript. The excerpt below appears as a number of non-contiguous chapters in Edmonson (1982), but is a contiguous passage in the original manuscript (folio 16). Also see Makemson (1951).

3 I have made my translation of the Chumayel excerpts from the transcription in Roys (1933) (CBC:20–22). These passages can also be found in Edmonson (1986: 107–11, 100–103, 143–49) and can be located in other editions, as well as the original man-

uscript in the Princeton University Library, through the concordance in Edmonson (1986: 267–68). I consulted and was assisted by the translations in Roys (1933), Bricker (1981), and Edmonson (1986).

4 I have made my translation of the Mani excerpts from the photostat of the original (as extant) manuscript in TLH; I also consulted the transcription in Solís Alcalá (1949), as well as his Spanish translation, which is translated into English in Craine and Reindorp (1979). An edition similar to Edmonson's Chumayel and Tizimin, complete with the full text in Maya and English, is sorely needed for the Codex Pérez/Mani book.

5 For this very brief excerpt I relied upon the transcription of the Maya text by Hires, also consulting her translation and notes (1981: 38, 196–97). Chan Kan is located southeast of Peto, in the southeast corner of the Mani region (see Map II; the *cah* does not appear on the Mani map that is Figure 7.1).

6 See Chapter 2 for further discussion of the Maya treatment of temporal linearity and cyclicity.

7 Edmonson (1982: xvi-xx; 1986: 3).

8 Edmonson (1982: xx).

9 In the Maya calendar, a *katun* was a unit of twenty 360-day years (there were three interlocking year cycles: the 260-day *tzolkin*, the 360-day *tun*, and the 365-day *haab*). Each *katun* was named after its final day, which was always Ahau (in the case of the *katun* above, 11 Ahau). As the *katunob* were only numbered up to thirteen, each *katun* would repeat every thirteen *katunob* (i.e. every 260 *tunob*, or 256 *haabob* or solar years). (Bricker 1981: 6–8; Sharer 1994: 559–75; see also Chapter 4.)

10 The meaning of the Maya term used here, *okbac*, is not clear; Edmonson's (1982: 55) suggestion of "wept" (from *okol*) seems more plausible than Roys's "prayed" (in Bricker 1981: 25).

11 *Ah tan tunobe*; Edmonson (1982: 55) suggests this may be a reference to the façade of the Mani church, but I would imagine that the reference is broader than that, reflecting a Maya observation of the Spanish preference for stone-fronted buildings. (One is reminded of the stone façade of the Montejo house [see Chapter 1, Figure 1.1], but it would be stretching it to suggest that the Mayas also had that image in mind.)

12 Edmonson's (1982: 63) translation of these phrases "There was the breaking of the lands; there was the shaking of the heavens" (*tan u pax cabal tan u sot canal*) better fits the grim mood of the passages to follow but is not as well supported by the lexical evidence.

13 *yuma u netzil uil*, literally "this lord, his reason [was] base/meager/stupid"; note, however, Edmonson's gloss: "These fathers of the waning moon" (1982: 64).

14 *Balam Ochil* and *Balam Chamacil*; Edmonson (1982: 64) notes that these were Maya military orders.

15 For a similar use of this metaphor, see the Title of Acalan-Tixchel (Chapter 3; TAT:72v).

16 This appears to be a play on his name: *ah kin*, "priest"; *xul*, "to end, finish"; Ah Kin Xuluc, "The Terminal Priest." This may be the same person as Ah Kul Xuluc, who appears several times in the Pech titles (Chapter 6).

17 *u chun*; which also means "origin, cause."

18 The Maya term *cumtan*, which I have translated as "crushing of people," literally means "to sit," but its meaning in the above context is not clear; Roys glosses it as "trampling on people" (1933: 79), Bricker as "witchcraft" (1981: 27), and Edmonson as "promotions" (1986: 110).

19 This would be a period from about the first century A.D. to shortly before the Spanish invasion.

20 This appears to be an altered Spanish place-name, possibly based on Cartagena. (Edmonson 1986: 101 proposes Constantinople.) I suggest that the specific reference is not important, as the name is being used as a metaphor for somewhere distant and foreign, similar to the use of Cozumel and West Zuyua in other texts (TAT:69v; TC:36; CBM:134; also see Chapter 1).

21 Roys suggests (1933: 80; echoed by Edmonson 1986: 101) that this may be "a reference to the battle on the day of San Bernabé at Merida"; as San Bernabé became the patron saint of Merida, it may also be a more general reference to Conquest-era encounters.

22 As *bobil*, which I have translated as "timber," can mean tree or stalk, it is possible that this is a reference to people being burnt at the stake. It is more likely, however, that it refers to the burning of the wooden structures atop the mounds that are the subject of this passage, thus making the sentence an account of the Conquest from the perspective of the history of the pyramids.

23 This is also an obscure name, which I take to play a similar role to Cartabona above; Edmonson (1986: 103) proposes that Viroa is a Maya reduction of Babylonia, which is certainly plausible and rather supports my interpretation; Roys (1933: 80) opts for Chacunescab as the name of a member of the Tutul Xiu *chibal*, which is also possible.

24 The Spanish-Maya agreement apparently being referred to here took place in 1542 or 1543; the Chilam Balam account tends to telescope the date of the initial arrival of Spaniards in Yucatan (1519) into the date of the founding of the colonial capital at Merida-Tiho (1542).

25 This is a reference to Yucatan's patron saint, the Virgin Mary of Izamal (the *pueblo* of Izamal was to the Mayas a *cah* named Itzmal).

26 Of the various prophecy passages in the Books of Chilam Balam, I have chosen this one because it precedes the better-known prophecies that appear in parallel sections in the Mani, Chumayel, and Tizimin manuscripts [see Roys (1933: 165) for an English translation and bibliographic references], as well as in a colonial Spanish form in Cogolludo (2, XI); furthermore, the English translation of this passage in

Craine and Reindorp (1979: 70–72) is itself a translation of the Spanish rendering by Solís Alcalá (1949: 143–47), and the latter is truncated and inaccurate.

27 A reference to 1527, the year that the elder Montejo first arrived in Yucatan (see Chapter 1).

28 The Maya phrase *hokol ich* can mean both "to show one's face" and "to germinate seedlings or grow crops in"; I expect the double meaning is intended here in order to suggest that these *batabob* both appear in the wrong places and do the wrong things.

29 Chuncaan was the pyramidal mound near the center of Ichcansiho; when the city became Merida (Tiho to the Mayas), the Franciscans built their monastery beside the mound. Also see the reference in the Pech titles (TY:4v; TCH:9).

30 In Maya culture the plumeria flower, *nicte*, had great ritual significance and thus the term had multiple usages and meanings; one was as a reference to flowers in general, especially flowers used ritually; another was a ritual relationship to the calendar cycle, which is the connection implied here by Solís Alcalá's translation (1949: 145). I suggest that the image is one of the deity Hunab Ku (literally "One Divine Being" or "One God") receiving flowers in a flower offering and also receiving the years as they passed (see Edmonson 1986: 163 for an interpretation of a Chumayel passage as equating flowers with years). The *nicte* was also associated with carnal vice, female sexuality, and sexuality and reproduction in general (Roys 1933: 104–5; Sigal 1995); note the references a few lines down to the opening of the plumeria in lustful times, an obvious image of female sexuality, and to the old women and old men of the plumeria—the sexually active elderly.

31 The Maya terms for mother and house are not the same (*na'* and *na*, respectively) but in colonial orthography they are written the same (*na*) and I suggest that a double meaning is intended here. The term is used earlier in the passage to clearly refer to the Virgin Mary and also to evoke the image of the houses of pre-Conquest Ichcansiho, and thus *kulbil na* now evokes the introduction of the worship of the Virgin (holy mother) in the new church (holy house).

32 This bird is the *chel*, the Yucatan Jay or Urraca, *Cissilopha* (*Cyanocorax*) *yucatanicus* (Barrera Vásquez 1980: 131; Swadesh et al. 1991: 46; Robin Restall, personal communication).

33 Tree symbolism played a role in Mesoamerican rulership imagery, so the trees [*che*] of this sentence could be taken as rulers; see Restall (1997a: 253, 413).

34 There are similar annals passages, or chronicles, in the Chilam Balam manuscripts from Chumayel and Tizimin (Roys 1933: 135–44; Edmonson 1982: 3–11; 1986: 51–64), but I have selected the Mani version here because it is by far the most substantial. Furthermore, published English translations of it are outdated and/or unsatisfactory; see, for example, the collection of the Chilam Balam chronicles in Brinton (1882: 81–185) and the rather unreliable copy and translation of the Mani chronicle included in some editions of John Lloyd Stephens's *Incidents of Travel in Yucatan* (whose first publication in New York in 1843 was the first appearance in print of any portion of the Chilam Balam literature).

35 The origin of Chacnouitan as a name for Yucatan is not clear. Of the other toponyms in this paragraph, Tulapan and Nonoual seem to refer to the central Mexican city of Tula and the adjacent mountain of Nonohual, while Zuyua is unidentifiable (see Chapter 1 and note 20 above); see also Brinton (1882: 109–24). Carmack (1981: 46) and Okoshi Harada (1993: 4) argue that Nonoual is the Chontal area.

36 That is, due to a breakdown of central authority; the context suggests that the phrase *mul tepal*, usually translated as "joint government," here refers to the acquisition of power by factions within the city in the face of outside attack (see the brief discussion of this phrase in Chapter 1).

37 I have translated the phrase *ah uitzil dzul*, but it could also be a personal name, making an alternative translation of "destroyed by Ah Uitzil Dzul from outside Mayapan *cah.*"

38 The Maya phrases here, *maya cimil* ("Maya death") and *noh kakil* ("great sickness") probably refer to the first wave of smallpox epidemics in the peninsula; see a similar reference in the Annals of Oxkutzcab (Chapter 4 above). The "great sickness" is also mentioned below in the entry for 1609.

39 Ah Pula means "the rain-bringer"; this would appear to be a reference to the Otzmal massacre, also mentioned in other sources presented here (see Chapters 4 and 8).

40 The reader should not be confused by this chronology: Fray Diego de Landa, the second bishop of Yucatan, died in 1579; his predecessor, fray Francisco de Toral, first arrived in the province in 1562. The chronology of the entries that follow is more or less accurate: for example, Diego de Quijada became governor in 1565 and was the ninth to occupy the office; there were indeed hangings in 1562, as part of Landa's campaign of persecution (see Chapter 1) and in the wake of the Tekax riot/revolt of 1610 (AGI-*Escribanía* 305a). A study of the Tekax affair is to be included in a book on colonial Yucatan which I am currently researching; brief summaries are also in Farriss (1984: 98–99, 193–94).

41 Because this date is given in Maya, not in Spanish (as is the previous date claiming to be that of the Conquest), it is tempting to see it as a date in the Maya calendar. However, as Hires (1981: 196–97) convincingly argues, that produces Maya dates which correspond to 1469 and 1864, the significance of which is unclear, whereas the European date of 1823 can be taken as that of the writing of this extant copy of the manuscript; a near-identical passage later in the Chan Kan text is clearly dated "*1832 años*" (CBCK:124; Hires 1981: 136, 356).

CHAPTER 8. *A Hybrid Perspective*

1 Doña Beatriz de Herrera is briefly discussed in Chapter 1. The Mani land treaty and its various extant records are referred to in Chapters 5 and 6. Nachi Cocom, baptized don Juan Cocom, the author of the murder of Chi's father twenty years earlier, was also supposed to participate in the survey, but, according to one version of the Mani treaty, reproduced in Roys (1943: 186), he sent a message saying he was sick.

2 For a discussion of the dating and authorship of the Xiu family tree see Cortez (1995: 69–81); note that circumstantial evidence suggests that Chi was the drawing's author, but we cannot be certain that he was. Gaspar Antonio and his mother, Ix Kukil Xiu, can be located at the top left-hand edge of the tree.

3 AGI-*Escribanía* 305a (the 1610 Tekax investigation records). For an excellent biography of Chi, see Karttunen (1994: 84–114, 308), upon which the preceding paragraphs are largely based (an older, briefer biography is Blom 1928).

4 AGI-*México* 105, 4.

5 Jakeman (1952: 2–5).

6 The Tiab y Tec *relación* was signed by Juan Bote, who acknowledged Chi's assistance (RY, I: 317–21); the Merida *relación* was signed by Martín de Palomar and signed and ghostwritten by Chi (RY, I: 65–84). It is possible that at some point Chi wrote up his own lengthy *relación* which has not survived. He did write a two-page "Report on some of the customs of the people of the provinces of Yucatan" for the governor of Yucatan in 1582, the original of which has survived, albeit in poor condition, in Seville, along with Chi's fifty-page 1580/1593 *probanza de mérito* (report of service to the Crown; AGI-*México* 105, 4); the 1582 report was copied almost verbatim by López de Cogolludo into his seventeenth-century history of the province (it is also published in Tozzer 1941: 230–32). Likewise, the similarity of some passages in Landa's *Relación* to entries ghostwritten by Chi in the *Relaciones de Yucatán* suggests that the Franciscan friar may have had access to an early Chi manuscript while writing his 1566 account in Spain. The *relaciones* excerpts included here were published by Jakeman (1952), but with English translations broken up into subject headings; I have made my own translations from the 1898 edition of the *relaciones*.

7 With the possible exception of Letter ix in Chapter 9.

8 These include Tutul Xiu's central Mexican-style crown, the Maya and central Mexican elements to his scepter or staff of office, the woman of Ticul's dress (more a central Mexican *huipil* than a Maya *ypil*), and the deer legs being ritually burned at the base of the drawing (Cortez 1995: 140–41, 161–71, 207–29).

9 For a more detailed discussion of these and other elements of the tree's iconography, see the superb dissertation on the subject by Cortez (1995).

10 As Felipe Fernández-Arnesto observes (personal communication), Chi seems here to be revealing the influence of his former mentor, Diego de Landa.

11 Despite the impression this sentence gives of Nachi Cocom's great antiquity, he was actually ruler of the Sotuta region at the time of the Spanish Conquest, afterwards remaining governor of Sotuta *cah*; indeed, although Chi was much younger than Cocom, and from a rival *chibal*, both men knew Diego de Landa well (Cocom is mentioned by Landa [XI] as a source for his *Relación*), and it is very likely that the two Maya nobles knew each other.

12 Both here and in Landa (XIII) the alleged central Mexican origins of the Xiu *chibal* of the Tutul Xiu region are played down, although note that the central Mexican iconographic elements in the Xiu family tree (Figure 8.1) suggest that Chi, if he was

indeed the artist, condoned this Xiu origin myth to some extent; I have argued above (Chapter 1) that while there is considerable evidence of centuries of central Mexican influence in pre-Conquest Yucatan, there is no proof beyond accounts such as this of the non-Yucatec origins of specific supposed foreign *chibalob*.

13 This was Napuc Chi, Gaspar Antonio Chi's father, as Chi makes explicit in his account of this murder in the 1593 cover-letter to his *probanza*, which features the additional detail that Ah Kulel Chi's tongue was cut out (AGI-*México* 105, 4: 2); *ah kulel*, as we have seen in previous chapters, was a title of office, indicating that Napuc Chi was a deputy to the Xiu *batab* of Mani. He is also referred to in some sources (the seventeenth-century chroniclers Cogolludo [3, VI] and Herrera; Tozzer 1941: 45) as a priest with the title Ah Kin Chi, and as a leader of the 1533 Xiu embassy that offered aid and allegiance to the Spaniards (testimony by Pedro Ku and Jorge Xiu in Chi's *probanza*)—which, some sources assert, inspired the Otzmal massacre three years later. Cogolludo (3, VI) is the only source to claim that Ah Kin Chi was blinded but not killed so that he could tell the Xiu what the Cocom had done.

14 Ah Mochan Xiu's name can be seen on the upper right-hand branch of the Xiu family tree (Figure 8.1).

15 This is presumably a reference to what modern scholars call the World Tree, an ornamented tree sometimes stone-carved in a cross shape representing in pre-columbian Maya iconography the central axis or pivot of the cosmos; the best-known example is at Palenque (Thompson 1970: 71–76; Schele and Miller 1986: 115, 282–83; Clendinnen 1987: 175; Schele and Freidel 1990: 67, 258). The World Tree does not bear a close resemblance to the Xiu family tree, but some iconographic connection may be inferred (see Cortez 1995: 112–27, for example).

16 In a subsequent letter to the Crown requesting a pension (the 1593 version of his *probanza* cited above), this list of aids given to the Spaniards is repeated by Chi in similar wording as services rendered to the Crown specifically by Chi's father, grandfather, uncles, and himself.

17 Although the original text uses the Spanish word *vino*, the reference is to the native drink *balche*; elsewhere in the *relaciones* Chi condemns Spanish wine for burning the liver and causing death (RY, I: 413, 427; Karttunen 1994: 110). There is also a *balche* reference in Letter viii in Chapter 9.

18 In the *relaciones* from Tecal; Dzidzantun; and Sisal and Chalante (whose Spanish authors recognize Chi as their ghostwriter), Chi comments, "the *encomienda* licences given to *encomenderos* and the books of baptisms and confirmations show that since this land was conquered its natives have continually diminished in number" (e.g., RY, I: 414); likewise, in four other *relaciones* acknowledged to have been written largely by Chi (those of Kisil and Sitilpech, Citilcum [Kitelcan] and Cabiche, Tekanto and Tepakan, and Izamal and Santa María), he remarks, "this land appears to have been well populated before now, and all over the land there are signs of it having been settled and cultivated; the natives say that it has been depopulated by famines and massacres" (e.g., RY, I: 198; passages pointed out by Jakeman 1952: 44–45).

CHAPTER 9. *The Politics of Conquest*

1 CDI: LXIX; LXX; Scholes and Adams (1938); Clendinnen (1987: 72–111); Karttunen (1994: 97–106).

2 Scholes and Adams (1938, 2: 68–73); Clendinnen (1987: 107).

3 Indeed, a recently discovered series of similar letters from the early eighteenth century may, upon further inspection, and with the potential support of letters from other decades, reveal that this genre was employed by Maya communities and their Spanish priests throughout the colonial period (AGI-*México*; Pedro Bracamonte, personal communication).

4 The following table lists all the letters to the king that have surfaced so far. I have designated each document by a Roman numeral (i–x), listed in chronological order, as well as a series letter (a or b). Under provenance I have listed the most prominent *cah* of origin, followed by the total number of origin *cahob*, and then given the dominant *chibal* of authorship, followed by the total number of signatories (mostly *batabob*, but in some cases—i.e. where the two numbers do not match—other officials also; likewise most names are of the dominant *chibal* but each letter features other patronyms too). Letter i is also in CDI: LXVI (transcription of Spanish text only); facsimile U (Maya and Spanish texts). Zimmerman (1970: 32–35) contains Letters i–vi (transcriptions of Maya and Spanish texts, variations noted, no translations, with photocopy-facsimiles of iii and v). Gates (1937: 114–15) presents Letter ii in facsimile (Maya text) with English translation. Letter viii is in González Cicero (1978: 232–34, edited Spanish text only) and Hanks (1996: 282–90, photocopy-facsimile of Maya text, with English translation of about a sixth of it). Letter ix is in CDI: LXXII (transcription of Spanish text); Zimmerman (1970: 36–37, transcription of Spanish text); Gates (1937: 115–17, English translation only). Letters vii and x do not seem to have come to the prior attention of scholars. A word about the series designations and intertextual similarities: series "a" letters are identical, save for the signatures, as are the series "b" pair; the letters of series "a" and "b" differ from each other only in ten minor single-word variations (listed by Zimmerman 1970: 33); Letters viii and x carry the same message but are textually quite distinct from the others; Letter ix is entirely different.

Letter	Series	Archival Location	Date	Provenance/Authors
i	a	AHN *caja* III	Feb. 11, 1567	Calkini (10)/Canul (10)
ii	a	AGI-*México* 367: 62	Feb. 12, 1567	Motul (13)/Pech (17)
iii	a	AGI-*México* 367: 64	Feb. 12, 1567	Dzidzantun (8)/Chel (9)
iv	a	AGI-*México* 367: 70	Feb. 21, 1567	Conkal (12)/Pech (16)
v	b	AGI-*México* 367: 67	February 1567	Champoton?/Couoh (6)
vi	b	AGI-*México* 367: 68	February 1567	Tixchel (1)/Paxbolon (7)
vii	a	AGI-*México* 367: 88	March 5, 1567	Itzmal (12)/Che (12)
viii		AGI-*México* 359	March 9, 1567	Merida (?)/Pech (25)
ix		AHN *caja* III	April 12, 1567	Mani (4)/Xiu (4)
x		AGI-*México* 104: 1	Jan. 7, 1580	Caucel (13)/Canul (13)

5 As mentioned above, Hanks has published transcriptions and translations of about a sixth of this letter (1986: 731, 736–38; 1996: 286, 288–90); however, he generously shared with me a photocopy of the original text, his transcription of it, and his translation of about half the letter, for which I am extremely grateful. Although Hanks's translation was very helpful indeed, the English version below, and any errors therein, are mine.

6 Gates (1937: 114–17); Tozzer (1941: 83–84); González Cicero (1978: 110–11, 194–95).

7 Gates (1937: 114).

8 *ca dziib tic huun tech tupach p^e frai gaspar de najera ah maya than.* A further point is that the signatures at the foot of some of the letters were clearly not signatures as such, having been written in the same hand as the document itself. This was taken to suggest that the "signators" were not really authors of the texts. However, most Mayas, including nobles and community officers, were illiterate; those who could sign, did, while others relied upon the notary or a colleague (for example, don Pablo Paxbolon seems to have signed all the names to the Tixchel letter). In fact, it is notable how many "real" signatures the letters feature; the vast majority of colonial-era records in Maya contain "signatures" written by notaries, with sometimes the *batab* writing his own name (Restall 1997a: 67–68, 229–50).

9 CDI: LXIX; CDI: LXX.

10 González Cicero (1978: 194). As Hanks has remarked (1986: 724), the anti-Franciscan letter appears to have been written only in Spanish, "but no one has adduced this as evidence of inauthenticity." Still more extant Spanish letters offer parallel political positions to those in the Maya petitions (AGI-*México* 367: various; Scholes and Adams 1938, 2: 83–84, 170–71, 378; González Cicero 1978: 194, 226–28; Hanks 1986: 725). It is possible that a Maya original is sitting in an archive waiting to be found by scholars. If not, the document's language prevents us from making certain kinds of philological analysis, but it does not, as Hanks points out, make it any less authentic. Mayas were aware that the king spoke no Maya, hence the translations of the pro-Franciscan letters (that is unless the Spanish versions came first). There is an interesting parallel of sorts in a corpus of twenty-one letters from Cakchiquel communities in the Valley of Guatemala written in Nahuatl in 1572 and addressed to the king; the petitions complained of the recent increase in tribute burdens. Nahuatl had been chosen as a *lingua franca* to bridge the gap between Spanish and Cakchiquel, but in 1576, when no relief to the tribute burden appeared to be in sight, the communities drew up their letters again—this time in Spanish (Dakin and Lutz 1996).

11 Land records are one example (Restall 1997a: 189–200); also see the land-survey section of the Title of Yaxkukul in Chapter 6. Repetition in such documents tends to be rhetorical rather than word-for-word copying, however.

12 Hanks (1986; 1996: 281–90). Hanks, a linguistic anthropologist specializing in the Yucatec Maya language, was the first to suggest that the letters to the king should not be dismissed as inauthentic.

13 Hanks (1996: 287).

14 There were indeed very few clergy in Yucatan in the late sixteenth century. Despite being decimated, the Maya population still stood at roughly two hundred thousand parishioners, who were served by a starting total of just four Franciscans in 1545, rising to only thirty-eight friars and seculars by 1580 (Farriss 1984: 93); numbers for 1567 were between these two, but were reduced, in effect, by the withdrawal of parish priests to half a dozen convent towns in the wake of the 1562 crisis. The Maya call for more priests was paralleled by similar requests in letters to the Crown from various Spanish officials (listed and cited in Hanks 1986: 725).

15 The meaning of the Maya term used here, *ahue*, which I have translated as "ruler," is not clear; it is possible that this is a Maya rendering of the Hebrew equivalent of Dios, Yahweh, but as the phrase *cech noh ahue* appears later in the letter as the more intelligible *cech noh ahau*, I suspect that the latter is intended.

16 The walls of Maya houses were made of wattle and daub, branches or sticks to which adobe was plastered; the image being evoked here is one of such poverty that even the plaster is gone from the walls.

17 The hanging was actually worse than this account suggests, as the victims had their hands tied behind their backs before being suspended from their wrists. The *burro* was not strictly speaking a rack, but more like a sawhorse, to which victims were tied and then beaten or otherwise abused. Victims of the water torture were forced to drink enormous amounts of water and then subjected to abuse such as being kicked in the swollen belly. These and the other tortures described were standard practices whenever torture accompanied Inquisition interrogations.

18 Quijada was removed by Céspedes (mentioned later in this letter) in 1565; it is ironic that Quijada, having been cajoled by Landa into supporting the 1562 campaign, was to suffer fines and imprisonment for his role while Landa received official exoneration (Clendinnen 1987: 102–108).

19 *Sant benitos* (as written in the text) were yellow capes with red crosses painted on them which the "guilty" were forced to wear as marks of shame (Scholes and Adams 1938).

20 A *receptor* was a notary specially appointed to record testimony outside the jurisdiction of Mexico City for courts responsible for indigenous affairs; the letter suggests that the *receptor* in question was appointed by the *audiencia*, or high court, of which there was one in Mexico City and one in Santiago de Guatemala.

CHAPTER 10. *Conquest as Negotiation*

1 *uchebal in ualic u okotba*; XC:10. The scenes on some pre-Conquest Maya polychrome ceramic vessels may depict petitionary presentations (Patricia McAnany, personal communication; for a possible example, see the rollouts in Schele and Miller 1986: 170–71).

2 Restall (1997a: 251–66).

3 Such language can also be seen in a sibling 1605 petition from Dzaptun (reproduced

in Restall 1997a: 323–24), as well as some late colonial examples (such as AGN-*Civil* 336, 1: 159–60; CCA-VIII, 1811, 9). Also see AGI-*México*, 367: 62; AGN-*Civil*, 2013, 1: 4–6; ANEY, 1736–37: c.400; and TT:33.

4 AGN-*Inquisición* 69, 5: 199.

5 The Xecpedz petition is also published in Restall (1998a), along with two other Maya petitions from the Andrés Mexía case file, two other documents translated from Spanish, and a brief analysis of the Inquisition investigation into Mexia (AGN-*Inquisición* 69, 5: 154–329).

6 AGN-*Civil* 2013, 1: 4–5.

7 These petitions are taken from a corpus of Maya-language documents known as the Xiu Chronicles (XC) or, more accurately, the Xiu Papers. The collection features petitions and records similar to those selected here and covering most of the colonial period (the only document which is really out of place, in terms of genre, is the one I have presented in Chapter 4 as the Chronicle of Oxkutzcab). The original documents are well preserved in TLH, and I was thus able to make my translations from them; this book includes facsimiles of five pages from the Xiu Papers and translations of five of its Maya-language documents (one in Chapter 4, three in the body of this chapter, and one in note 14 below). Also of much help, and likewise housed in TLH, was a partial transcription and a full translation by Ralph Roys, and an accompanying study of the papers by Roys and Sylvanus Morley, none of which was ever published (Roys 1941).

8 Remote communities like Xecpedz, far from Merida-Tiho (see Map II), seldom saw Spaniards and thus viewed visiting priests as useful economic contacts; priests in turn engaged in economic enterprise to supplement income through tithes, fees, and tribute in the form of local produce (to which the petition also refers). Priests sometimes abused this relationship; in another document in the same case file as this petition, Xecpedz accused Mexía of visiting the *cah* only twice, each time demanding goods for which he failed to pay. Note the similarity between the phrasing and content of the complaints here and the grievances against the secular clergy aired in the petition that is Letter viii in Chapter 9.

9 This is a reference to Mexía saying mass in Latin or Spanish and to his inadequate grasp of Yucatec Maya. The investigation into Mexía turned up complaints from other *cahob* that he would neither preach nor hold confession in the tongue of his parishioners; furthermore, in September 1573 (forty days after Xecpedz wrote up their complaint), Mexía was reprimanded by the civil authorities in Valladolid for not preaching or giving confession in Maya. Maya communities continued to complain, even as late as the 1830s, that the priests assigned to their parishes spoke Maya poorly. The colonial Church, of course, never ordained non-Spaniards (Restall 1997a: 162; 1998a).

10 Having already been decimated in the first half of the century, the Maya population was again halved between the censuses of 1549 and 1580–86 due to a further series of famines and epidemics (Cook and Borah 1974: 1–179; Farriss 1984: 57–65; Restall 1997a: 173–76). In stating "there's nobody here" the petitioners are probably

referring to population loss through flight as well as mortality; in times of crisis the so-called *despoblado* regions (see Chapter 1) offered refuge and alternative sources of food for Mayas from the colony.

11 The *cah* of Tahnab was located on the highway or *camino real* between Merida and Campeche (see Map II).

12 *danta meyah cokol* uses the Spanish loanword *tanda* and the equivalent Maya phrase to create a bilingual semantic couplet, a common stylistic device in colonial Maya texts (Restall 1997a: 241–42, 300–301).

13 Yaxakumche or Yaxa was a tiny *cah* subordinated to Oxkutzcab during the colonial period, as the xc documents show. Although Yaxa still had its own *batab* in the 1780s (Bracamonte 1994: 32), it is not even included in the Mani maps (see Figure 7.1), in which Oxkutzcab can be seen to the right of Mani.

14 A number of these documents, probably most of them, are preserved in the xc corpus. Here, for example, is my translation of a record written in Maya just eight years before doña Catalina's petition and surely one of the papers to which she refers: "Here in the *cah* of San Juan Yaxa adjacent to the *cah* of San Francisco Oxkutzcab, on the seventeenth of the month of December, the year 1624, we have received into our possession the edict of our lord, the *señor* governor [i.e. the Spanish governor of Yucatan], in which we are told to give a corn field [*col*], with a fieldhand [*ak kab*], to don Alonso Xiu and a record of possession [*u pach u bulla*] in which we say we will give these things just as we have been told. When we saw the edict of our lord, we placed it between our heads, kissed it, and gave our names in order to ratify it. Captain don Fernando Camal, [*batab*]; Francisco Couoh, notary; Melchor Uz, alcalde; Juan Tec, Diego Noh, *regidores*" (xc:9). Note that the overwhelming majority of colonial-era Maya documents, like this one and the first two petitions presented in this chapter, were *cah* products authored by some or all of the community's political authorities; petitions from individuals, a genre more commonly associated with Spanish practices, were rare, and a petition from a woman (such as doña Catalina Cime) rarer still.

15 A *tomín* was a *real*, eight of which made up a *peso*. The term (written here, as was usual, *tumín*) also meant "coin" in Nahuatl and Maya.

16 This is the same don Juan Xiu who wrote and signed the surviving copy of the Annals of Oxkutzcab (Chapter 4). Note too that this same don Juan added his name to the Xiu family tree, thereby updating the tree from the late sixteenth to the late seventeenth century and providing a visual parallel to the *probanza* documents among which the drawing was preserved; the addition can be seen on the far left edge of the drawing (Figure 8.1 in Chapter 8; Cortez 1995: 70–73).

17 This is a reference to the *procurador* and the *defensor* (both Spanish terms are used in the document) of "the Indians," Spanish officials designated to provide legal services to Maya communities. A single attorney sometimes held both posts, as was the case in 1640 with Martín de Meñaca, who then went on to petition the governor on behalf of don Juan and his sisters.

18 I.e. not just a Maya noble (*almehen*), but a Maya noble granted the Spanish noble designation of *hidalgo* and thus recognized by the colonial authorities; it is this status that the Xiu petitions sought, with considerable success, to maintain.

19 *coon maya uinice*; this is a rare example of the use of the term "Maya" as an ethnic designation, and an even rarer example of it as a self-reference. I have argued elsewhere that the Mayas used the word primarily as an adjective to describe things other than people—mostly the Yucatec language—and that its usage as an ethnic reference was viewed before the nineteenth century as archaic or literary or possibly even denigratory (Restall 1997a: 14–15). The latter interpretation would fit the usage above, as the petitioner adopts the self-deprecating stance typical of Maya petitionary discourse. Although there are a few examples of the term in the quasi-notarial documents presented in previous chapters, the only other use of "Maya" in this sense in a mundane notarial document is from the same decade as the Xiu petition and employs the same phrase (AGI-*Escribanía*, 317a, 2: 147; a *cabildo* petition of 1669 from Baca) suggesting that it may be specific to the late seventeenth century.

20 The Spanish interpreter loosely translated the petition, which he states don Juan Xiu then signed, on May 30, 1662 (XC:36); that same day or the one after, the *defensor*, Francisco Crespo de Morales, repeated the request in his name (XC:37); on June 1, the office of the governor of the province, don Joseph Campero de Sorrevilla, acknowledged receipt of the petitions; on June 2, the governor granted the musket license. The speed with which the request was processed suggests that it lacked controversy; indeed we know from colonial Maya wills that indigenous men who were not even nobles owned shotguns (Restall 1997a: 180).

21 *ah tepp cheob*; literally, those covered by trees. This is a reference to the Mayas living in the more-forested areas of the peninsula to the southeast of the colony, the region the Spaniards misnamed *despoblado* or "uninhabited" (see Chapter 1).

22 This is a reference to events of the 1620s. The story begins with the 1604 Paxbolon-Maldonado expedition of conquest against the indepedendent Mayas to the east of Acalan-Tixchel (see Chapter 3); the campaign resulted in a number of families being brought under colonial rule, but many more remained outside the colony. Furthermore, while communities continued to be forcibly moved (there was a major relocation of Mayas to Sahcabchen in 1615, for example), there was a steady countermigration out of the colony's margins and into the unconquered area. The issue would not be resolved until the Spanish Conquest of the Peten Itza in 1697. Meanwhile, in 1614 the Maya ruler, Canek, sent an embassy to Merida; partly as a result, friars Fuensalida and Orbita attempted to set up a mission in 1618, followed by another friar named Delgado in 1621. Delgado's apparent success at a *cah* called Sacalum encouraged an expedition of "pacification" led by Francisco de Mirones in 1622, which resulted by 1624 in the deaths of Delgado, Mirones, and other Spaniards. The provincial governor decided to use Mayas from the colony to punish the "rebels" from the south. Thus later in 1624 a force of armed Mayas from Oxkutzcab, led by their *batab* don Fernando Camal (named above in note 14), was sent to the region. There they killed some twenty "delinquent Indians" (as a

Spanish report described them) and captured another fifty, bringing them back into the colony along with the religious items that Delgado had used in his mission in Sacalum. The Oxkutzcab participants were rewarded with tribute exemptions for them and their children. Although don Juan Xiu's ancestors are not listed in the 1624 petition requesting confirmation of this reward (Scholes and Adams 1991: 42–44), Xiu is able to claim the legacy of the Mirones' revenge to justify his musket license. (See Scholes and Adams 1991, an English-language edition of archival documents relating to the Mirones affair; also see Jones 1989: 155–87.)

23 As Roys (1941: 658) suggests, the sense here is probably, "I am not that sort of person."

Glossary of Maya and Spanish Terms

adelantado (Sp)
Title granted to a Spaniard to indicate his possession of a royal license to conquer and colonize a specified territory on behalf of the Crown; a successful *adelantado* expected to be confirmed as governor (*gobernador*) of the new imperial province.

ahau (M)
Ruler, senior lord.

alcalde (Sp)
Magistrate; an officer of a Spanish or a Maya *cabildo*; an *alcalde mayor* was a Spanish colonial official with regional authority (although Mayas occasionally used the term to denote the senior *alcalde* of their *cabildo*).

audiencia (Sp)
Judicial high court and administrative authority; Yucatan fell variously in the sixteenth century into the jurisdiction of the *audiencias* in Guatemala and Mexico City, ending up under the authority of the latter.

batab (M)
(plural: *batabob*) The Maya municipal governor or ruler of a *cah*.

cabildo (Sp)
The municipal council, Spanish or Maya; each *cah* was governed by a *cabildo*, subordinated to the *batab*.

cah (M)
(plural: *cahob*) The self-governing municipal community (village or town) of the Yucatec Maya; included both residential core and concomitant lands; primary focus of Maya identity, along with the *chibal*.

chibal (M)
The Maya patronym-group, lineage, or extended family; primary focus of Maya identity, along with the *cah*.

defensor (Sp)
In the context of this book, a reference to the Defender of the Indians, aka Protector of the Indians, a Spanish lawyer assigned to represent indigenous interests before colonial administrators and magistrates.

doctrina (Sp)
Christian teaching; also a parish of indigenous Christians.

dzul (M)

Foreigner; usually meaning Spaniard in the colonial period; also a *chibal* name; written as ꜩul in colonial orthography.

encomienda (Sp)

A royal grant of the inhabitants of one or more indigenous communities, licensing a Spaniard to receive their labor and tribute; held by an *encomendero*.

estancia (Sp)

Rural estate devoted to agriculture and / or cattle ranching; held by an *estanciero*.

halach uinic (M)

"True man"; regional ruler, chief ruler; this highest Maya office title was usually used after the Conquest to refer to the Spanish provincial governor.

hidalgo (Sp)

Nobleman; *indio hidalgo* was a level of indigenous nobility recognized by colonial authorities and carrying certain privileges, such as tribute exemption, not accorded to other Maya nobles (*almehenob*).

nuc uinic (M)

Elder, or one of the principal men of a *cah*, including colonial-era *cabildo* members.

-ob (M)

The plural suffix in Yucatec Maya.

oidor (Sp)

Judge and member of an *audiencia*.

probanza (Sp)

"Proof"; an official report and record of merits and services to the Crown.

regidor (Sp)

Councilman; an officer of a Spanish or a Maya *cabildo*.

relación (Sp)

Account, report; sometimes part of a *probanza*.

título (Sp)

In the context of this book, a primordial title; a document drawn up by indigenous *cabildos*, usually a late colonial compilation of records going back to the Conquest period or before. A *título* typically features an account of the Conquest and an assertion of the early colonial confirmation both of the social status and political office of ruling families and of the territorial boundaries of the community or region.

List of Historical Figures

Canche, Napot
Batab of Calkini when the *cah* submitted and first paid tribute to Montejo; father of Alonso Canche, the putative author of sections of the Title of Calkini (Chapter 5).

Chi, Gaspar Antonio
(c.1532–1610) Nobleman of the Chi *chibal* through his father and the Xiu *chibal* through his mother; brought up by Franciscans; at various points in a long career he was assistant to fray Diego de Landa, interpreter to Bishop Toral, Interpreter General of Yucatan, and governor of Mani; source of various Spanish *relaciones* (Chapter 8) and probable creator of the Xiu family tree (Figure 8.1).

Cocom, Nachi
Regional ruler of Sotuta at the time of the Spanish Conquest; allegedly ordered 1536 massacre of Xiu ambassadors at Otzmal; despite opposing Spaniards to late 1540s, was baptized Juan Cocom and remained ruler of Sotuta; died shortly before the 1562 anti-idolatry campaign but was posthumously condemned; some sources have two Nachi Cocoms, with he of the 1530s as grandfather of Nachi/Juan Cocom of the 1540s (Chapters 4 and 8).

Cortés, Hernán
(1485–1547) Spanish conquistador of central Mexico (Chapter 3).

Cuauhtemoc
The last ruler or *tlatoani* of the Mexica empire centered on Tenochtitlan; taken captive by Cortés in 1521 and hanged by him in Acalan in 1525 (Chapter 3).

Landa, Diego de
(1524–1579) Head of the Franciscans in Yucatan and later bishop; best known for his violent persecution of Maya "idolaters" in 1562 and for his 1566 *Relación*, a history and ethnography of the Yucatec Mayas (Chapters 8 and 9).

López, Tomás
An *oidor* (judge) of the *audiencia* (imperial High Court) in Guatemala, which had jurisdiction over Yucatan at the time of López's official visit in 1552–53, when he ordered a number of reforms, of which tribute reduction is mentioned most often in Maya-language accounts (Chapters 3 and 6).

Montejo, Francisco de
Three Francisco de Montejos, father, son, and nephew, led expeditions of conquest into the Yucatan peninsula; references in Maya accounts to the captain Montejo and the *adelantado* are usually to the son, who succeeded in founding

the colony of Yucatan in the 1540s, although it was the father who officially held the title of *adelantado* and who became the colony's first governor (Chapters 5 and 6).

Paxbolonacha and Paxbolon

Paxbolonacha was ruler of the Chontal Mayas of the Acalan region (eastern Tabasco and southern Campeche) in the early sixteenth century and received Cortés in 1525; his grandson and namesake, christened don Pablo Paxbolon (born 1543), ruled Acalan from 1566 to his death in 1614/15 (Chapters 3 and 9).

Pech

Noble *chibal* who ruled most of the *cahob* in the northwest region named after them (Ceh Pech) before and after the Conquest; still dominant in the region in late colonial times; early allies of the Spaniards, and thus beneficiaries of *indio hidalgo* status (Chapters 6 and 9).

Xiu, don Juan

Seventeenth-century Maya nobleman, head of the Xiu family in Yaxakumche, a small *cah* subordinated to Oxkutzcab; copyist of the Annals of Oxkutzcab (Chapter 4) and author of a series of petitions to maintain *indio hidalgo* rights (Chapter 10); added his name to the Xiu family tree (Figure 8.1).

Xiu, Tutul

Name given to the dominant noble *chibal* of the Mani region and sometimes to the regional ruler (*halach uinic*); following the supposed founder of the dynasty (also called Hun Uitzil Chac Tutul Xiu), whom various sources have as a migrant from Mexico and/or ruler of Uxmal and/or Mayapan; the Tutul Xiu in 1542 traveled to Merida-Tiho to offer his allegiance to Montejo, helping win *indio hidalgo* status for Xiu nobles; the last Tutul Xiu *halach uinic* of Mani, Ah Kukum Xiu, was baptized don Francisco de Montejo Xiu (Chapters 4 and 7–10).

Bibliography

PUBLISHED AND SECONDARY SOURCES

Ancona, Eligio. 1878–80. *Historia de Yucatán desde la época mas remota.* 4 vols. Merida, Yucatan.

Alvaro Hermann, Manuel. 1996. "Algunas alternativas metodológicas para la interpretación de las glosas del Códice Muro" (Paper presented at the Third International Symposium on Codices and Documents, Puebla, Mexico).

Ávila, Manuel Encarnación. 1864. Unpublished handwritten Spanish translation of the Title of Chicxulub.

Barrera Vásquez, Alfredo. 1957. *Códice de Calkiní.* Campeche: Biblioteca Campechana.

———. 1965. *Libro de los Cantares de Dzitbalche.* Mexico City: Instituto Nacional de Antropología e Historia (Reprinted in Garza 1980).

———. 1980. *Diccionario Maya.* Merida, Yucatan: Cordemex.

———. 1984. *Documento No. 1 del Deslinde de Tierras en Yaxkukul, Yucatán.* Mexico City: INAH (Colección científica, Linguistica 125).

Barrera Vásquez, Alfredo, and Silvia Rendón, eds., 1948. *El libro de los libros de Chilam Balam.* Mexico City: Fondo de Cultura Económica.

Berlin, Heinrich. 1950. "La Historia de los Xpantzay." In *Antropología e Historia de Guatemala* 2(2).

Blom, Frans. 1928. "Gaspar Antonio Chi, Interpreter." In *American Anthropologist* 30, 250–62.

———. 1936. *The Conquest of Yucatan.* Cambridge, MA: Riverside Press.

Boone, Elizabeth Hill, and Walter D. Mignolo. 1994. *Writing Without Words: Alternative Literacies in Mesoamerica and the Andes.* Durham: Duke University Press.

Borah, Woodrow. 1991. "Yet Another Look at the Techialoyan Codices." In *Land and Politics in the Valley of Mexico: A Two Thousand Year Perspective*, H. R. Harvey, ed. Albuquerque: University of New Mexico Press.

Bracamonte, Pedro. 1994. *La memoria enclaustrada: historia indígena de Yucatán, 1750–1915.* Mexico City: CIESAS.

Bricker, Victoria. 1981. *The Indian Christ, the Indian King: The Historical Substrate of Maya Myth and Ritual.* Austin: University of Texas Press.

Brinton, Daniel G. 1882. *The Maya Chronicles.* Philadelphia (Library of Aboriginal American Literature).

———. 1885. *The Annals of the Cakchiquels.* Philadelphia (Library of Aboriginal American Literature).

Burkhart, Louise M. 1996. *Holy Wednesday: A Nahua Drama from Early Colonial Mexico.* Philadelphia: University of Pennsylvania Press.

Burns, Allan F. 1991. "The Language of Zuyua: Yucatec Maya Riddles and Their Interpretation." In *Past, Present, and Future: Selected Papers on Latin American Indian Literatures,* Mary H. Preuss, ed. Lancaster, CA: Labyrinthos.

Carmack, Robert. 1973. *Quichean Civilization: The Ethnohistoric, Ethnographic, and Archaeological Sources.* Berkeley: University of California Press.

———. 1981. *The Quiché Mayas of Utatlán: The Evolution of a Highland Guatemalan Kingdom.* Norman: University of Oklahoma Press.

———. 1995. *Rebels of Highland Guatemala: The Quiché-Mayas of Momostenango.* Norman: University of Oklahoma Press.

Carmack, Robert M., and James Mondloch. 1983. *El Título de Totonicapán: Su texto, traducción, y comentario.* Mexico City: Universidad Autónoma de México, Centro de Estudios Mayas.

———. 1989. *El Título de Yax, y otros documentos quichées de Totonicapán, Guatemala.* Mexico City: Universidad Autónoma de México, Centro de Estudios Mayas.

Carmack, Robert M., and Alonso Efraín Tzaquitzal Zapeta. 1993. *Título de los Señores de Coyoy.* Guatemala City: CIGDA.

Carrasco, Pedro. 1997. "Indian-Spanish Marriages in the First Century of the Colony." In *Indian Women of Early Mexico,* Susan Schroeder, Stephanie Wood, and Robert Haskett, eds. Norman: University of Oklahoma Press.

Carrillo y Ancona, Crescencio. 1880. *Catecismo de Historia y de Geografía de Yucatán.* Merida, Yucatan: Libreria Catolica.

Cartas de Indias. 1877. Madrid: Ministerio de Fomento.

Chamberlain, Robert S. 1948. *The Conquest and Colonization of Yucatán.* Washington, DC: Carnegie Institution.

Chance, John K. 1989. *Conquest of the Sierra: Spaniards and Indians in Colonial Oaxaca.* Norman: University of Oklahoma Press.

Christensen, Alexander F. 1996. "Cristóbal del Castillo and the Mexica Exodus." In *The Americas* 52 (4), 441–64.

Clendinnen, Inga. 1987. *Ambivalent Conquests: Maya and Spaniard in Yucatán, 1517–1570.* Cambridge: Cambridge University Press.

———. 1991. "'Fierce and Unnatural Cruelty': Cortés and the Conquest of Mexico." In *Representations* 33, 12–47.

Cline, Howard. 1975. *Guide to Ethnohistorical Sources,* part 4. *Handbook of Middle American Indians,* vol. 15. Austin: University of Texas Press.

Cline, S. L. 1988. "Revisionist Conquest History." In *The Work of Bernardino de Sahagún, Pioneer Ethnographer of Sixteenth Century Aztec Mexico,* Jorge Klor de

Alva et al., eds. Albany and Austin: SUNY-Albany Institute for Mesoamerican Studies and University of Texas Press.

Coe, Michael D. 1993. *The Maya*, 5th ed. New York: Thames and Hudson.

Coggins, Clemency Chase. 1987. "New Fire at Chichén Itzá." In *Memorias del Primer Coloquio Internacional de Mayistas*. Mexico City: Universidad Nacional Autónoma de México.

Cogolludo, Diego López de. 1957. *Historia de Yucatán* [1654]. Mexico City: Editorial Academia Literaria.

Colección de documentos inéditos relativos al descubrimiento, conquista y colonización de las antiguas posesiones españolas en América y Oceanía sacados de los Archivos del Reino y muy especialmente del de Indias. 1864–84. Madrid: Real Academía de la Historia.

Colón, Hernando. 1947. *Vida del Almirante don Cristóbal Colón escrita por su hijo Hernando Colón*. Ramón Iglesias, ed. Mexico City: Fondo de Cultura Económica.

Cook, Sherburne F., and Woodrow Borah. 1974. *Essays in Population History: Mexico and the Caribbean*, vol. 2. Berkeley and Los Angeles: University of California Press.

Craine, Eugene R., and Reginald C. Reindorp, eds. 1979. *The Codex Pérez and the Book of Chilam Balam of Maní*. Norman: University of Oklahoma Press.

Culbert, T. Patrick, ed. 1973. *The Classic Maya Collapse*. Albuquerque: University of New Mexico Press.

Culbert, T. Patrick, and Don S. Rice, eds. 1990. *Precolumbian Population History in the Maya Lowlands*. Albuquerque: University of New Mexico Press.

Cummins, Thomas B. F. 1991. "We Are the Other: Peruvian Portraits of Colonial Kurakakuna." In *Transatlantic Encounters: Europeans and Andeans in the Sixteenth Century*. Kenneth Andrien and Rolena Adorno, eds. Berkeley: University of California Press.

Dakin, Karen, and Christopher H. Lutz. 1996. *Nuestro pesar, nuestra aflicción: Memorias en lengua náhuatl enviadas a Felipe II por indígenas del Valle de Guatemala hacia 1572*. Mexico City: Universidad Nacional Autónoma de México and Centro de Investigaciones Regionales de Mesoamérica.

Díaz del Castillo, Bernal. 1963. *The Conquest of New Spain*. New York: Penguin.

Dumond, Don E. 1997. *The Machete and the Cross: Campesino Rebellion in Yucatan*. Lincoln: University of Nebraska Press.

Early, James. 1994. *The Colonial Architecture of Mexico*. Albuquerque: University of New Mexico Press.

Edmonson, Munro S. 1982. *The Ancient Future of the Itza: The Book of Chilam Balam of Tizimin*. Austin: University of Texas Press.

———. 1986. *Heaven Born Merida and Its Destiny: The Book of Chilam Balam of Chumayel*. Austin: University of Texas Press.

Elliott, J. H. 1989. "The Mental World of Hernán Cortés" [1967], in *Spain and Its World, 1500–1700: Selected Essays*. New Haven: Yale University Press.

Farriss, Nancy M. 1984. *Maya Society Under Colonial Rule: The Collective Enterprise of Survival*. Princeton: Princeton University Press.

——. 1987. "Remembering the Future, Anticipating the Past: History, Time, and Cosmology among the Maya of Yucatan." In *Journal for the Comparative Study of Society and History* 29, 566–93.

Fernández-Arnesto, Felipe. 1995. *Millennium: A History of the Last Thousand Years*. New York: Scribner.

Florescano, Enrique. 1994. *Memory, Myth, and Time in Mexico from the Aztecs to Independence*. Austin: University of Texas Press.

García Bernal, Manuela Cristina. 1978. *Yucatán: Población y encomienda bajo las Austrias*. Seville: Escuela de Estudios Hispano-Americanos.

——. 1979. "El Gobernador de Yucatán Rodrigo Flores de Aldana." In *Homenaje al Dr. Muro Orejón*. Seville: Escuela de Estudios Hispano-Americanos.

——. 1985. "Garcia de Palacio y sus ordenanzas para Yucatan." In *Temas Americanistas* 5, 1–12

Garza, Mercedes de la, ed. 1980. *Literatura Maya*. Caracas: Biblioteca Ayacucho.

Gates, William, ed. 1935. *The Maya Calkini Chronicle, or Documents concerning the Descent of the Ah-Canul, or Men of the Serpent, their Arrival and Territory*. Baltimore: The Maya Society.

——. 1937. *Yucatan Before and After the Conquest, by Friar Diego de Landa*. Baltimore: The Maya Society (Reprinted by Dover, 1978.)

Gibson, Charles. 1964. *The Aztecs Under Spanish Rule: A History of the Indians of the Valley of Mexico, 1519–1820*. Stanford: Stanford University Press.

Gillespie, Susan D. 1989. *The Aztec Kings: The Construction of Rulership in Mexica History*. Tucson: University of Arizona Press.

González Cicero, Stella María. 1978. *Perspectiva religiosa en Yucatán, 1517–1571*. Mexico City: El Colegio de México.

Gruzinski, Serge. 1993. *The Conquest of Mexico: The Incorporation of Indian Societies into the Western World, 16th-18th Centuries*. Cambridge, UK: Polity Press.

Gubler, Ruth, with David Bolles. 1997. *The Book of Chilam Balam of Na*. Lancaster, CA: Labyrinthos.

Hanks, William F. 1986. "Authenticity and Ambivalence in the Text: A Colonial Maya Case." In *American Ethnologist* 13 (4), 721–44.

——. 1987. "Discourse Genres in a Theory of Practice." In *American Ethnologist* 14 (4), 668–92.

——. 1989. "Rhetoric of Royal Address in Sixteenth-Century Yucatec Maya." Unpublished manuscript.

——. 1996. *Language and Communicative Practices*. Boulder: Westview Press.

Haskett, Robert. 1992. "Visions of Municipal Glory Undimmed: The Nahuatl Town Histories of Colonial Cuernavaca," in *Colonial Latin American Historical Review* 1 (1), 1–36.

———. 1996. "Paper Shields: The Ideology of Coats of Arms in Colonial Mexican Primordial Titles." In *Ethnohistory* 43 (1), 99–126.

Hassig, Ross. 1992. "Aztec and Spanish Conquest in Mesoamerica." In *War in the Tribal Zone: Expanding States and Indigenous Warfare*, R. Brian Ferguson and Neil L. Whitehead, eds. Santa Fe: School of American Research Press.

Helms, Mary W. 1993. *Craft and the Kingly Ideal: Art, Trade, and Power.* Austin: University of Texas Press.

Hernández Pons, Elsa. 1997. "La ceiba, el árbol sagrado." In *Arqueología Mexicana* 5 (28), 68–73.

Hill, Robert M., II. 1992. *Colonial Cakchiquels: Highland Maya Adaptation to Spanish Rule, 1600–1700.* Fort Worth: Harcourt Brace.

Hires, Marla Korlin. 1981. "The Chilam Balam of Chan Kan." Ph.D. dissertation, Tulane University.

Izquierdo, Ana Luisa. 1997. *Acalán y La Chontalpa en el siglo XVI: su geografía política.* Mexico City: Universidad Nacional Autónoma de México.

Jakeman, M. Wells. 1952. *The "Historical Recollections" of Gaspar Antonio Chi: An Early Source-account of Ancient Yucatan.* Provo: Brigham Young University, Publications in Archaeology and Early History 3.

Jones, Grant D. 1989. *Maya Resistance to Spanish Rule: Time and History on a Colonial Frontier.* Albuquerque: University of New Mexico Press.

Jones, Lindsay. 1995. *Twin City Tales: A Hermeneutical Reassessment of Tula and Chichén Itzá.* Niwot: University Press of Colorado.

———. 1997. "Conquests of the Imagination: Maya-Mexican Polarity and the Story of Chichén Itzá." In *American Anthropologist* 99 (2), 275–90.

Justeson, John S., and George A. Broadwell. 1996. "Language and Languages in Mesoamerica." In *The Legacy of Mesoamerica: History and Culture of a Native American Civilization*, Robert M. Carmack, Janine Gasco, and Gary H. Gossen, eds. Upper Saddle River, NJ: Prentice Hall.

Karttunen, Frances. 1985. *Nahuatl and Maya in Contact with Spanish.* Austin: University of Texas, Dept. of Linguistics and Center for Cognitive Science, Texas Linguistic Forum 26.

———. 1994. *Between Worlds: Interpreters, Guides, and Survivors.* New Brunswick: Rutgers University Press.

———. 1997. "Rethinking Malinche." In *Indian Women of Early Mexico.* Susan Schroeder, Stephanie Wood, and Robert Haskett, eds. Norman: University of Oklahoma Press.

Kicza, John E. 1992. "A Comparison of Spanish and Indian Accounts of the Conquest of Mexico." In *Five Centuries of Mexican History*, vol. 1. Virginia Guedea and Jaime E. Rodriguez O., eds. San Juan Mixcoac, Mexico: Instituto Mora and University of California, Irvine.

———. n.d. *Patterns in Spanish Overseas Encounters to 1600: The Factors Underlying Success and Failure in Warfare Against Non-Western People.* Manuscript. Albuquerque: University of New Mexico Press.

Klor de Alva, J. Jorge. 1992. "El discurso nahua y la apropriación de lo europeo." In *De palabra y obra en el Nuevo Mundo, vol. 1: Imágenes interétnicas.* Miguel León-Portilla, Manuel Gutiérrez Estévez, Gary H. Gossen, and J. Jorge Klor de Alva, eds. Mexico City: Siglo Veintiuno.

Knaut, Andrew L. 1995. *The Pueblo Revolt of 1680: Conquest and Resistance in Seventeenth-Century New Mexico.* Norman: University of Oklahoma Press.

Koning, Hans. 1993. *The Conquest of America: How the Indian Nations Lost their Continent.* New York: Monthly Review Press.

Kramer, Wendy. 1994. *Encomienda Politics in Early Colonial Guatemala, 1524–1544: Dividing the Spoils.* Boulder: Westview Press.

Kubler, George. 1961. "Chichén Itzá y Tula." In *Estudios de Cultura Maya* 1, 47–59.

Landa, Fray Diego de. 1959. *Relación de las cosas de Yucatán* [1566]. Mexico City: Editorial Porrúa. (Citations of this work are to chapter numbers, to enable the reader to find the reference in any of the many editions.)

Las Casas, Bartolomé de. 1988. *Brevisima Relación de la Destrucción de las Indias* [c. 1550]. Merida, Yucatan: Editorial Dante. (English trans. by Herma Briffault, *The Devastation of the Indies: A Brief Account.* Baltimore: Johns Hopkins University Press, 1992.)

Le Clézio, J.M.G. 1993. *The Mexican Dream. Or, The Interrupted Thought of Amerindian Civilizations.* Chicago: University of Chicago Press (from *Le rêve mexicain, ou la pensée interrompue* [Gallimard, 1988]).

Leibsohn, Dana. 1993. "The Historia Tolteca-Chichimeca: Recollecting Identity in a Nahua Manuscript." Ph.D. dissertation, University of California, Los Angeles.

León-Portilla, Miguel. 1992. *The Broken Spears: The Aztec Account of the Conquest of Mexico* (rev. ed.). Boston: Beacon Press.

Lockhart, James. 1972. *The Men of Cajamarca: A Social and Biographical Study of the First Conquerors of Peru.* Austin: University of Texas Press.

———. 1991. *Nahuas and Spaniards: Postconquest Central Mexican History and Philology.* Stanford and Los Angeles: Stanford University Press and UCLA Latin American Center.

———. 1992. *The Nahuas After the Conquest: A Social and Cultural History of the Indians of Central Mexico, Sixteenth through Eighteenth Centuries.* Stanford: Stanford University Press.

———. 1993. *We People Here: Nahuatl Accounts of the Conquest of Mexico.* Berkeley: University of California Press (Repertorium Columbianum, vol. 1).

————. 1994. "Sightings: Initial Nahua Reactions to Spanish Culture." In *Implicit Understandings: Observing, Reporting, and Reflecting on the Encounters between Europeans and Other Peoples in the Early Modern Era*. Stuart B. Schwartz, ed. Cambridge: Cambridge University Press.

López Portillo y Pacheco, José. 1992. *They Are Coming . . . : The Conquest of Mexico*. Denton: University of North Texas Press.

Lowe, J.G.W. 1985. *The Dynamics of Apocalypse: A Systems Simulation of the Classic Maya Collapse*. Albuquerque: University of New Mexico Press.

Makemson, Maud Worcester. 1951. *The Book of the Jaguar Priest: A Translation of the Book of Chilam Balam of Tizimin, with Commentary*. New York: Schuman.

Marcus, Joyce. 1992. *Mesoamerican Writing Systems: Propaganda, Myth, and History in Four Ancient Civilizations*. Princeton: Princeton University Press.

————. 1993. "Ancient Maya Political Organization." In *Lowland Maya Civilization in the Eighth Century A.D.*, Jeremy A. Sabloff and John S. Henderson, eds. Washington DC: Dumbarton Oaks.

Marks, Richard Lee. 1994. *Cortés: The Great Adventurer and the Fate of Aztec Mexico*. New York: Knopf.

Martínez Hernández, Juan. 1909. *Chilam Balam de Maní o Códice Pérez*. Merida, Yucatan: Colegio San José de Artes y Oficios.

McAnany, Patricia A. 1996. *Living with the Ancestors: Kinship and Kingship in Ancient Maya Society*. Austin: University of Texas Press.

————. 1998. "Ancestors and the Classic Maya Built Environment." In *Function and Meaning in Classic Maya Architecture*. Stephen Houston, ed. Washington DC: Dumbarton Oaks.

Mitchell, J. Leslie. 1935. *The Conquest of the Maya*. New York: Dutton.

Molina Solís, Juan Francisco. 1896. *Historia de Yucatán durante la dominación española*. 3 vols. Merida, Yucatan: Imprenta de la Lotería del Estado.

Morley, Sylvanus G. 1920. *The Inscriptions at Copán*. Washington, DC: Carnegie Institution, Publication 219.

————. 1946. *The Ancient Maya*. Stanford: Stanford University Press.

Mullen, Robert J. 1997. *Architecture and its Sculpture in Viceregal Mexico*. Austin: University of Texas Press.

Nobles, Gregory H. 1997. *American Frontiers: Cultural Encounters and Continental Conquest*. New York: Hill and Wang.

Okoshi Harada, Tsubasa. 1993. "Los Canules: analisis etnohistorico del Codice de Calkiní." Ph.D. dissertation, Universidad Nacional Autónoma de México, Mexico City.

————. 1994. "Ecab: Una revisión de la geografía política de una provincia maya yucateca." In *Memorias del Primer Congreso Internacional de Mayistas*. Mexico City: Universidad Nacional Autónoma de México.

Oviedo y Valdés, Gonzálo Fernández de. 1959. *Historia general y natural de las Indias* [1547]. Madrid: Atlas.

Pagden, Anthony, trans. and ed. 1986. *Hernán Cortés: Letters from Mexico*. New Haven: Yale University Press.

Patch, Robert W. 1991. "Decolonization, the Agrarian Problem, and the Origins of the Caste War, 1812–1847." In *Land, Labor, and Capital in Modern Yucatan*. J.T. Brannon and G.M. Joseph, eds. Tuscaloosa: University of Alabama Press.

———. 1993. *Maya and Spaniard in Yucatán, 1648–1812*. Stanford: Stanford University Press.

Pérez Martínez, Héctor. 1936. *Ah Nakuk Pech: Historia y Crónica de Chac-Xulub-Chen*. Mexico City: Secretaria de Educación.

Pollock, H.E.D., Ralph L. Roys, T. Proskouriakoff, and A. Ledyard Smith, eds. 1962. *Mayapan, Yucatan, Mexico*. Washington DC: Carnegie Institution.

Quezada, Sergio. 1993. *Pueblos y Caciques Yucatecos, 1550–1580*. Mexico City: El Colegio de México.

Recinos, Adrián. 1984. *Cronicas Indígenas de Guatemala* [1957]. Guatemala City: Academia de Geografia e Historia de Guatemala.

Recinos, Adrián, and Delia Goetz. 1953. *Annals of the Cakchiquels and the Title of the Lords of Totonicapán*. Norman: University of Oklahoma Press.

Relaciones de Yucatán. 1898. Vols. 1 and 2 published as vols. 11 and 13 in *Colección de documentos inéditos relativos al descubrimiento, conquista y organización de las antiguas posesiones españoles de ultramar*. Madrid: Real Academía de la Historia.

Restall, Matthew. 1995a. *Life and Death in a Maya Community: The Ixil Testaments of the 1760s*. Lancaster, CA: Labyrinthos.

———. 1995b. "'He Wished It in Vain': Subordination and Resistance among Maya Women in Post-Conquest Yucatan," in *Ethnohistory* 42 (4), 577–94.

———. 1997a. *The Maya World: Yucatec Society and Culture, 1550–1850*. Stanford: Stanford University Press.

———. 1997b. "Heirs to the Hieroglyphs: Indigenous Writing in Colonial Mesoamerica," in *The Americas* 54 (2), 239–67.

———. 1998a. "The Telling of Tales: Six Yucatec Maya Communities and Their Spanish Priest." In *Colonial Lives: Documents on Latin American History, 1550–1850*. Geof Spurling and Richard Boyer, eds. New York: Oxford University Press.

———. 1998b. "Interculturation and the Indigenous Testament in Colonial Yucatan." In *Dead Giveaways: Indigenous Testaments of Colonial Mesoamerica and the Andes*. Susan Kellogg and Matthew Restall, eds. Salt Lake City: University of Utah Press.

———. 1998c. "The Ties that Bind: Social Cohesion and the Yucatec Maya Family in Colonial Mexico," *Journal of Family History* 23(4).

Riese, Frauke Johanna. 1981. *Indianische Landrechte in Yukatan um die Mitte des 16.*

Jahrhunderts: Dokumentenanalyse und Konstruktion von Wirklichkeitsmodellen am Fall des Landvertrages von Mani. Hamburg: Hamburgischen Museum für Völkerkunde.

Ringle, William M. 1990. "Who Was Who in Ninth-Century Chichén Itzá?" In *Ancient Mesoamerica* 1, 233–43.

Romero Frizzi, María de los Angeles. 1994. "Indigenous Mentality and Spanish Power: The Conquest in Oaxaca." In *Caciques and Their People: A Volume in Honor of Ronald Spores.* Ann Arbor: University of Michigan Museum of Anthropology.

Roys, Ralph L. 1929. "Crónica de Calkini." Unpublished transcription of the Title of Calkini.

———. 1933. *The Book of Chilam Balam of Chumayel.* Washington, DC: Carnegie Institution (Reprinted by University of Oklahoma Press, 1967).

———. 1940. "Personal Names of the Maya of Yucatan." In *Contributions to American Anthropology and History* 6, 31–48. Washington, DC: Carnegie Institution.

———. 1941. "The Xiu Chronicle." Unpublished book manuscript, including partial transcription and translation, TLH.

———. 1943. *The Indian Background to Colonial Yucatán.* Washington, DC: Carnegie Institution.

———. 1946. "The Book of Chilam Balam of Ixil." In *Notes on Middle American Archaeology and Ethnology* 75. Washington DC: Carnegie Institution.

———. 1957. *The Political Geography of the Yucatán Maya.* Washington, DC: Carnegie Institution.

———. 1962. "Literary Sources for the History of Mayapan." In *Mayapan, Yucatan, Mexico.* H.E.D. Pollock, Ralph L. Roys, T. Proskouriakoff, and A. Ledyard Smith, eds. Washington DC: Carnegie Institution.

Rubio Mañé, Ignacio. 1941. *La Casa de Montejo en Mérida de Yucatán.* Mexico City: Imprenta Universitaria.

Rugeley, Terry. 1996. *Yucatán's Maya Peasantry and the Origins of the Caste War.* Austin: University of Texas Press.

Sabloff, Jeremy A. 1990. *The New Archaeology and the Ancient Maya.* New York: Freeman.

Sabloff, Jeremy A., and E.W. Andrews V, eds. 1986. *Late Lowland Maya Civilization: Classic to Postclassic.* Albuquerque: University of New Mexico Press.

Sabloff, Jeremy A., and John S. Henderson, eds. 1993. *Lowland Maya Civilization in the Eighth Century A.D.* Washington DC: Dumbarton Oaks.

Sahagún, fray Bernardino de. 1978. *The War of the Conquest: How It Was Waged Here in Mexico* [1579], trans. Arthur J. O. Anderson and Charles E. Dibble. Salt Lake City: University of Utah Press.

Schele, Linda, and Mary E. Miller. 1986. *The Blood of Kings.* New York: George Braziller.

Schele, Linda, and David A. Freidel. 1990. *A Forest of Kings*. New York: W. Morrow & Co.

Scholes, France V., and Eleanor Adams, eds. 1938. *Don Diego Quijada, Alcalde Mayor de Yucatán, 1561–1565*, 2 vols. Mexico City: Editorial Porrua.

————. 1991. *Documents Relating to the Mirones Expedition to the Interior of Yucatan, 1621–24* [1936]. Lancaster, CA: Labyrinthos.

Scholes, France V., Carlos R. Menéndez, J. Ignacio Rubio Mañé, and Eleanor B. Adams, eds. 1936–38. *Documentos para la historia de Yucatán*, 3 vols. Merida, Yucatan: Compañía Tipográfica Yucateca.

Scholes, France V., and Ralph L. Roys. 1938. "Fray Diego de Landa and the Problem of Idolatry in Yucatan." In *Cooperation in Research*. Washington, DC: Carnegie Institution.

————. 1948. *The Maya Chontal Indians of Acalan-Tixchel*. Washington, DC: Carnegie Institution (Reprinted by University of Oklahoma Press, 1968).

Schroeder, Susan. 1995. "Looking Back at the Conquest: Nahua Perceptions of Early Encounters from the Annals of Chimalpahin." In *Chipping Away on Earth: Studies in Prehispanic and Colonial Mexico*. Eliose Quiñones Keber, ed. Lancaster, CA: Labyrinthos.

Schumann, Otto. 1985. "Consideraciones históricas acerca de las lenguas indígenas de Tabasco." In *Olmecas y mayas en Tabasco: cinco acercamientos*. Lorenzo Ochoa, ed. Villahermosa: Gobierno del Estado de Tabasco.

Sharer, Robert J. 1994. *The Ancient Maya*, 5th ed. Stanford: Stanford University Press.

Sigal, Pete. 1995. "Passions of the Mind: Yucatecan Maya Thoughts on the Body, Pleasures, Sexuality, and the Self, Sixteenth to Eighteenth Centuries." Ph.D. dissertation, University of California, Los Angeles.

Smailus, Ortwin. 1975. *El Maya-Chontal de Acalan: Análisis lingüístico de un documento de los años 1610–12*. Mexico City: Universidad Nacional Autónoma de México (Centro de Estudios Mayas, 9).

Solís Alcalá, Ermilo. 1949. *Códice Pérez*. Merida, Yucatan: Imprenta Oriente.

Stern, Steve. 1987. "New Approaches to the Study of Peasant Rebellion." In *Resistance, Rebellion, and Consciousness in the Andean Peasant World*. Steve Stern, ed. Madison: University of Wisconsin Press.

Stephens, John Lloyd. 1988. *Incidents of Travel in Yucatan* [1841]. Mexico City: Panorama Editorial. (Citations of this work are to chapter numbers to enable the reader to find the reference in any of the many editions.)

Stuart, David. 1993. "Historical Inscriptions and the Maya Collapse." In *Lowland Maya Civilization in the Eighth Century A.D.* Jeremy A. Sabloff and John S. Henderson, eds. Washington DC: Dumbarton Oaks.

Swadesh, Mauricio, María Cristina Álvarez, and Juan R. Bastarrachea. 1991. *Diccionario de elementos del maya yucateco colonial*. Mexico City: Universidad Nacional Autónoma de México.

Tedlock, Barbara. 1992. *Time and the Highland Maya*, 2d ed. Albuquerque: University of New Mexico Press.

Tedlock, Dennis. 1985. *Popol Vuh. The Mayan Book of the Dawn of Life*. New York: Touchstone.

———. 1993. "Torture in the Archives: Mayans Meet Europeans." In *American Anthropologist*, 91 (1), 139–52.

Terraciano, Kevin. 1994. "Ñudzahui History: Mixtec Writing and Culture in Colonial Oaxaca." Ph.D. dissertation, University of California, Los Angeles.

Terraciano, Kevin, and Lisa Sousa. 1992. "The 'Original Conquest' of Oaxaca: Mixtec and Nahua History and Myth." In *UCLA Historical Journal* 12, 29–90.

Thomas, Hugh. 1993. *Conquest: Montezuma, Cortés, and the Fall of Old Mexico*. New York: Simon & Schuster.

Thompson, J. Eric S. 1956. *The Rise and Fall of Maya Civilization*. London and Norman: Victor Gollancz and University of Oklahoma Press.

———. 1970. *Maya History and Religion*. Norman: University of Oklahoma Press.

Todorov, Tzvetan. 1984. *The Conquest of America*. New York: Harper & Row.

Tozzer, Alfred M. 1941. *Landa's relación de las cosas de Yucatán*. Cambridge, MA: Peabody Museum of Archaeology and Ethnology, Papers 28.

———. 1957. *Chichén Itzá and Its Cenote of Sacrifice: A Comparative Study of Contemporaneous Maya and Toltec*. Memoirs of the Peabody Museum, 11–12. Cambridge: Harvard University Press.

Trexler, Richard C. 1995. *Sex and Conquest: Gendered Violence, Political Order, and the European Conquest of the Americas*. Ithaca: Cornell University Press.

Warren, Benedict J. 1985. *The Conquest of Michoacán: The Spanish Domination of the Tarascan Kingdom in Western Mexico, 1521–1530*. Norman: University of Oklahoma Press.

Wells, Allen. 1985. *Yucatán's Gilded Age: Haciendas, Henequen, and International Harvester*. Albuquerque: University of New Mexico Press.

Whitecotton, Joseph W. 1990. *Zapotec Elite Ethnohistory: Pictorial Genealogies from Eastern Oaxaca*. Nashville: Vanderbilt University, Publications in Anthropology.

Wood, Stephanie. 1984. "Corporate Adjustments in Colonial Mexican Indian Towns: Toluca Region." Ph.D. dissertation, University of California, Los Angeles.

———. 1989. "Don Diego García de Mendoza Moctezuma: A Techialoyan Mastermind?" in *Estudios de Cultura Náhuatl* 19, 245–68.

———. 1991. "The Cosmic Conquest: Late-Colonial Views of the Sword and the Cross in Central Mexican Títulos." In *Ethnohistory* 38(2).

———. 1998. "Testaments and Títulos: Conflict and Coincidence of Cacique and Community Interests," in Susan Kellogg and Matthew Restall, eds., *Dead*

Giveaways: Indigenous Testaments of Colonial Mesoamerica and the Andes. Salt Lake City: University of Utah Press.

Wright, Ronald. 1992. *Stolen Continents: The Americas Through Indian Eyes Since 1492.* New York: Houghton Mifflin.

Yáñez, Agustín. 1939. *Crónicas de la conquista de México.* Mexico City: Universidad Nacional Autónoma de México, Biblioteca del Estudiante Universitario 2.

Zeitlin, Judith Francis. 1997. "Remembering Kings: History, Text, and Ethnicity in Colonial Tehuantepec, Mexico" (Paper presented at the New England Council of Latin American Studies Meeting, Mount Holyoke, MA).

Zeitlin, Judith Francis, and Lillian Thomas. 1992. "Spanish Justice and the Indian Cacique: Disjunctive Political Systems in Sixteenth-Century Tehuantepec." In *Ethnohistory* 39 (3), 285–315.

Zimmerman, Günter. 1970. *Briefe der indianischen Nobilität aus Neuspanien an Karl V und Philipp II um die Mitte des 16. Jahrhunderts.* Munich: Kommissionsverlag Klaus Renner.

Index